A Dramatic Reinvention

A Dramatic Reinvention

German Television and Moral Renewal after National Socialism, 1956–1970

Stewart Anderson

berghahn
NEW YORK • OXFORD
www.berghahnbooks.com

First published in 2020 by
Berghahn Books
www.berghahnbooks.com

© 2020, 2026 Stewart Anderson
First paperback edition published in 2026

All rights reserved. Except for the quotation of short passages
for the purposes of criticism and review, no part of this book
may be reproduced in any form or by any means, electronic or
mechanical, including photocopying, recording, or any information
storage and retrieval system now known or to be invented,
without written permission of the publisher.

Library of Congress Cataloging-in-Publication Data

Names: Anderson, Stewart, 1979- author.
Title: A dramatic reinvention : German television and moral renewal after National Socialism, 1956-1970 / by Stewart Anderson.
Description: New York : Berghahn, 2020. | Includes bibliographical references and index.
Identifiers: LCCN 2019048107 (print) | LCCN 2019048108 (ebook) | ISBN 9781789206449 (hardback) | ISBN 9781789206456 (ebook)
Subjects: LCSH: Television broadcasting--Germany--History--20th century. | Television broadcasting--Moral and ethical aspects--Germany. | Television broadcasting--Social aspects--Germany. | Television programs--Germany--History--20th century. | Variety shows (Television programs)--Germany--History--20th century.
Classification: LCC PN1992.3.G4 A64 2020 (print) | LCC PN1992.3.G4 (ebook) | DDC 791.450943/09045--dc23
LC record available at https://lccn.loc.gov/2019048107
LC ebook record available at https://lccn.loc.gov/2019048108

British Library Cataloguing in Publication Data
A catalogue record for this book is available from the British Library

EU GPSR Authorized Representative
LOGOS EUROPE, 9 rue Nicolas Poussin, 17000, LA ROCHELLE, France
Email: Contact@logoseurope.eu

ISBN 978-1-78920-644-9 hardback
ISBN 978-1-83695-380-7 paperback
ISBN 978-1-83695-381-4 epub
ISBN 978-1-78920-645-6 web pdf

https://doi.org/10.3167/9781789206449

Contents

Acknowledgments vi
List of Abbreviations viii

Introduction 1

Chapter 1. Navigating History: Historical Consciousness, International Cooperation, and Redemption 31

Chapter 2. Crafting Political Role Models: The Righteous Fugitive and the Man (or Woman) of Conscience 61

Chapter 3. Managing Prosperity: Moderation, Empathy, and Christianity 93

Chapter 4. Resetting Gender Roles: Women's Equality, Reinvented Masculinity, and the Nuclear Family 122

Chapter 5. Embracing Diversity: Racial Tolerance and Integration 153

Conclusion 183

Epilogue 188

Appendix 1. Television Programs Referenced 190

Appendix 2. West German Television Stations 194

Appendix 3. Television Licenses/Subscriptions, 1958–1970 195

Bibliography 197
Index 209

Acknowledgments

Historians often prefer to work in solitude; nonetheless, this book would not exist were it not for a host of collaborators and supporters. Chief among them is my former dissertation adviser Wulf Kansteiner, whom I would like to thank for his steadfast support of my work, for his patience with my idiosyncratic ways of thinking and communicating, and for our long, engaging, fruitful conversations about the peculiar logic of German television history. I will also forever be indebted to Jean Quataert, from whom I learned how to properly question, criticize, edit, and think. I will always treasure her advice, which she continued to offer even under great personal stress and hardship. I am grateful to Howard Brown and Heather DeHaan for their helpful suggestions during the early stages of this project.

I must acknowledge the pioneering efforts and critical advice of other German television historians within the Anglo-American academy, especially Heather Gumbert, Henning Wrage, and Joe Perry. Likewise, I would like to thank Christoph Classen, Nora Hilgert, Knut Hickethier, Nicolai Hannig, and the late Inge Marszolek, my continental colleagues in German television and radio history, for their perspectives and interventions. And, while they may not realize their significance in this project, Maria Mitchell, Judith Becker, and Benjamin Pearson offered important theoretical perspectives on church institutions in the Federal Republic.

Though their input occurred more than a decade ago, the core inspiration for this book developed in Binghamton, New York, among my fellow graduate students, including (among many others) Kristin Bertrand, Jaime Wadowiec, Angela Haas, David Gutman, Daniel Gashler, and Megan Talmadge McKinney. I am especially indebted, however, to Todd Goehle and Shelley Rose, both of whom were, in ways too numerous to recount here, role models, colleagues, and friends.

This book would have been impossible without the tireless help of archivists. Joerg-Uwe Fischer at the Deutsches Rundfunkarchiv in Babelsberg was professional, courteous, and accommodating, to say nothing of his intellectual guidance as I first began my foray into television history. Veit

Scheller and his assistant Birgit Otto at the ZDF Unternehmensarchiv were wonderfully enthusiastic and polite, making my critical—and time-consuming—research at the ZDF a pleasurable experience. I owe a personal debt to Hans Müncheberg, both for his willingness to allow me access to a number of important files at the Archiv Müncheberg and for his own primary-source impressions of the East German television system during the 1960s. I must similarly thank Rudi Kurz for a memorable interview in which I learned more about the motivations of television producers than I often did at the archives themselves. I am also grateful to Petra Witting-Nöthen for granting me access to the Westdeutscher Rundfunk Historisches Archiv, Bernd Brettschneider for his help at the Norddeutscher Rundfunk in Hamburg, and Dethlef Arnemann for helping me sort through the NDR holdings at the Staatsarchiv Hamburg. Further thanks go to Ulf Rathje at the Bundesarchiv, the library staff at the Hochschule für Funk und Fernsehen in Babelsberg, Andreas Dan at the Deutsches Rundfunkarchiv in Frankfurt, and Jana Behrendt at the SWR in Baden-Baden.

While not technically collaborators, I would be remiss if I did not offer heartfelt thanks to the Fulbright Commission for their generous support of my research. I am likewise indebted to Irene Dingel at the Institute for European History for the opportunity to study, research, and write while in residence at the Institute's haunts in Mainz.

My colleagues at Brigham Young University have provided constant support and encouragement. Special thanks are due to Paul Kerry, Eric Dursteler, Craig Harline, Sarah Reed, Jeff Hardy, Mark Choate, Wade Jacoby, and Rob McFarland.

Many parents push and goad their children on to personal, professional, and even academic success. I am grateful to my parents for *not* pushing too hard. From a very young age, they afforded me a great deal of autonomy and agency, supporting rather than smothering, observing rather than intervening. I count their parenting philosophy among the chief reasons I found the perseverance to see this project to completion. Finally, I would like to acknowledge the deep debt I owe to my wife, Michelle. Full of candor, wit, and common sense, her contributions to this project, while they may not be directly reflected in any academic or historiographical sense, have been far-reaching.

ABBREVIATIONS

ARD	Arbeitsgemeinschaft der öffentlich-rechtlichen Rundfunkanstalten der Bundesrepublik Deutschland (Association of Public Broadcasters of the Federal Republic of Germany)
BR	Bayerischer Rundfunk (Bavarian Broadcasting)
CDU	Christlich Demokratische Union (Christian Democratic Union of Germany)
DEFA	Deutsche Film Aktiengesellschaft ([East] German Film Company)
DFF	Deutscher Fernsehfunk ([East] German Television Broadcasting)
epd	*Evangelischer Pressedienst*
FDJ	Freie Deutsche Jugend (Free German Youth)
FRG	Federal Republic of Germany (Bundesrepublik Deutschland)
GDR	German Democratic Republic (Deutsche Demokratische Republik)
HR	Hessischer Rundfunk (Hesse Broadcasting)
MfS	Ministerium für Staatssicherheit (Ministry of State Security)
NDR	Norddeutscher Rundfunk (North German Radio)
NWDR	Nordwestdeutscher Rundfunk (Northwest German Radio)
NWRV	Nord- und Westdeutscher Rundfunkverband (North and West German Broadcasting Association)
RB	Radio Bremen
SA	Sturmabteilung (Storm Division)
SDR	Süddeutscher Rundfunk (South German Radio)
SED	Sozialistische Einheitspartei Deutschlands (Socialist Unity Party of Germany)
SFB	Sender Freies Berlin (Radio Free Berlin)
SPD	Sozialdemokratische Partei Deutschlands (Social Democratic Party of Germany)
SR	Saarländischer Rundfunk (Saarland Broadcasting)
SS	Schutzstaffel (Protection Squadron)
SWF	Südwestfunk
WDR	Westdeutscher Rundfunk (West German Broadcasting)
ZDF	Zweites Deutsches Fernsehen (Second German Television)

INTRODUCTION

In 1963, Germans on both sides of the East/West divide commemorated the twenty-fifth anniversary of Carl von Ossietzky's death. Ossietzky was every bit as controversial a figure in postwar Germany as he had been in the Weimar Republic. A famous pacifist and journalist, he had exposed the Republic's clandestine attempts to remilitarize in 1931, suffered internment at the hands of the Nazis in 1933, and been awarded the Nobel Peace Prize in 1935. Many, particularly in the Federal Republic of Germany (FRG), considered Ossietzky a still-convicted traitor. Rudolf Augstein, founder and owner of *Der Spiegel*, in 1958 scathingly declared him a "Thersites . . . an evil and ugly hack . . . who could not bring himself, even in prison, to utter a word of praise for the nation."[1] He was more widely celebrated in the German Democratic Republic (GDR), but here, too, his memory was not without controversy. Publishers, for example, readily reproduced and annotated his famous articles for the left-leaning *Weltbühne*, but omitted his sharp criticisms of the Communist Party.[2] Even though he had leaned toward the political left and courageously defied National Socialism, the authorities would not allow his works to appear in print unfiltered.

Discussions about Ossietzky would remain fraught until at least the 1980s, but starting with the 1963 anniversary, a wider number of politicians and intellectuals chose to single him out for public recognition. Their reasons for doing so varied, but these events were almost universally colored by the Cold War. The GDR Peace Council, for example, created a "Carl von Ossietzky Medal" in January 1963 as a sort of analogue to the Nobel Peace

Prize for left-leaning pacifists. Notable recipients included Bertrand Russell and Wilhelm Elfes. That same month, Max Suhrbief, leader of the Liberal Democratic Party in the GDR, organized a rally for Ossietzky at his graveside in Berlin-Niederschönhausen. He used the opportunity to accuse the "reactionary [West German] state" of persecuting the working class in much the same way as it had Ossietzky.[3] In August, West German students and peace activists erected a monument to Ossietzky and other prisoners at the Esterwegen concentration camp near Oldenburg in the FRG. Local authorities refused to countenance it, however, complaining Ossietzky had been a traitor and that in any event, the vast majority of victims buried there had been common criminals.[4] Numerous revisionist biographies also appeared.[5]

Perhaps the most significant rehabilitations of Ossietzky's memory, however, were those broadcast directly to German living rooms in the form of television plays, or teleplays.[6] In September 1963, for example, the East German station Deutscher Fernsehfunk (DFF) aired a play entitled *Carl von Ossietzky*.[7] Like other East German television programs of the era, it dramatizes a large swath of the title character's adult life, depicting his initial doubts about revealing state secrets, his subsequent change of heart and heroic reporting, his cruel imprisonment in 1931, and his eventual conversion to socialism while in the concentration camp system. What differentiates this particular narrative from print biographies and commemorative speeches, however, are the visual and aural cues afforded by the medium itself. In the office of the reactionary judge who rules against the hero, for instance, the camera lingers on a bust of Otto von Bismarck, the architect of German unification and the symbol par excellence of Prussian militarism.[8] The program also features the violent suppression of a combined Social Democratic and Communist demonstration and Ossietzky sarcastically responding to police interrogations with the militaristic "Jawohl!" (Yes, sir!). Finally, the program begins and ends with a scene of Ossietzky's wife, Maud, standing in front of her husband's tombstone. In both instances, a narrator proclaims, "Everywhere else in the world, his name is held in honor. But not here."

On the one hand, these cues help advance the plot by marking certain characters as heroes (Ossietzky), villains (the judge), and victims (Maud). On the other, they serve the political concerns of the present. The association between an immoral judge and Prussian militarism aligns with the East German elites' claim that conservatism, capitalism, and fascism went hand in hand. The depicted alliance between the Social Democrats and Communists whitewashed the very real hostilities between the two parties during the Weimar period and therefore provided an after-the-fact justification for their forced merger in 1947. Ossietzky's responses to questioning dramatically underline the show's broader claim that he was a man of real conviction and courage, even under the threat of torture. The image of the grieving wife, draped in black and shedding silent tears for her dead husband, invites the viewer to consider the reasons why the title character died for his convictions. Moreover, the scene also references the present inasmuch as it was filmed at Ossietzky's actual grave in Berlin-Niederschönhausen (in East Berlin), subtly suggesting to the viewer that Ossietzky's story still matters in the ongoing struggle between communist and capitalist Germany. Indeed, at least one newspaper critic, Otto Bonhoff at the conservative *National-Zeitung* in East Berlin, noted, "*Carl von Ossietzky* might help us to recognize and master the here and today."[9]

Less than six months after the East German production aired, the West German station Norddeutscher Rundfunk (NDR) broadcast a rival play entitled *Der Prozess Carl von Ossietzky* (The trial of Carl von Ossietzky).[10] This production, as the title suggests, covers a much shorter time frame, starting with the specific events that triggered Ossietzky's arrest and trial in 1931 and culminating with his imprisonment. The bulk of the plot revolves around arguments for and against the type of hard-hitting investigative journalism that led to Ossietzky's trial. The dialogue is cerebral and nuanced; it encourages the viewer to think carefully about the philosophical and moral implications of Ossetizky's actions and whether, by implication, they could be justified in the present day. Similar to the East German version, it paints the hero as courageous and moral. When given the opportunity to leave the country before his sentencing, for example, Ossietzky elects to stay despite death threats, rocks thrown through his apartment window, and the repeated, impassioned admonitions of his colleagues. Like its counterpart, the NDR play draws a connection between Prussian militarism and National Socialism. The reactionary judge overtly lauds Hitler, and members of the audience at the official court hearing are dressed in SA uniform. It diverges, however, in other details. One otherwise conservative military officer and witness at the court proceedings makes an impassioned plea for democracy and tolerance. He declares, "Democracy isn't a bad thing . . . people can even win wars with it." This implies the pre–World War II German military system was not completely rotten; instead, it followed a common West German narrative, that National Socialism nurtured the darker aspects of German military culture. Press reviews embraced this interpretation. Contributors at the *Evangelischer Pressedienst* (*epd*), for instance, lauded the play for demonstrating the Nazis' underhanded tactics to members of the younger generation who did not personally live through the regime.[11] The largely positive response must have gratified—and perhaps surprised—the play's writers, Maria Matray and Answald Krüger, who understood their depiction of Ossietzky as a controversial political statement, framed within an at times ambivalent, at times hostile attitude toward Weimar-era resistance figures.[12]

The two dramas, so different in ideological origin and political context yet so similar in purpose, throw several important questions into sharp relief. Why had Ossietzky been transformed from traitor to hero in the public discourse? How did the two German states, with such contrasting visions of political and moral righteousness, come to valorize and commemorate the same figure? What did they have to gain from resurrecting a hero who embodied neither West nor East German ideals? And why did these changes occur in 1963/1964 and not earlier? While these questions do not lend themselves to simple answers, they speak to one of the most visible unresolved tensions of the postwar era: what to do with the Nazi past. Faced with such a catastrophe as the failed Third Reich, German intellectuals and writers heavily employed the "sick man" metaphor. They equated the nation with a diseased patient, stricken with fascism and intolerance.[13] Popular representations repeatedly invoked the image of the doctor, come to heal a physically and mentally ill nation.[14] Faced with a figurative convalescence, Germans now debated whether to reach back into the past in an attempt to restore their impressive pre-1933 (or pre-1919) culture or to reinvent their intellectual and moral world from the ground up.[15] Responses to this perceived tension varied widely, both in and between the two states. The contemporary historian Friedrich Meinecke, for one, felt much of what he termed the "German catastrophe" could be treated by rediscovering the land of Goethe and Beethoven.[16] Some West German politicians and social critics came to construct a "modernization under conservative auspices," in which intellectual, technological, and even moral progress was achieved within the context of a society skeptical of democracy itself.[17] Other conservatives, including Chancellor Konrad Adenauer and President Theodor Heuss, embraced the restoration of Western European Christendom (the *Abendland*). For them, it would be manifest as an interconfessional alliance with bourgeois underpinnings.[18] In a similar vein, many clerics and other pious Germans favored a more overt re-Christianization as the most effective antidote to Nazism.[19] Still others preferred a more grandiose, far-reaching reconstruction of German identity, memory, and morality. For instance, the left-leaning Catholic publisher of the *Frankfurter Hefte*, Walter Dirks, railed against the "vacuum" he saw in both West Germany and more broadly in Europe. This continent of "deficiency and failure," he argued, did not need nostalgia or restoration; it required a "Third Way" between Washington and Moscow.[20] Indeed, for Dirks and his frequent collaborator, the former concentration camp prisoner Eugen Kogon, nothing less than a complete reinvention of the nation and its values would suffice to purge Germany's guilt.[21]

Communist elites in the GDR publicly played down such self-criticism and soul-searching, proclaiming the bulk of former fascists now lived in the Nazi state's natural successor, the capitalist FRG. Yet, such declarations did not prevent many East Germans, ranging from high-ranking party members to average citizens, from engaging in a far-reaching discourse about their recent past and how to master it. On the one hand, intellectuals and politicians in the immediate postwar years identified, exaggerated, and celebrated left-leaning anti-Fascists. Over time, authorities began to see some of these individuals and groups as rivals and moved to trim the list of approved heroes.[22] Nevertheless, the trope of communist resistance remained a pillar of the regime's self-proclaimed legitimacy. On the other hand, the GDR cultivated an official socialist moral vision, as encapsulated in government-approved documents such as "The Ten Commandments of Socialism."[23] Such manifestos advocated normative adherence to Marxist doctrine, class consciousness, and egalitarian principles. Like elites in the FRG, then, the Sozialistische Einheitspartei Deutschlands (Socialist Unity Party of Germany—SED) and its allies explored both abstract and concrete ways to diagnose and treat Germany's condition.

These various discussions were not merely about crafting political speeches, controlling historical narratives, and manipulating commemorations, as important as these steps may have been in terms of dealing with the Nazi legacy. Many perceived the nation's deficiencies as widespread and very real. Though observers and elites in both East and West disagreed on the treatment, they agreed Germany had suffered through a fundamental, all-encompassing sickness and now needed a physician's care.[24] This book explores how such concerns played out on a moral level. The nation's buildings and infrastructure had been severely damaged, its political institutions destroyed, and its leaders humbled. But the inescapable question for all prospective rebuilders was, "How do we prevent this from happening again?" The question of restoring, reasserting, reconstructing, reformulating, and/or reinventing morality in Germany constantly loomed in the background, a common thread between conservative, liberal, socialist, and communist solutions to overcoming the Nazi past. I argue that television emerged as one of the most important mediums for presenting, discussing, and working through the question of remoralizing Germany. Popular television plays, in particular, provided an ideal platform for Germany's moral reinvention, one that easily transcended state boundaries and gave producers and writers the ability to ease viewers into a consideration of difficult, painful topics via dramatic representations. Executives, producers, and writers repeatedly privileged moral instruction over entertainment in prime-time television fiction. Viewers and critics helped shape the direction and tenor of moral representations in letters to the stations, newspaper reviews, and viewer ratings. In this atmosphere, a multivariate discourse emerged. Television fiction acted as both a pulpit and a sounding board for East and West Germans as they engaged with the Nazi past and reinvented their moral world.[25] And, despite the ideological gulf between West and East, a significant number of common post-Nazi values emerged: all agreed, for example, a good German should be tolerant, family-centered, democratic, moderate, brave, and thoughtful. The makers of German television, East and West, followed broadly similar paths to moral reinvention and renewal, even as each side's end goal, respectable liberal democratic nation in the FRG and triumphant Marxist utopia in the GDR, differed significantly.

Television was far from the first institutional response to the perceived moral vacuum left behind by the Nazis, of course; it was the heir to a long-standing, uneven rebuilding process which had many different facets. The first step in Allied denazification—purging the political structure of Nazi officials—began almost immediately after the war ended. It germinated in the offices and boardrooms of Allied commanders, continued with the Nuremberg Trials and each zone of occupation's denazification policies, and largely concluded in the consolidation of institutional power after 1949 under Konrad Adenauer in the West and Walter Ulbricht in the East, respectively. These initial processes focused mainly on high-ranking leaders, not on the rank and file, who often continued to serve in bureaucratic functions. The process of identifying and removing Nazis lost much of its focus over the next several decades; in both German states, wartime emotions and passions had become irrelevant and dangerous.[26] Memories of violence and German complicity in a program of mass murder were simply not expedient in the Cold War climate. Despite its short duration, denazification has become perhaps the most well-studied and visible symbol of how Germans overcame Nazism.[27] Another strategy for overcoming Nazism was political reeducation for the masses, which occurred frequently on both sides of the German-German divide and has likewise received a great deal of scholarly attention. Most notably, histories written during and after the cultural turn have highlighted the serious—and enduring—contributions made by cultural artifacts such as films, music, and literature on both sides of the border.[28] In the same vein, the role of youth culture in remembering and correcting the past has also come under the historian's microscope.[29] Some recent works on reconstruction have expanded the scope of analysis to include the reinvention of morality, sexuality, race, and even civilization generally.[30]

Overall, however, cultural historians have tended to treat media representations as singular examples within what they see as a broader discourse of reconstruction. Particularly juicy media products such as the films *Toxi* (1952) and *Die Mörder sind unter uns* (*Murderers Among Us*, 1946), as well as the television play *Gottes zweite Garnitur* (*The Lonely Conqueror*, 1967), to name just a few that have received scholarly attention, often appear as fodder for an article or a chapter-length case study but are usually only one component among many in the concomitant monograph.[31] In a similar vein, scholars often use television programming as a quick and easy way to explore how the masses responded to the rapid pace of social and cultural change.³² There are notable exceptions to this pattern, of course, as some well-known historical monographs employ mediatic sources (usually films) as the centerpiece of a full-length study.³³ But very few scholars—historians or otherwise—have conceptualized television fiction as a tool for reinventing the nation or as a means for grappling with and overcoming the past.³⁴ In this book, I postulate that television became much more than a mirror; it emerged as a significant agent of change in its own right.

Of course, Anglo-American cultural historians are not the only group to have studied German television through a historical lens. Television history also has a long, rich tradition within the German academy, with studies devoted to television programming from both institutional and political perspectives. Television's prominent place as a heated ideological battleground during the Cold War also (rightly) receives an enormous amount of attention. In this historiographical tradition, television from the 1950s and 1960s has been fruitfully employed in a wide variety of historiographical contexts but only rarely as a lens for examining Germans' attempts to grapple with and overcome their past. There are two possible reasons for this. First, despite the Nazis' famous attempts to popularize the medium in the 1930s, television did not become a truly mass medium in Germany until the late 1950s, at the very earliest. While American and British consumers purchased sets in droves during the late 1940s, test programming in the two German states did not begin until 1952, and regular broadcasts not before 1956 (for the most part because of technical limitations).³⁵ Chronologically speaking, television does not fit neatly into the intense 1940s debates Germans had about denazification, collective guilt, and reconstruction. It is certainly true that the tenor of these discussions had changed before viewers began snapping up sets by the millions in the early 1960s. Despite the fifteen-year interim, however, the painful German past had not disappeared. For the elites charged with producing television dramas, at least, the moral imperative to heal and rehabilitate the German nation in the wake of such crimes persisted throughout the 1950s and 1960s. From station directors such as Klaus von Bismarck, Hans Bausch, and Heinz Adameck to producers and writers such as Rudi Kurz, Helmut Sakowski, and Rolf Hädrich, television's makers conceived of their task as one of moral renewal. As I demonstrate throughout this volume, television representations from the late 1950s and 1960s reflect this overriding concern.

Furthermore, in a broader sense, television executives, producers, and writers frequently employed a terminology of newness and originality in describing the significance of their medium. Consider, for instance, the long-time Westdeutscher Rundfunk (WDR) producer Günter Rohrbach's claim that television represented a new, more sophisticated epoch in theater history, or the enthusiast Kurt Wilhelm's giddy stipulation that the medium would in fact permanently replace radio and film.[36] Günter Kaltofen, an early East German writer and enthusiast, expressed similar sentiments in his extended essay *Das Bild das deine Sprache spricht*.[37] Adolf Grimme, station director at Nordwestdeutscher Rundfunk (NWDR), even proclaimed in 1952 that television would become a panacea for Germany's broader ills.[38] The East German council over television dramas apparently agreed, stating in 1962, "It is in the first place [imperative] that our viewers be made aware, through the means of the television play, that the German Democratic Republic is the rightful German state . . . [and] that new lifestyles and ways of thinking are required." This amounted to more than a Cold War statement: producers aimed to connect the power of dramatization with the remaking of entire "lifestyles" and "ways of thinking."[39]

Television set manufacturers, too, contributed to the discourse of the new by pitching TV as a medium of the future.[40] Though difficult to quantify, this enthusiasm clearly extended to the viewing public, as conversations about television became common in both public discourse (in newspapers, on street cars, in doctors' offices) and in living rooms around the nation. What percentage of the public owned a set? Figures for the West German criminal thriller *Das Halstuch* (The scarf, 1962) are instructive.[41] WDR estimated more than 90 percent of the existing West German television sets tuned into the last three episodes of the series.[42] Following a formula developed concurrently in both East and West, one television set accounted for approximately three people during the evening hours.[43] There were 8.5 million registered television sets in West Germany at the time, which means that if these numbers are reasonably accurate, more than twenty-three million West Germans had tuned in.[44] This does not account for unregistered sets, East German viewers (there were roughly three million registered sets in the GDR in 1962), or the strong possibility that more than three viewers were watching any given set on this particular evening. However, given a West German population of around fifty-seven million, this means more than 40 percent of the population tuned in, even though there was only one set for every seven people. To give a sense of how quickly television ownership rose during the period in question, according to the GDR statistical almanacs, the number of authorized sets in the East soared from 70,607 in 1956 to almost 4.5 million in 1970 (Appendix 3). Given the medium's huge popularity with the masses and its perceived importance among political, intellectual, and even church elites, television occupied an important intersection between institutional and cultural rebuilding efforts.

Such rhetoric of course did not mean television was the first dramatic medium that attempted to educate or instruct the masses. Friedrich Schiller, for instance, crafted many of his famous plays as concrete examples of what he saw as a basis for the moral enlargement of the individual.[45] The cinema (and theater) of the late imperial period and the Weimar Republic continued this tradition, and German-produced films often differed starkly from their Hollywood counterparts in that they offered deeper moral and aesthetic instruction. In some ways responding to cultural critics such as Franz Pfemfert, who warned of cinema's potential "soullessness" and lack of imagination but also extolled its potential to educate and enhance, filmmakers in Germany crafted didactic, thought-provoking pieces such as *Tagebuch einer Verlorenen* (*Diary of a Lost Girl*, 1929), *Die Geächteten* (The Outlaws, 1919), and *M* (1931).[46] Despite some initial resistance, social critics and educators in turn came to expect cinema to refine the nation's tastes and moral sensibilities. Radio plays had likewise long reflected German media's implicit mandate to combine dramatic tension, entertainment, and education, from Bertolt Brecht's *Mann ist Mann* (*Man Equals Man*, 1926) to Wolfgang Borchert's *Draußen vor der Tür* (*The Man Outside*, 1947).[47] Television should thus be understood as the heir to an older, broader tradition of didactic theater unique to Germany, and later extended to cinema and radio. The latter media forms, however, had been tainted by association with National Socialism. Well-known radio play writers such as Günter Eich had tailored their programs to the Nazis' ideological agenda.[48] Conservative voices criticized radio for "intellectual emptiness" and for an undesirable "mechanization of culture."[49] Likewise, many German elites now understood the film industry, which remained a highly successful and profitable institution after the war, as somewhat suspect. Regulators and censors saw "unregulated film as potentially more dangerous than radio or the press to German reconstruction because of its visual immediacy and potent appeal to certain 'vulnerable' sectors of the population."[50] National Socialist propagandists had made heavy use of the medium in the 1930s, and, within the discourse of reconstruction and renewal, this rendered it problematic.[51]

While authorities in the Third Reich had little trouble harnessing radio and cinema in their propaganda efforts, they were unable to tap into television as a foundational mass medium. When commercial electronic television first seemed viable in the 1930s, Joseph Goebbels insisted Germany should take advantage. Hitler lent his support to the project, and by 1935, the Nazis had found the necessary personnel and technical capacity to start test programming.[52] Despite their leaders' grand vision, however, the Nazis found themselves limited by technical constraints. Prohibitive costs and a lack of infrastructure meant the regime could establish only a few dozen television parlors in Berlin. This setting attracted a relatively large number of viewers for the 1936 Olympics, but viewership beyond this event never amounted to much. Moreover, a directive from the Führer himself soon placed the entire industry under the command of the air force, which wanted to develop the new broadcasting technology for military purposes. Very few individuals purchased sets in the late 1930s, and during the war, television functioned almost exclusively as a way to keep wounded soldiers in Berlin up to speed with events on the front.[53] Because it never achieved widespread popularity, then, television did not figure among the media requiring reform and restructuring after 1945. This does not mean, however, that its creators and enthusiasts failed to see its potential for renewing and reviving the nation; indeed, its very status as something new and fresh made it an ideal engine for reformulating Germany's moral compass. At the same time, a small set of dissenting voices in the 1960s saw television as a potentially detrimental innovation, with one describing it as a "Trojan horse" containing crass materialism that could be inserted directly into the German living room.[54] However, such criticism, usually originating in church circles, was relatively rare in West Germany until the 1970s and almost entirely nonexistent (at least in any public forum) in the East. Earlier postwar criticisms about radio's intellectual deficiencies do not seem to have been made about television when it appeared a decade later. The consensus surrounding television's potential as a moral medium may not have been absolute, but it was strong.

A second possible reason that historians have not often contextualized television as part of the postwar moral or intellectual rebuilding process is that older grand narratives about the trajectory of collective memory after 1945 emphasized the 1950s and early 1960s as a period of relative cultural silence. This narrative traces its origins to the 1968 student protests and found wide currency among scholars until the late 1990s.[55] This view is no longer fashionable, however. Cultural anxieties about returning POWs, the resurgence of consumer culture, and, by the early 1960s, the appearance of southern European guest workers (reminiscent of forced labor during the war) manifested themselves in newspaper editorials, election rallies, radio discussion programs, and even some films. Far from a memory wasteland of *Heimatfilme* and lederhosen, the period between the late 1940s and the early 1960s saw the persistence of postwar dilemmas and uncertainties. Contemporaries viewed television as a new, exciting medium but also as much more than a novel curiosity or as an extension of the rising culture of consumption. They saw television, which never caught on as the public form of consensus-building the Nazis had intended, as an ideal means by which to complete the process of rehabilitation and reconstruction. Television enthusiasts, including members of the station directorates, proclaimed television could simultaneously provide a "window on the world" and a carefully regulated fulcrum for domestic and civic morals.[56] Accordingly, the two German governments earmarked funds for the medium well ahead of the first broadcasting dates, and producers on both sides spent considerable time and effort crafting their own programs (rather than merely acquiring licenses for American or Soviet productions). To be sure, television's pioneers in Germany recognized entertainment and relaxation would play a prominent role as well. Right as television began to emerge as a truly mass medium in 1960, for example, 33 percent of West German programming hours consisted of entertainment (*Unterhaltung*) and sports. Television dramas, documentaries, and films, which could be both entertaining and instructive, made up 31 percent, various types of news broadcasts 14 percent, children's and women's programs 15 percent, and religious programs 1 percent.[57] An overview of programming for the same year in the GDR yields similar numbers: entertainment and sports accounted for 31 percent of the total; dramas, documentaries, and films 36 percent; children's programs 11 percent; and news programs 16 percent.[58] Such statistics demonstrate television existed to serve a broad range of interests and tastes. Two types of programs, however, dominated both the station budget and viewership shares: variety shows (a staple of early television across the globe) and television plays.

The parallel development of original, innovative, didactic dramas on both sides of the German-German border went beyond a merely structural resemblance; despite the glaring ideological differences between the two sides, East and West German programs often spoke to the same moral issues and themes. From addressing gender inequality and racism to fretting about materialism and political apathy, these productions often featured a common denominator. One of the chief aims of this book is to relate and explain the striking thematic similarities between the two sets of programs. I argue that German television fiction from this era needs to be understood as part of a common, German-wide discourse. Moreover, this discourse encompassed much more than an antagonistic set of attacks and counterattacks. Many representations advanced moral lessons independent of the Cold War struggle. Such a reevaluation of German television history is the natural result of the broader historiographical trend toward nuanced, relational histories of the early Cold War. Historians no longer assume a binary, antagonistic relationship between the two states.[59] They also recognize that even the most ideologically intransigent members of the two regimes, East and West, did not perceive of the German-German divide as permanent.[60] While the amount of scholarship that examines transborder trends during the Cold War has expanded, few studies to date have attempted to compare East and West German television programs, perhaps because they operated under such divergent systematic constraints. In the GDR, the state assumed full authority for the creation and distribution of television programming, largely operating as a centralized system. Authorities reserved their tightest censorship for news broadcasts and documentaries, but teleplays attracted attention as well. They borrowed technology and equipment from the Soviet Union, but only occasionally looked to the East for guidance on programming. In the FRG, television followed a heavily decentralized, public service model. Here, writers and producers worked for regional stations (e.g., in Hamburg or Stuttgart), and each station was allowed broadcasting slots on the national channel. In this relatively unique system, producers sometimes looked to other European and even American stations for guidance on technological standards and to help fill some morning and afternoon slots with syndicated content; nonetheless, West German television, as in the East, largely followed its own path and created German-specific content.

Heretofore, most historical analyses of German television have mirrored the reality of the division between East and West. Two of the most expansive projects in German television history—the Deutsche Forschungsgemeinschaft (German Research Foundation—DFG) Sonderforschungsbereich 240, a 1990s research node that produced monographs and edited volumes on various aspects of West German television history, and the more recent DFG Forschungsgruppe Programmgeschichte des DDR-Fernsehens, which systematically (often statistically) catalogued and interpreted East German television programs and their viewers—demonstrate the separateness of the audiences, ideological assumptions, and archival structures of the two systems. Some scholars have demonstrated the weak points in this narrative, in terms of both cross-border institutional exchange and similarities in viewer tastes.[61]

These common tastes were not coincidental; many viewers on both sides of the divide could watch the other state's programs. Of course, this is not to imply every viewer in the two German states could receive all German signals. The almost legendary Tal der Ahnungslosen ("Valley of the Clueless") in the southern GDR, an area in which television viewers, for technical reasons, could not receive either West German channel, certainly existed. But some have argued the cultural and social effects of this "isolation" have been greatly exaggerated.[62] More importantly, there is abundant evidence that East Germans watched West German television, and, in a phenomenon that has not been given enough attention by historians, West Germans *could*, and frequently *did*, watch East German shows.[63] This ensured a relational development in the rise of moral television, even as the two systems competed for the hearts and minds of the German public. Producers, aware of the concurrent programs, copied examples from the other state. The popular DFF program *Gewissen in Aufruhr* (Conscience up in arms, 1961, see chap. 1), for example, was a direct reaction to the West German *So weit die Füße tragen* (As far as your feet can carry you, 1959). Perhaps even more telling, the DFF four-part program *Wolf unter Wölfen* (*Wolf among Wolves*, 1964), adapted from a Hans Fallada novel of the same name, achieved viewer and critical success in both the East, where DFF produced it, and the West, where Zweites Deutsches Fernsehen (ZDF) broadcast it three years later despite a general boycott against GDR programs.[64] Viewers and critics fawned over the excellent acting and objective depictions in *Wolf unter Wölfen*, ignoring the fact that it had been produced in an ostensibly tainted Eastern studio.[65] In fact, one critic went so far as to say, "To boycott such artistic films, television plays, or documentaries is—there is no better word—immoral and culture-hating."[66]

Another example of the way television transcended state boundaries can be seen in the way viewers wrote letters to the other side's stations. One viewer in the GDR who sent his letter to Sender Freies Berlin (SFB) through two other Eastern cities to escape detection by the authorities commented, as any other "Western" viewer might, that while they really liked the film *Der Teufel spielt Balalaika* (*Until Hell Is Frozen*, 1961), it would have been better if the Russian dialogue had been translated into German.[67] Other letters to SFB spoke to the political situation more directly but did not necessarily agree with the GDR's position. One viewer from an unidentified village noted "more than 75 percent of all the villagers here watch Western television," a statement that clearly demonstrates sympathy for the FRG.[68] But he follows up this observation with a somewhat less political request: "Please change the dance programs to Sunday afternoon. I especially like westerns and criminal thrillers." Viewers in the East seem to have felt a sense of ownership over Western television despite the political barriers. A similar trans-state dynamic existed among Western viewers who watched East German programs. One viewer wrote to DFF: "Keep it up. That should assure all of you that you are also gladly heard and seen beyond your state's borders."[69] This and similar West German letters, occasionally cited in DFF's internal report *Der Fernsehzuschauer* (The television viewer), sent a clear message to the East German producers: if you make quality programs, we will watch them.[70] Viewers had diverse reasons for writing to the "enemy" state's broadcasters, including political consternation, pleas for a respite from dictatorship, and simple entertainment. But the fact that they wrote at all suggests a television culture that transcended state boundaries. And write they did, in surprisingly large numbers. SFB preserved fifty to one hundred letters from the East per year, receiving many more but not keeping them because of content repetition, while the other West German stations seem to have received (though not necessarily preserved) even more, especially in Cologne and Hamburg.[71] These are not huge numbers, but given the difficulty in getting a letter across the border, especially to such a conspicuous institution as a television station (SFB) whose very existence seemed to depend on the continued desire of the West German government to destabilize the GDR, these sources are highly significant.

More visible instances of trans-state exchange also occurred at the institutional level. With *Irrlicht und Feuer* (Ghost light and fire, 1966), for example, DFF's decision to use a non-Communist, contemporary West German author's (Max von der Grün) work as the basis for a prime-time drama seemed a controversial decision. However, *Irrlicht und Feuer* became an instant success with viewers.[72] When officials saw how the program incited nonparty viewers to heap criticism on the West, they quickly moved to appropriate it, including it among the "highlights" of an already highlight-strewn summer.[73] Then, in 1968, Südwestfunk (SWF) bought the rights to broadcast the program in a West German primetime slot. This broadcast, which drew a moderate number of viewers (it was unfavorably paired with a popular ZDF game show, so it had little chance of reaching the 80 percent level commanded by the most popular plays, such as the aforementioned beloved criminal thrillers), drew a +3 qualitative rating, an outstanding number considering the controversial subject matter and Western viewers' general distaste for overtly modernist, avant-garde pieces. Critics also embraced the program.[74] Even after the SWF event, letters continued to pour in from both East and West asking for a rebroadcast.[75] The popularity of *Irrlicht und Feuer* affords a glimpse into television-viewing habits and tastes, which clearly transcended political barriers and taboos. What constituted a "good" teleplay had more to do with the values and morals that viewers and critics in each state had in common than with those that were different.

As SWF's apparent autonomy in the purchase of *Irrlicht und Feuer* demonstrates, the notion of two distinct "sides" in Cold War–era German television is fundamentally flawed. Because of fundamental differences in the four postwar occupation zones, the reality of the Cold War, and the persistence of the dream of unification, German television developed in a unique—and highly confusing—manner. In 1945, the four Allied occupiers repurposed the old state-run radio broadcasting facilities as instruments of their own propaganda campaigns. From the start, the organizational structure among the four zones varied wildly. The Soviets created a highly centralized, state-dependent broadcaster. The British and French, after the model of the BBC, likewise established single stations within their respective zones (NWDR and SWF). Unlike the Russians, however, they disassociated their respective broadcasting stations from the state. The Americans, in contrast to the other powers, decided to seed multiple, independent stations: Radio Bremen (RB), Hessischer Rundfunk (HR), Bayerischer Rundfunk (BR), and Süddeutscher Rundfunk (SDR).[76] This aligned with some early advisers' vision of a decentralized Germany. By 1948, control over these stations had been largely transferred to German authorities, even before the foundation of the Federal Republic of Germany and the German Democratic Republic. After the Berlin Airlift of 1948/1949, it became clear that two distinct states would coexist for the foreseeable future. With a united anti-communist front in mind, the Americans had agreed German radio should follow the British model of public service broadcasting, rather than the Americans' favored commercial system. But the Allies insisted the stations should be kept separate from the state institutions; to ensure this, they made it clear that continued decentralization was a precondition of German ownership over broadcasting facilities.[77] As a result, smaller stations from the American zone, like RB, operated alongside much larger broadcasters, like the enormous NWDR. Over time, two new organizations joined their ranks: Saarländischer Rundfunk (SR), created in 1947 but transferred to the FRG after a 1955 referendum firmly established the Saarland region as part of West Germany, and SFB, established in the divided city of Berlin in 1953. In 1956, NWDR split into two stations: Norddeutscher Rundfunk, seated in Hamburg, and Westdeutscher Rundfunk, centered in Cologne. This network of regional stations, so divergent in origin and size, would eventually assume responsibility for introducing television in the FRG.

While following a mirrored timeline in terms of inception and growth, radio broadcasters were never assigned primary responsibility for creating television in the Soviet zone. The East German government itself, under direction from Moscow, began preparing for television in 1948. They envisioned this new project as an extension of the inter-German struggle for territory and influence. For SED authorities, television was first and foremost a technical challenge. As such, it fell to the postal service to first conceptualize and administer the nascent medium. As Heather Gumbert has argued, this attitude toward television meant writers and producers of fictional programming enjoyed considerable creative autonomy, in sharp contrast to other artists in the GDR.[78] Over the course of the 1960s, and in no small part as a result of ideological heterogeneity in the rapidly expanding genre of television fiction, the SED moved to corral and eventually instrumentalize television.[79] Even with the end of such autonomy, however, DFF continued to produce vibrant and sometimes unorthodox programs throughout the Ulbricht era (which lasted until 1971). For example, various aspects of bourgeois morality—the nuclear family, consumer culture, and frugal living—coexisted with and even complemented Marxist ideology.[80] The protagonist's extramarital affair in the well-publicized *Sommer in Heidkau* (Summer in Heidkau, 1964), for instance, sparked a backlash among both viewers *and* members of the SED's inner circle. Moreover, the SED appropriated the bourgeois imperative of order and the rule of law by using print media to disseminate the notion that crime rates had decreased under socialism and that this trend would inevitably continue.[81] Multipart epic teleplays such as *Gewissen in Aufruhr* and *Geboren untern schwarzen Himmeln* (Born under black skies, 1962) reinforced this objective by visualizing prewar and wartime criminality and then offering an orderly, sanitized version of the same locations, now accustomed to a positive Marxist influence.[82]

The West German government did not directly control the broadcasting industry; nonetheless, directors at the largest station, NWDR, in consultation with British occupation authorities, began preparing the way for television in 1948 by creating task forces and purchasing technical equipment. The other radio stations followed suit. In 1950, an FRG-wide work group known as the Arbeitsgemeinschaft der öffentlich-rechtlichen Rundfunkanstalten der Bundesrepublik Deutschland (Association of Public Broadcasters of the Federal Republic of Germany—ARD) agreed that television should be a national institution, that they should begin with a single channel, and that airtime should be shared by prearrangement among the regional stations (see Appendix 2 for a diagram illustrating the relationship between the various West German stations). Test programming in both East and West began in 1952. By the mid-1950s, West Germany's economy and infrastructure had largely recovered from the ravages of the war. Konrad Adenauer, the FRG's chancellor and a hugely popular conservative figure, favored an American (commercial) model for television. When it became clear he could not reverse the radio stations' decision to pattern their new TV station after the BBC, he attempted to drum up support for a second television station, controlled by the federal government instead of the radio stations and their allies, the state governments. His "Deutschland-Fernsehen," later incorporated as "Freies Fernsehen GmbH," found considerable support among German companies but was fiercely opposed by the existing stations and the Social Democrats.[83] A famous Constitutional Court decision in 1960 put an end to Adenauer's vision, declaring that only the existing stations had the authority to create a second channel. In 1963, the state governments and ARD gave life to ZDF, similarly a public service broadcaster but providing a contrast to the first channel.

Together, the German stations produced more than three thousand teleplays between 1956, the start of regular daily programming in both East and West, and 1970, the last year before sharp funding decreases (a result of a recession in the West and changing viewer tastes in both states) affected dramatic programming both in East Germany and at ZDF. This sheer number attests to the popularity of television plays in the 1950s and 1960s. It also makes it difficult for historians to offer a comprehensive survey of the types of themes, tropes, and moral lessons that appeared during this time. Some studies have approached this issue by employing quantitative methods.[84] While extremely valuable to future researchers, such explanations tend to group programs and themes according to predetermined, superficial categories. In this model, the researcher typically relies on definitions offered by the writers and producers themselves. This approach foregoes the opportunity to explore the nuances of each production in greater detail. Quantitative analyses therefore exclude discussions about any given play's mise-en-scène, its particular use of image and sound, and the actors' ability to shape and redirect the piece's underlying meaning by means of inflection and subtle cues. Other studies offer a corrective to this by employing a fine-grained, qualitative approach.[85] Here, the scholar typically offers a close reading of one or two programs, which, in turn, either correspond to or offer a surprising contrast to other productions from the same era. The weakness here is that a qualitative study might not be particularly representative of what viewers are consuming as a whole. Any given program might be an anomaly.

If plotted on the continuum between these two poles (quantitative and qualitative), my approach in this book falls closer to the latter. Nevertheless, inasmuch as this book discusses a wide variety of dramas, it aims to be more comprehensive than a set of case studies. I focus primarily on productions that resonated most deeply with the viewing public. In purchasing a television set and paying a compulsory annual tax, many viewers demonstrated a certain commitment toward or investment in the new medium. Advertising brought little revenue, and, particularly in the early years, families might well have decided *not* to purchase a set and pay the tax if they did not approve of the programming. But the notion of viewer investment can be seen even more clearly in how they assessed specific programs. In 1962, for example, the WDR production *Das Halstuch* aired in the West. A six-part mystery series by the British author Francis Durbridge, *Das Halstuch* captivated a huge percentage of the German population; more than 90 percent of all existing television sets were tuned in to the last three episodes of the series. When the actor Wolfgang Neuss prematurely revealed the identity of the murderer in a newspaper interview, he unleashed a "storm of indignation" in the FRG.[86] Strong negative reactions to particular programs also show the high level of viewer investment, such as the angry West German letters sent to the NDR about the avant-garde drama *Schlachtvieh* (*Lambs to the Slaughter*, 1963) and the equally vicious response to the experimental East German opera film *Fetzers Flucht* (Fetzer's flight, 1962, see chap. 2).

Indeed, response letters provide a particularly valuable source of information about viewers' preferences and expectations. As noted earlier, each station received thousands of letters a year.[87] Unfortunately, many of the letters to West German stations were destroyed. Some have been preserved in regional archives and a select few in the Deutsches Rundfunkarchiv (German Broadcasting Archive), an institution that has locations in Babelsberg (for the now defunct DFF) and in Frankfurt (for the ARD). However, stations only started diligently filing and preserving these letters in the 1970s, and there are few extant viewer letters from the 1950s and 1960s. They are referenced in official documents, but such reports rarely reveal much about the letters' specific content. Moreover, obtaining access to such documents at West German archives is extremely difficult, in part because of the decentralized nature of the ARD, in part because the institutions have chosen to restrict large numbers of documents to internal users only.[88] The situation on the East German side is similarly frustrating, but for different reasons. Michael Meyen, who has studied DFF viewer information extensively, notes, "Opinion research in the GDR was embedded in the ideological monopoly of the SED and was subject to the politics of the day."[89] Thus, the number of letters preserved by the stations at the time depended more on political expediency than on the resonance the program actually had among viewers. Even setting aside the problem of preservation and station politics, it is unclear to what extent the letters—on either side of the Wall—can be seen as representative of the viewing public. Because they are unsolicited (unlike the responses collected by ratings agencies), they may well reflect a particular agenda or concern. To give one small example of this, the overwhelming majority of letters surviving for *Gottes zweite Garnitur* are fan letters, requesting contact information for the charismatic lead, Jimmy Powell (an African American actor who had trained in Vienna before taking the ZDF job, his first major role). Moreover, the archives preserve very little in terms of demographic data. Some records reproduce the writers' names and mailing addresses, but other potentially useful information such as age, political affiliation, and so on is impossible to divine unless the writers mention it themselves.

Nonetheless, viewer letters, as well as opinions collected by television correspondents, provide valuable glimpses into the programs viewers preferred; in some cases, responses even forced the East Germans to collect viewer data after the fact. The DFF multipart series *Dr. Schlüter* (1965), for instance, became one of the most popular television broadcasts of the decade—and it caught the authorities completely by surprise. Letters that probably would have otherwise been destroyed were preserved and even bound together in a self-congratulatory book circulated among the station executives. Clearly, viewers took their viewing experiences seriously, and those plays that elicited a strong public reaction (positive or negative) are included in this study.

Anecdotal evidence and small sets of viewer letters are not the only ways to gauge viewer participation, however. Though inconsistently gathered and in many ways incomplete, ratings statistics and social scientific surveys about viewing preferences are largely untapped gold mines for television historians. Starting in 1963, for example, the two West German channels (ARD and ZDF) contracted a private company called Infratest GmbH to collect viewer statistics and data.[90] Infratest monitored every program during the evening, using both quantitative (Infratam) and qualitative (Infratest) measuring sticks. The former was merely a percentage of the total number of viewers, taken from a sampling of one thousand installed machines that reported back to Infratest every five minutes. The latter assigned a rating between −10 (low) and +10 (high) to every program based on six hundred viewers' responses. In addition, the Infratest portion of the report included a sampling of comments made at the time of the survey, designed to give decision-makers a more nuanced feel for how audiences felt about the show, along with Infratest's own interpretation of the data. Though this method of collecting data seems inadequate by today's standards, Infratest continued using this system until 1974, and it evoked little criticism until after 1970.[91] In the East, too, authorities collected information about how many people tuned in to each program. This was never as systematic as in the West, and there are significant gaps in the late 1950s and early 1960s. For the purposes of deciding which programs to look at more closely in this volume, however, these gaps and silences are perhaps just as significant as the actual numbers. Authorities assigned special significance to and collected data for certain programs. Advertising for these select productions began weeks, sometimes even months, ahead of the actual broadcast date(s). This in turn doubtless led to heightened viewer anticipation and reactions (exceptions such as *Dr. Schlüter* notwithstanding).

Television critics, writing chiefly in newspapers, magazines, and other print publications, also invested themselves in dramatic productions. Some critics, especially in the smaller daily newspapers (both West and East) and in the Springer publication *Hörzu*, aligned themselves with what they felt were the entertainment demands of viewers. One excellent example of this is a *Bild-Zeitung* critique of the 1970 ZDF criminal thriller *11 Uhr 20* (11:20), in which the comments of a variety of viewers, including even the show's director, Wolfgang Becker (though these were seemingly taken out of context), offer the same criticism: the show was "boring."[92] Such commentators gave special attention to criminal thrillers, especially those written by the English author Francis Durbridge, and expressed their likes or dislikes according to criteria such as novelty, surprise, and excitement. Larger daily newspapers like the *Süddeutsche Zeitung*, the *Frankfurter Allgemeine Zeitung*, and, on the East German side, *Neues Deutschland* emphasized artistic and aesthetic innovations. These critics thought television stations had a mandate to produce intellectually stimulating material and that viewers had a right to expect educational, thought-provoking dramas.[93] Finally, the *epd—Kirche und Fernsehen*, published by the Protestant *Evangelischer Pressedienst*, and the *Funk-Korrespondenz*, a Catholic trade publication, based their assessments on both intellectual and moral criteria. Sometimes the commentaries in the two church-related papers openly decried moral degradation and promoted the positive influence of Christianity, but normally the two church publications carefully embedded moral observations in intellectual or aesthetic critiques.[94] As the complex patchwork of newspaper reviewers neatly demonstrates, television spoke to a broad, heterogeneous set of viewers. Because of this, the societal critiques advanced by the writers and producers of teleplays, responding as they did to the critics' reactions, often exhibited substantial complexity and nuance.[95]

While multifaceted, the project of moral reinvention through television fiction did follow particular themes. Some of these topics, moreover, transcended the German-German divide. The five chapters in this book correspond with what I see as the most prominent themes that received substantial attention in both the FRG and the GDR. The first chapter focuses on representations of the Nazi era, from Wehrmacht soldiers and collaborators to rescuers and victims during the Holocaust. The purpose and tenor of representations varied, but in general, they served the needs of the present: marginalizing Nazi perpetrators as exceptional, and constructing heroes by displaying the valor and/or courage in resisting the regime and its crimes. A few programs broke this mold by challenging the "resistance" narrative or by complicating viewers' relationship with the past, but in large measure, fictional dramatic programs that provided instruction on the past did so as a way to justify the present, whether communist or liberal democratic. Chapter 1 explores the rationale behind this decision, as well as the voices of dissent that would eventually find greater expression in the wake of the 1968 student uprisings.

Chapter 2 examines televisual lessons on politics and morality. From the start, German elites on both sides of the border recognized the need for political reorientation and reeducation in the wake of the Nazi dictatorship. As television matured into a mass medium, bringing popular dramatic programming into viewers' living rooms, concerned producers and decision-makers such as Klaus von Bismarck, Heinz Adameck, and Christian Geißler invested heavily in moral-political programs. East German citizens learned about the evils of the FRG—the pseudo-democratic heir to the Third Reich—and the origins of a unified Socialist Party that could represent all workers' interests. West Germans watched as, for example, East German border guards were forced to shoot their fleeing comrades. In both states, programs promoted abstract ideals such as democracy and civil society, as well as more specific responses to political oppression, such as daring escapes across the border and quixotic struggles against the "other" German regime. These programs indoctrinated viewers on Cold War politics, but they also provided a platform for overcoming Nazi attitudes about the state.

Historical and political reeducation were perhaps the most obvious solutions to the moral wasteland left behind by the Nazis, but they were by no means the only fronts. In Chapter 3, I examine anti-materialist efforts in the two German states. In the West, the major churches, Catholic and Protestant, had been enmeshed in broadcasting institutions and politics since the Allies allowed stations to restart radio programming in 1946. The stations allotted significant airtime for church broadcasts, and, even more significantly, clerics and laymen from both confessions sat on station advisory boards, advocating church-approved programs and occasionally censoring material they considered objectionable. The intersection between the churches and public service broadcasting in the FRG constitutes a vast, underexplored site of postwar rebuilding, cultural change, and political contestation. This site was by no means homogeneous, and leaders did not always agree on which themes, tropes, or strategies to pursue. However, one topic runs like a red thread through the church representatives' plans and, more broadly stated, through FRG broadcasting as a whole: the relentless battle against materialism and worldliness. Decision-making bodies at each of the stations, under the sometimes subtle, sometimes overt influence of church bishops and authorities, conflated general postwar fears about rising materialism with what they saw as the hedonism and moral depravity of the Nazi era. This became even more imperative after the start of the economic miracle (1948–1966). Other strategies for reestablishing the Christian milieus, such as the Ruhr Valley industrialists' apprenticeship system, had proved ineffective.[96] Television, the emergent mass medium of the mid-twentieth century, became an important arena for corrective West German representations of anti-materialist values such as frugality, restraint, and even religiosity. Ironically, television plays in the FRG sometimes even included the television set itself as part of the problematic culture of materialism.[97] East German producers, ever mindful of DFF's ability to broadcast in the West (and of their own citizens' knowledge of West Germany's superior economy), similarly crafted moral lessons on materialism, often loosely rooted in Marxism but likewise sensitizing viewers to nonmaterialist modes of happiness. Religion played a more minor role here, but, despite vastly disparate ideological foundations and goals, the two sides employed strikingly similar tropes.

Chapter 4 looks at the reformulation and reinvention of gender norms. The Third Reich's defeat had left German masculine ideals and stereotypes, based heavily on aggression and militarism, in tatters. Moreover, women began to enter the workplace in large numbers, particularly in the East (where the regime, seeking to shore up its legitimacy, forged an uneasy partnership with women).[98] This situation raised the question of women's equality. Television fiction stepped in to address these perceived issues with new role models and ideal behaviors. Other gendered concerns, such as family relations, raising children, and the proper limitation of (especially female) sexuality also featured heavily. Authorities certainly never reached any kind of consensus on gender politics, a fact reflected by the colorful variety of programs during the 1950s and (especially) the 1960s, which present heterogeneous visions of gender relations.

Finally, in chapter 5, I explore the issue of race and ethnicity in postwar Germany. A central platform of the Nazi *Volksgemeinschaft* (people's community) had been the exclusion of non-Germans and minority groups such as homosexuals, Jehovah's Witnesses, and the "work-shy." Despite the ambiguous and dubious nature of Nazi racial categories and laws, most Germans adopted some level of prejudice and approved of the separation of Aryans and non-Aryans. These attitudes, as television authorities knew full well, persisted after the war ended. A major task of moral rebuilding, then, particularly in an era of guest workers, political reconciliation, and Europeanization, was overcoming racist attitudes. Television plays sometimes provided viewers with strong non-German protagonists, but more commonly, they presented progressive, anti-racist versions of tolerance and acceptance.

Notes

1. Jens Daniel (one of Augstein's pseudonyms), "Er spricht nicht mit Thersites," *Der Spiegel* 26, 25 June 1958.
2. Franz Baumer, *Carl von Ossietzky* (Berlin: Colloquium Verlag, 1984), 10.
3. Ruth Greuner and Reinhart Greuner, *Ich stehe links: Carl von Ossietzky über Geist und Ungeist der Weimarer Republik* (Berlin: Buchverlag der Morgen, 1963), 44–45.
4. Elke Suhr, *Carl von Ossietzky: Eine Biographie* (Cologne: Kiepenheuer & Witsch, 1988), 17.
5. Kurt R. Grossmann, *Ossietzky: Ein deutscher Patriot* (Berlin: Kindler, 1963); Greuner and Greuner, *Ich stehe links*.
6. The usual translations for *Fernsehspiel*, "television play" or "teleplay," respectively connote a stage play and a screenplay in modern American English usage. But while some of these television programs adapted material from the theater, none were actually performed on stage. More closely akin to films, but not the same as the "made-for-TV-movie" introduced by NBC in 1964, the German *Fernsehspiel* (some critics and authors preferred the term *Fernsehfilm*) constitutes a unique genre. Television consciously aimed to promote itself as a separate artistic category from film, and some techniques from the early experimental days remained ensconced even as the *Fernsehspiel* started to technologically resemble cinema. The *Fernsehspiel* was shorter than a standard film, the actors' faces occupied a much larger percentage of the screen, and many productions were broken up into multiple episodes.
7. Lothar Creutz, Carl Andrießen, and Günter Kaltofen, *Carl von Ossietzky*, dir. Richard Groschopp (DFF, 1 September 1963). Appendix 1 contains a list of all the television plays referenced in this book, organized chronologically and by station.
8. In the 1980s, the East German regime would move to appropriate Bismarck's legacy as part of the broader German socialist tradition (as well as other figures such as Martin Luther). In the 1960s, however, Bismarck remained something of a villain, in stark contrast to celebrated cultural "heroes" such as Goethe and Schilling. See Alan L. Nothnagle, *Building the East German Myth: Historical Mythology and Youth Propaganda*

in the German Democratic Republic, 1945–1989 (Ann Arbor: University of Michigan Press, 1999), 187–188.
9. Otto Bonhoff, "Jahre eines wunderbaren Lebens," *National-Zeitung* (14 August 1963).
10. Maria Matray and Answald Krüger, *Der Prozess Carl von Ossietzky*, dir. John Olden (NDR, 11 February 1964).
11. *epd—Kirche und Fernsehen* 7, 15 February 1964, 11.
12. See the May 1963 letter from the writers to the director in the Staatsarchiv Hamburg, NDR 621-1 144 1060, "Carl von Ossietzky." Matray and Krüger worried conservative voices would take issue with their decision to valorize such a divisive figure. The question of Ossietzky's legacy was indeed long contested in the Federal Republic, as evidenced by a 1992 court decision to uphold his conviction. Large has shown that West German rejection of resistance groups and figures was not at all uncommon, especially in the 1950s. See David Clay Large, "'A Beacon in the German Darkness': The Anti-Nazi Resistance Legacy in West German Politics," *Journal of Modern History* 64, Supplement (1992): 174.
13. Kapczynski has extensively traced the genesis of this trope, in the National Socialists' obsession with biology and in its development after the war. Intellectuals as diverse as Karl Jaspers, Friedrich Meinecke, Thomas Mann, and Bertolt Brecht gave voice to the metaphor, and it remained popular for decades. The imagery found currency in so many circles because it simultaneously conveyed the notion that something was terribly wrong with the German body and, at the same time, absolved the nation from any real guilt, infected as it was with a foreign disease (National Socialism). See Jennifer M. Kapczynski, *The German Patient Crisis and Recovery in Postwar Culture* (Ann Arbor: University of Michigan Press, 2008), 22–23, 27.
14. Most notably in Wolfgang Staudte's *Murderers Among Us* (1946), Thomas Mann's *Doctor Faustus* (1943), and Peter Lorre's *The Lost One* (1951).
15. Or they resisted the polarizing restoration-reinvention discussion by pragmatically harnessing previous cultural patrimonies to a "counter-elitist political vision." Sean Forner, "Reconsidering the 'Unpolitical German,' Democratic Renewal and the Politics of Culture in Occupied Germany," *German History* 32, no. 1 (2014): 76–78.
16. Friedrich Meinecke, *Die deutsche Katastrophe* (Zürich: Brockhaus, 1946), 170.
17. Christoph Kleßmann, "Ein stolzes Schiff, und krächzende Möwen: Die Geschichte der Bundesrepublik und ihre Kritiker," *Geschichte und Gesellschaft* 4 (1985): 480; Axel Schildt, *Zwischen Abendland und Amerika Studien zur westdeutschen Ideenlandschaft der 50er Jahre* (Munich: Oldenbourg Verlag, 1992), 7. It is important to note Schildt embraces such terms because they capture various conservatives' motivations in the postwar period. My research in television similarly suggests that various competing visions of Germany's reconstruction had much in common.
18. West German politicians heavily employed the restoration concept in speeches from the late 1940s and early 1950s. For a thorough exploration of the term and its manifold uses, see Jeffrey Herf, "Multiple Restorations: German Political Traditions and the Interpretation of Nazism, 1945–1946," *Central European History* 26, no. 1 (1993): 21.
19. See Ewald Frie, "The Catholic Church in Germany after the End of the War: Its Failure as a Force for Shaping Society," *German History* 13, no. 3 (1995).
20. Quoted in Ulrich Bröckling, "Der 'Dritte Weg' und die 'Dritte Kraft': Zur Konzeption eines sozialistischen Europas in der Nachkriegspublizistik von Walter Dirks," in *Siegerin in Trümmern: Die Rolle der katholischen Kirche in der deutschen Nachkriegsgesellschaft*, ed. Joachim Köhler and Damian van Melis (Stuttgart: Kohlhammer, 1998), 77. Eugen Kogon, Dirks's coeditor of the *Frankfurter Hefte*, also wrote extensively about Germany's

moral vacuum after the Third Reich. See esp. Eugen Kogon, "Gericht und Gewissen," *Frankfurter Hefte* 1, no. 1 (1946).
21. Historians, too, sometimes employ "vacuum" to describe the process of cultural and moral rebuilding in the postwar period. Werner Faulstich, for example, asserts a "Wertevakuum" arose in the late 1940s and especially in the 1950s, in which mass media emerged as a major engine for social change and diversification. Werner Faulstich, *Die Kultur der 50er Jahre* (Munich: Wilhelm Fink Verlag, 2002), 8.
22. Gregory Wegner, "In the Shadow of the Third Reich: The 'Jugendstunde' and the Legitimation of Anti-Fascist Heroes for East German Youth," *German Studies Review* 19, no. 1 (1996): 128–129.
23. As Young-sun Hong argues, the GDR started "building socialism" in earnest in the late 1950s. Young-sun Hong, "Cigarette Butts and the Building of Socialism in East Germany," *Central European History* 35, no. 3 (2002): 328.
24. It is true that political leaders in postwar Germany, in particular Catholic and Protestant bishops, argued against any massive political and moral reckoning, particularly regarding war crimes trials. Frank Buscher neatly sums up this counterpoint when he asks, rhetorically, "if Germany's political and moral leadership did not think that the German people were in need of reorientation, why should the average man in the street think otherwise?" Frank Buscher, *The U.S. War Crimes Trial Program in Germany, 1946–1955* (New York: Greenwood Press, 1989), 3. However, while this iteration of the "restoration" position indeed found deep resonance among conservatives, it also belies the fact that those same religious elites repeatedly bemoaned Germany's deep-rooted materialism and lack of political virtue. For the bishops and their allies, then, the question was not whether National Socialism had sparked a nationwide illness (it had), but what sort of treatment was now needed.
25. Niklas Luhmann, *The Reality of the Mass Media*, trans. Kathleen Cross (Boston: Polity, 2000), 80.
26. Jeffrey Herf, *Divided Memory: The Nazi Past in the Two Germanys* (Cambridge, MA: Harvard University Press, 1997), 8.
27. Institutional histories forged the way in the Anglo-American academy: James F. Tent, *Mission on the Rhine* (Chicago: University of Chicago Press, 1982); Arthur Hearnder, ed., *The British in Germany: Educational Reconstruction after 1945* (London: Hamilton, 1978). Somewhat more recently, see Thaddeus Stephen Jackson, *Civilizing the Enemy: German Reconstruction and the Invention of the West* (Ann Arbor: The University of Michigan Press, 2006); Brian M. Puaca *Learning Democracy: Education Reform in West Germany, 1945–1965* (New York: Berghahn Books, 2009).
28. Robert Moeller, ed., *West Germany under Construction: Politics, Society, and Culture in the Adenauer Era* (Ann Arbor: University of Michigan Press, 1997).
29. Uta Poiger, *Jazz, Rock, and Rebels: Cold War Politics and American Culture in a Divided Germany* (Berkeley: University of California Press, 2000); Jaimey Fisher, *Disciplining Germany: Youth, Reeducation, and Reconstruction after the Second World War* (Detroit: Wayne State University Press, 2007).
30. Konrad Jarausch, *After Hitler: Recivilizing Germans, 1945–1995*, trans. Brandon Hunziker (New York: Oxford University Press, 2006); Paul Betts, "Manners, Morality, and Civilization: Reflections on Postwar German Etiquette Books," in *Histories of the Aftermath: The Legacies of the Second World War in Europe*, ed. Frank Biess and Robert G. Moeller (New York: Berghahn, 2010).
31. Heide Fehrenbach, "Narrating 'Race' in 1950s' West Germany: The Phenomenon of the *Toxi* Films," in *Not So Plain as Black and White: Afro-German Culture and History,*

1890–2000, ed. Patricia Mazón and Reinhild Steingröver (Rochester, NY: University of Rochester Press, 2005), 136–160; Ulrike Weckel, "The *Mitläufer* in Two German Postwar Films: Representation and Critical Reception," *History and Memory* 15, no. 2 (2003); Michelle René Eley, "Anti-Black Racism in West German Living Rooms: The ZDF Television Film Adaptation of Willi Heinrich's *Gottes zweite Garnitur*," *German Studies Review* 39, no. 2 (2016).

32. E.g., in Brian C. Etheridge, *Enemies to Allies: Cold War Germany and American Memory* (Lexington: University Press of Kentucky, 2016), 208–209.
33. Jennifer M. Kapczynski, "Postwar Ghosts, 'Heimatfilm' and the Specter of Male Violence. Returning to the Scene of the Crime," *German Studies Review* 33, no. 2 (2010); Heide Fehrenbach, *Cinema in Democratizing Germany Reconstructing National Identity after Hitler* (Chapel Hill: University of North Carolina Press, 1995).
34. Perhaps the most notable attempt to show the importance of television in the context of Germany's attempts to deal with its past is Christina von Hodenberg, who argues television itself played a pivotal role in the development of a critical public sphere in the FRG. Christina von Hodenberg, "Mass Media and the Generation of Conflict: West Germany's Long Sixties and the Formation of a Critical Public Sphere," *Contemporary European History* 15, no. 3 (2006): 386.
35. Knut Hickethier and Peter Hoff, *Geschichte des deutschen Fernsehens* (Stuttgart: Metzler, 1998), 66–67.
36. Günter Rohrbach, "Bildungstheater oder Zeittheater: Probleme der Fernsehspieldramaturgie (1966)," in *In guter Gesellschaft: Günter Rohrbach, Texte über Film ud Fernsehen*, ed. Hans Helmut Prinzler (Berlin: Bertz & Fischer Verlag, 2008), 86; Kurt Wilhelm, *Fernsehen: Abendteuer im Neuland* (Cologne: Grotesche Verlagsbuchhandlung, 1965), 46.
37. Günter Kaltofen, *Das Bild das deine Sprache spricht: Fernsehspiele* (Berlin: Henschelverlag, 1962), 10.
38. Quoted in Gerhard Schäffner, "'Das Fenster in die Welt': Fernsehen in den fünfziger Jahren," in Faulstich, *Die Kultur der 50er Jahre*, 92. Note that there is a certain tension between Grimme's ambitious concept of a panacea and former BBC head Hugh Carleton Greene's original vision for NWDR, when it was first created as a radio station in 1945, that "a German station [should] inform and entertain and diffuse democratic values simply by exemplifying them." David Welch, "Priming the Pump of German Democracy: British 'Re-education' Policy in Germany after the Second World War," in *Reconstruction in Postwar Germany: British Occupation Policy and the Western Zones*, ed. Ian D. Turner (New York: Berg, 1989), 229.
39. Bundesarchiv, DR 8 25, "Kollegiumsvorlage 14/62," 19 February 1962.
40. E.g., Joe Perry, "Healthy for Family Life: Television, Masculinity, and Domestic Modernity during West Germany's Miracle Years," *German History* 25, no. 4 (2007): 560.
41. Francis Durbridge and Marianne de Barde, *Das Halstuch*, dir. Hans Quest (WDR, 3, 5, 7, 10, 13, 17 January 1962).
42. Hickethier and Hoff, *Geschichte des deutschen Fernsehens*, 158.
43. *Infratest Wochenbericht*, January 1963.
44. Knut Hickethier, *Das Fernsehspiel der Bundesrepublik: Themen, Form, Struktur, Theorie und Geschichte, 1951–1977* (Stuttgart: J. B. Metzlersche Verlagsbuchhandlung, 1980), 17.
45. Michael John Kooy, *Coleridge, Schiller, and Aesthetic Education* (New York: Palgrave, 2002), 1.

46. Franz Pfemfert, "Kino als Erzieher," *Das Blaubuch* 23 (1909): 548–550.
47. Adelheid von Saldern, "*Volk* and *Heimat* Culture in Radio Broadcasting during the Period of Transition from Weimar to Nazi Germany," *Journal of Modern History* 76, no. 2 (2004): 315–317.
48. Glenn R. Cuomo, *Career at the Cost of Compromise: Günter Eich's Life and Work in the Years 1933–1945* (Atlanta: Rodopi, 1989), 5, 46. Likewise, Stuart Andrew Bergerson has argued in his study of radio in Hildesheim between 1923 and 1953 that while listeners found ways to constitute their own listening experiences in a constant dialectic with producers, reflecting Alf Lüdtke's concept of *Eigensinn*, the medium had become untrustworthy after its pivotal role in the creation of the Nazi *Volksgemeinschaft*. Andrew Stuart Bergerson, "Listening to the Radio in Hildesheim, 1923–53," *German Studies Review* 24, no. 1 (2001): 107.
49. Clemens Münster, "Zur Kulturgeschichte des Augenblicks," *Frankfurter Hefte* 5 (1950): 45.
50. Heide Fehrenbach, "The Fight for the 'Christian West': German Film Control, the Churches, and the Reconstruction of Civil Society in the Early Bonn Republic," in Moeller, *West Germany under Construction*, 321–322.
51. Of course, the German film industry—in particular, the West German side—had other difficulties. They were essentially unable to export their products in the 1950s, and American productions provided stiff competition, even within the FRG. See Irmela Schneider, *Film, Fernsehen & Co: Zur Entwicklung des Spielfilms in Kino und Fernsehen* (Heidelberg: Carl Winter, 1990), 32–33.
52. Hickethier and Hoff, *Geschichte des deutschen Fernsehens*, 38.
53. Konrad Dussel, *Deutsche Rundfunkgeschichte*, 3rd ed. (Konstanz: UVK, 2010), 112–121.
54. Gerhard Hildmann, *Fernsehen—ein Trojanisches Pferd?* (Stuttgart: Neske, 1963), 5–11. See also Ernst Emrich, *Wir Schalten um* (Ravensburg: Ravensburger Taschenbücher, 1965); Otto Walter Haseloff, "Über Wirkungen des Fernsehens," in *Wirkungen des Fernsehens*, ed. Otto Arzt, Bruno Krammer, and Bernhard von Watzdorf (Mainz: Zweites Deutsches Fernsehen, 1972), 5–25. Even these dissenting voices are tempered and cautious, readily admitting the medium could also be a positive influence.
55. Historians still recognize the late 1960s as a period of major transformation in terms of Holocaust memory. But as Moeller concludes in a 2002 review article, referencing scholars such as Ute Frevert, A. D. Moses, and Detlef Siegfried, the 1968er generation seemed for a time unable to recognize the fact that some Germans did critically confront the past before 1968. Robert G. Moeller, "What Has 'Coming to Terms with the Past' Meant in Post–World War II Germany? From History to Memory to the 'History of Memory,'" *Central European History* 35, no. 2 (2002): 236.
56. Bernt Rhotert, "Das Fernsehspiel: Der Gang einer Fernsehspielproduktion (1959)," in *Theorie des Fernsehspiels*, ed. Claus Beling (Heidelberg: Quelle & Meyer, 1979), 48–51.
57. As listed in Hickethier and Hoff, *Geschichte des deutschen Fernsehens*, 134. The remainder included announcements, pauses, and advertisements.
58. Ibid., 192. What constituted "news" and what "documentary" in the GDR seems to have been unclear.
59. As one example of this, see Steven M. Schroeder, *To Forget It All and Begin Anew: Reconciliation in Occupied Germany, 1944–1954* (Toronto: University of Toronto Press, 2013).
60. Martin Sabrow, "Der Apfel von Weibelskirchen: Plädoyer für einen entgrenzten Blick auf die deutsche Teilungsgeschichte," in *Mehr als eine Erzählung: Zeitgeschichtliche*

Perspektiven auf die Bundesrepublik, ed. Frank Bajohr, Anselm Doering-Manteuffel, Claudia Kemper, and Detlef Siegfried (Göttingen: Wallstein, 2016), 69.

61. See esp. Thomas Beutelschmidt, "Von West nach Ost—von Ost nach West: Irrlicht und Feuer," in *Alltag: Zur Dramaturgie des Normalen im DDR-Fernsehen*, ed. Henning Wrage (Leipzig: Leipziger Universitätsverlag, 2006), 25–30. Also, Heather Gumbert has mentioned how (referencing Michael Meyen's work on East German television viewers) "viewers generally watched the same kinds of programmes on both East and West channels." Heather Gumbert, "Split Screens? Television in East Germany, 1952–89," in *Mass Media: Culture and Society in Twentieth-Century Germany*, ed. Karl Christian Führer and Ross (London: Palgrave, 2006), 148.

62. Hans-Jörg Stiehler, "Das Tal der Ahnungslosen: Erforschung der TV-Rezeption zur Zeit der DDR," in *Medienrezeption seit 1945: Forschungsbilanz und Forschungsperspektiven*, ed. Walter Klinglers, Gunnar Roters, and Maria Gerhards (Baden-Baden: Nomos Verlag, 1999), 193–208.

63. This fact was bemoaned, for example, by Emil Dovifat, a journalist and member of the NWDR *Verwaltungsrat* (governing board), in an internal memorandum prepared for his fellow television executives in Hamburg. Cited in Axel Schildt, "Der Beginn des Fernsehzeitalters: Ein neues Massenmedium setzt sich durch," in *Modernisierung im Wiederaufbau: Die westdeutsche Gesellschaft der 50er Jahre*, ed. Axel Schildt and Arnold Sywottek (Bonn: Verlag J. H. W. Dietz, 1993), 492.

64. Hans Fallada and Klaus Jörn, *Wolf unter Wölfen*, dir. Hans-Joachim Kasprzik (DFF, 14, 16, 18, 21 March 1965). Re-broadcast on 6, 8, 10, 11 March 1968 on the ZDF.

65. See, e,g., *Infratest Wochenbericht*, March 1968, 27. As the editors point out, the fact that the program was produced in the East is not reflected in the viewer comments at all.

66. Joachim Holm, *Die Andere Zeitung*, 21 March 1968. *Die Andere Zeitung* is admittedly a left-leaning publication and may harbor more sympathy for East German programming than other West German news outlets. The "boycott" refers to Ernst Lemmer's instructions to the West German press not to print DFF's program schedule or else risk being labeled as purveyors of communist propaganda. See Woo-Seung Lee, *Das Fernsehen im geteilten Deutschland (1952–1989): Ideologische Konkurrenz und programmliche Kooperation* (Potsdam: Verlag für Berlin-Brandenburg, 2003), 53–54.

67. Deutsches Rundfunkarchiv-Babelsberg (DRA-B), SFB 362/31/11/04/05-06, 6946/1, "Zuschauerpost et al aus der DDR, 1961–1980," 1966 letter, anonymous.

68. Ibid., 1965 letter, anonymous.

69. *Der Fernsehzuschauer* 6, Hauptabteilung Kunst und Kultur Brief und Kritik Zuschriften, November–December 1965, letter, anonymous, 2.

70. Thomas Lindenberger asserts West German viewers began to lose interest in productions from the East after 1961, creating an asymmetrical relationship. Thomas Lindenberger, "Looking West: The Cold War and the Making of Two German Cinemas," in Führer, *Mass Media, Culture and Society*, 125. This is doubtless some truth to this, but, as this book demonstrates, teleplays continued to unpack political and moral lessons in a relational fashion.

71. DRA-B, SFB 362/31/11/04/05-06, 6946/1, "Zuschauerpost et al aus der DDR, 1961–1980."

72. A survey of two thousand viewers reported an average of 54.1 percent of GDR households tuned in and that, on a scale of 1 to 5, where 1 is the highest possible score, viewers gave it an average score of 1.96. DRA-B H-048-01–04/0183, Sehbeteiligungskartei.

73. Marianne Lange, "Die Künste im 26. Gesamtsystem der ideologischen Arbeit," *Theorie und Praxis* 35–36 (1967): 25.

74. *epd—Kirche und Fernsehen* 25, 22 June 1968, 9.
75. DRA-B, Dramatische Kunst—Fernsehspiele II—Programmunterlagen nach Sendedatum (A13, 395), 3. October 1966.
76. Hickethier and Hoff, *Geschichte des deutschen Fernsehens*, 65.
77. Ibid., 64.
78. Heather Gumbert, *Envisioning Socialism: Television and the Cold War in the German Democratic Republic* (Ann Arbor: University of Michigan Press, 2014), 12.
79. Notable events along this timeline include the negative public response to two 1962 modernist dramatic programs, *Fetzers Flucht* and *Monolog für einen Taxifahrer*, the 1963 Kafka Conference in Prague, the second Bitterfeld Conference in 1964, and the 11th Party Plenum in 1965. See Peter Hoff, "Das 11. Plenum und der Deutsche Fernsehfunk," in *Kahlschlag: Das 11. Plenum des ZK der SED 1965, Studien und Dokumente*, ed. Günter Agle (Berlin: Aufbau Taschenbuch, 1991).
80. Thomas Großbölting, *SED-Diktatur und Gesellschaft: Bürgertum, Bürgerlichkeit und Entbürgerlichung in Magdeburg und Halle* (Halle: Mitteldeutscher Verlag, 2001), 416.
81. Richard Millington, "'Crime Has No Chance': The Discourse of Everyday Criminality in the East German Press, 1961–1989," *Central European History* 50, no. 1 (2017): 61–62.
82. Jutta Bartus and Rudolf Böhm, *Geboren unter schwarzen Himmeln*, dir. Joachim Hübner (DFF, 21, 23, 25, 28, 30 October 1962).
83. Hickethier and Hoff, *Geschichte des deutschen Fernsehens*, 117.
84. Hickethier, *Das Fernsehspiel der Bundesrepublik*; Claudia Dittmar and Susanne Vollberg, eds., *Zwischen Experiment und Etablierung: Die Programmentwicklung des DDR-Fernsehens 1958 bis 1963* (Leipzig: Leipziger Universitätsverlag, 2008).
85. Nora Hilgert, *Unterhaltung, aber sicher! Populäre Repräsentation von Recht und Ordnung in den Fernsehkrimis "Stahlnetz" und "Blaulicht," 1958/59–1968* (Bielefeld: Transcript, 2013).
86. Hickethier and Hoff, *Geschichte des deutschen Fernsehens*, 158.
87. DRA-B, SFB 362/31/11/04/05-06.
88. I explore the challenges of navigating German television archives in Stewart Anderson, "Modern Viewers, Feudal Television Archives: How to Study German *Fernsehspiele* of the 1960s from a National Perspective," *Critical Studies in Television* 5, no. 2 (2010).
89. Michael Meyen, ed., *Einschalten, Umschalten, Ausschalten? Das Fernsehen im DDR-Alltag* (Leipzig: Leipziger Universitätsverlag, 2003), 13.
90. Karin Bacherer, *Geschichte, Organisation und Funktion von Infratest* (Munich: Infratest, 1987), 31. Infratest was founded as a rough analogue to the American company Gallup, and would come to use many of the same measurement technologies and techniques as the (also American) Nielsen ratings.
91. Ibid., 182–188.
92. *Bild-Zeitung*, 13 January 1970; Herbert Reinecker, *11 Uhr 20*, dir. Becker (ZDF, 8, 9, 11 January 1970).
93. It must be noted that critics writing for most East German newspapers, including the highly visible, state-run *Neues Deutschland*, were tightly constrained by the SED's official Marxist ideology. Nonetheless, they regularly criticized broadcasts, even those that members of the Politburo had carefully vetted and instrumentalized.
94. See, e.g., the *epd*'s predictable delight and moralizing of the 1967 WDR program *Wie verbringe ich meinen Sonntag?* (How do I spend my Sunday?), which discusses the emptiness of most people's Sunday activities. *epd—Kirche und Fernsehen* 11, 18 March 1967.

95. In fact, the plays' thematic and moral complexities distinguish them from many other mediatic representations in postwar Germany. The American occupation authorities, for instance, insisted that theater pieces with a contemporary setting should stick to simple, positive depictions and lessons. See Ralph Willett, *The Americanization of Germany, 1945–1949* (New York: Routledge, 1989), 64. After the heavy-handed policies in the early occupation ended, theater resumed its place as an arbiter of social and cultural issues. Nevertheless, some of the most lauded playwrights, such as Karl Wittlinger and Leopold Ahlsen, switched to television in the late 1950s, both reflecting and precipitating a move toward safer classical theater productions. See Knut Hickethier, "Das Theater der Bundesrepublik," in Faulstich, *Die Kultur der 50er Jahre*, 47.
96. Mark Roseman, "The Organic Society and the 'Massenmenschen': Integrating Young Labour in the Ruhr Mines, 1945–58," *German History* 8, no. 2 (1990): 163–166.
97. E.g., in Helmut Pigge, *Wie verbringe ich meinen Sonntag?* dir. Rainer Wolffhardt (WDR, 16 March 1967).
98. Donna Harsch, *Revenge of the Domestic: Women, the Family, and Communism in the German Democratic Republic* (Princeton, NJ: Princeton University Press, 2007), 8.

Chapter 1

NAVIGATING HISTORY

Historical Consciousness, International Cooperation, and Redemption

In December 1965, the East German DFF broadcast a multipart television play called *Dr. Schlüter*.¹ The play follows the life of a gifted chemist, his Faustian pact with National Socialism, and his eventual redemption in the GDR. Written by Karl-Georg Egel and directed by Achim Hübner, it had been stuck in various stages of production since 1961. Even within the relatively slow-moving world of television fiction, where limited airtime and censorship backlogs could delay the filming and approval processes for a year or more, this was a long time. Gone were the days of live plays and improvisation, common in the late 1950s. Gone, too, was the experimentation and ideological heterogeneity of pieces from the early 1960s, when political authorities were less concerned about minute censorship. High-ranking SED authorities criticized DFF for what they perceived to be decadence and an unacceptable sympathy with the West. In 1962, for example, the head of the Politburo Commission on Agitation and Propaganda, Albert Norden, complained to the head of state broadcasting, Gerhard Eisler, that a comedian for the popular variety show *Da lacht der Bär* (The laughing bear), Eberhard Cohrs, had gone too far in criticizing the state: "When he shoots off political jokes and directs them *exclusively* against the GDR, then it's obnoxious."² In 1965, shortly before *Dr. Schlüter* aired, the Politburo member Erich Honecker would express his frustrations with even greater bluntness, criticizing the domestic media of representations of "anti-humanism." He explained further, "The GDR was a clean country . . . [with] immovable standards of ethics and morality . . . [but] these artists focus on the representation of supposed deficiencies and mistakes in the GDR."³ For Honecker and others in the GDR's political elite, the artistic license characteristic of early television had gone too far. The regime slowly began to see television as a unique, powerful medium for producing propaganda, rather than merely as a space to be occupied.⁴ They shuffled personnel at the station and implemented a tighter system of pre-broadcast censorship and scrutiny. The new, more rigid relationship between television and East German politics gradually deepened in the wake of the Berlin Wall's erection in 1961 (which solidified polarizing Cold War inclinations) and the Eleventh Party Plenum in 1965 (where the SED openly denounced artists who had deviated from Party norms).⁵

Dr. Schlüter, which the station director Heinz Adameck envisioned as a successor to the popular 1961 play *Gewissen in Aufruhr* (Conscience up in arms), struggled to pass muster in this new climate. The producers were forced to make multiple changes to the script.⁶ When it finally aired, few press outlets in the GDR announced the series. Daily newspapers such as the *Berliner Zeitung* and *Neues Deutschland*, which regularly promoted upcoming television dramas with full-page features and interviews with the director, remained oddly silent. The station's own programming guide for journalists and reporters, the *Fernsehdienst*, contained no pictures, descriptions, or announcements in the weeks leading up to the broadcast. The day before the first installment, the government's press agency, the Allgemeine Deutsche Nachrichtendienst (ADN), sent out a relatively small note that the broadcast was scheduled to air the next day.⁷ Thus, despite a large production budget, a respected writer, and a seasoned director, *Dr. Schlüter* aired on 4 December with almost no fanfare.

Within a few days, however, this silence changed to near universal acclaim. On 5 December, the ADN reported the phone lines at the television studio rang without pause during and immediately after episode 1. *Dr. Schlüter* elicited more than eighty spontaneous positive responses within an hour. One woman from Berlin called and invited her neighbors (who did not own TV sets) once she realized how good the show was.⁸ Viewership numbers for the first night were above average, and subsequent installments came close to breaking ratings records.⁹ *Neues Deutschland* finally wrote about *Dr. Schlüter* on 6 December, the same date as the second episode.¹⁰ The right-leaning (but still subject to SED censorship) *National-Zeitung* in Berlin followed suit on 7 December, with the television critic Lothar Schmidt-Renny claiming the play was "the most significant DFF production since *Gewissen in Aufruhr*."¹¹ By 10 December, two days after the last installment had aired (until a much-delayed episode 5 was finally broadcast in March 1966), the print media was absolutely bubbling with excitement over the program. Celebratory reviews began to appear in the regional and local papers. Egel even appeared at numerous lectures and forums, explaining how he came to write *Dr. Schlüter* and fielding questions from students and workers. In short, Egel and Hübner seemed to defy the odds: they had created an exceptionally popular television play without the regime's full support.

How did *Dr. Schlüter* overcome these massive obstacles? Given the censors' initial skepticism and the press echo before 4 December, the reasons for this about-face must be sought in the program itself. One of the most readily apparent strengths in *Dr. Schlüter* is its majestic presentation and epic mode, a hallmark of the most popular East German television films from the early 1960s. The opening scene in episode 1 includes a panoramic view of the ocean and a grand orchestral number. A narrative voice-over explains that what will follow is a "journey . . . much the same as countless other Germans have faced in our Republic." The opening scenes in subsequent installments similarly combine a full-throated score with sweeping landscape shots. Episode 2 surveys the general devastation of a concentration camp (viewers later discover this is Auschwitz). Episode 3 shows the title character and an unknown companion reposing in the mountains above a lake. The camera slowly pans out, revealing a rugged landscape in the Soviet Union. The evocative sounds and images at the start of each episode connote outsized significance. They also likely appealed to a mass audience. Earlier East German epics, popular with viewers and authorities alike, had employed similar musical and cinematographic techniques. Hübner's decision to recycle this stylistic recipe for success made *Dr. Schlüter* seem comfortable and familiar to viewers.

But panoramic shots and classical music surely do not, in and of themselves, explain the program's popularity. *Dr. Schlüter* also attracted viewers with a nuanced, deeply conflicted protagonist. The title character, a gifted chemist named Martin Schlüter, is first presented as an intelligent but otherwise unremarkable graduate student. During the 1930s, however, he is recruited by a large company that contributes directly to Germany's remilitarization campaign. He wants to resign his position but is blackmailed into accepting a supervisor position and eventually finds himself overseeing production at a concentration camp. After a brief internment in a Siberian POW camp, he returns to Germany, choosing to live in the FRG. But he becomes disillusioned with the West, migrating to the GDR and finding work as a university professor. He does not embrace communism, and his continued love of material comforts represents a sharp contrast to the protagonists in similar multipart East German epics. All the same, however, Schlüter has rejected fascism, West Germany, and, in general terms, the "old order." By the final installment, he has embraced socialism and become a valued member of East German society.

Egel and Hübner's redemption story resonated far more powerfully in the mid-1960s than it might have just a few years earlier. In part, the erection of the Berlin Wall had indirectly altered the programs. No longer could the authorities insist on a Manichean dichotomy between good socialists and evil capitalists; because the Wall had largely stopped movement between the two German states, the regime was forced to recognize that complicated figures and non-socialists might also want to find a home in the GDR.[12] In this new atmosphere, the redemption story exerted a powerful pull on East Germans' imaginations. Yet, this pull had another cause. *Aktion Ochsenkopf* (Operation Ox Head), an early 1960s Freie Deutsche Jugend (Free German Youth—FDJ)–led attempt to root out and eliminate the viewing of West German television in the GDR, had failed miserably. East German viewers regularly watched dramas from the West. With this in mind, DFF felt obliged to match the narrative sophistication and ideological nuance on offer in the FRG.[13] The popularity of redemption stories thus reflected both the realities of the newly reinforced German-German border and the television directorate's growing recognition that it would need to cultivate more believable heroes to keep East German viewers from tuning in to the West German stations.[14]

Television's use of nuanced characters and moral complexity in describing the Nazi past was by no means limited to *Dr. Schlüter*. Though generated within very different memory regimes—the increasingly contested narrative of Nazi exceptionality and German reliability cultivated in the FRG versus the robust valorizing of wartime Communists as anti-fascist heroes and Nazi victims in the East—teleplays in both East and West Germany gradually began to challenge taboos and discursive silences regarding the Holocaust and other crimes committed during the Third Reich.[15] Indeed, television's ascension as a mass medium roughly corresponded with some of the most visible events in post-Holocaust history: the Adolf Eichmann trial in 1961 and the Frankfurt Auschwitz trials between December 1963 and August 1965. While the trials did not necessarily usher in a new era of memory culture, they placed some dark, unsavory truths about German complicity in the public's eye. In both West and East, German institutions such as the Communist Party, the Catholic and major Protestant churches, and even industrialists had portrayed the German public as the "first" victims of Nazi aggression.[16] Complex, sometimes morally dubious characters such as Martin Schlüter appeared more regularly and challenged Germans' assumptions about their own victimhood. References to the murder of six million Jews became more explicit. During the 1960s, in short, German television fiction invited viewers to reassess the recent past, a stark contrast to the mediatic silence common (though not universal) during the 1950s.[17] Moreover, television plays couched these reevaluations in didactic terms. In representing storm troopers, officers, and partisan fighters, television producers aimed to inoculate German viewers from a repeat of the Nazi catastrophe by casting the Third Reich and its atmosphere as a moral proving ground.

As television matured, three types of moral lessons associated with the recent German past became most prominent. First, television plays taught viewers a heightened sense of historical consciousness. The silences and taboos surrounding the Third Reich and its crimes, so common in other media forms from the early 1950s, were supplanted by the notion that knowledge about history could be a value unto itself. From its inception, television executives and producers consciously sought to represent themes from German history. This included the National Socialist era, though the types of thoughtful, self-critical representations that have come to mark German media since the 1970s, embodied in ZDF documentaries from the 1970s and 1980s, were at that point rare.[18] Far more common were representations of individual interactions with the Third Reich. Camp guards, high-ranking Nazi officials, and future West German leaders featured most prominently. Rescue and resistance stories were also quite common. While such tales were certainly designed to entertain viewers, they also served a decidedly moral purpose. Modern-day Germans were exhorted to empathize with and emulate the protagonists, and the Nazi past was condemned in straightforward terms.

Second, dramatic broadcasts exhorted viewers to consider the merits of international cooperation. On both sides of the German-German divide, the ideal protagonist was simultaneously a German patriot and part of a larger, more virtuous international front against fascism. Few adult viewers had been part of such resistance movements, and the intended lesson was clear: international cooperation and unity was paramount in present-day Europe. Moreover, while most of these representations did not explicitly couch the need for cooperation in the nation's collective guilt, they did correspond with a wider trend to look beyond German suffering and victimhood, and consider the havoc wrought by the Third Reich on other people, be they Jews, Poles, or even Englishmen.[19] These types of depictions became more common in the wake of the Eichmann trial in 1961.[20]

Third, after 1965 and the Frankfurt Auschwitz trials, historical pieces increasingly told stories of redemption (as noted with *Dr. Schlüter*).[21] Millions of Germans had been fascists, collaborators, or fellow travelers. Television broadcasts during this era made no attempt to draw any particular attention to this fact, but they nonetheless offered redemption to both individual citizens and, in a broader sense, to the German nation itself.[22] To gain said redemption, protagonists and viewers needed to learn (or relearn) the value of democracy and tolerance. West German producers and directors such as Klaus von Bismarck and Rolf Hädrich steered television discourse about the legacy of the Third Reich toward what Jeffrey Olick has recently called the narrative of the "moral nation," in contrast to the dominant narrative of the FRG as a "reliable nation" in the 1950s.[23] Redemptive story arcs played a crucial role in elites' efforts to reshape narratives and collective memories about the past. Even writers and producers in the GDR seemed to favor the redemption narrative by the mid 1960s, partly because the two broadcasting systems were locked in a dialectic struggle, and DFF therefore mimicked rhetorical strategies from West German broadcasts, and partly because the Berlin Wall had rendered emigration from the West impossible (at least in the public eye).

Despite careful planning on the part of producers, dramatic references and allusions to the past are not always easy to decode. Producers had various intentions when they crafted such representations, sometimes playing the role of historian—even inviting professional historians to advise them—but sometimes using the past for other reasons. Of course, in the broadest sense, every depiction of the past can be considered historical, particularly within the narrative structure of television fiction. But in a more specific sense, some plays used themes and issues from the past more consciously, and hence more heavily or intricately, than others. As might be expected, the flavor of the East German shows with historical themes differed in many ways from their West German counterparts. East German productions tended to cover multiple periods of the recent German past in epic form.[24] In some cases, the director even went so far as to change the appearance of the lead actors to account for the passage of up to thirty years of history. Analogous West German programs or "epics" did not cut through multiple periods; rather, they focused on an individual's journey within a more singular context. Moreover, East German television often created histories that corresponded with Marx's understanding of historical materialism in mind. Sinister capitalist circles are shown to drive the financial woes of the day, and Communist workers' fronts come across as the only obstacle standing between industrialists and utter exploitation. In other words, the programs crafted a teleology or history of the present by drawing a line between the exploitation of capitalism and the salvation found in the modern GDR. Such triumphalist histories rarely, if ever, appeared in the FRG.

Nonetheless, the similarities between East and West German versions of history on dramatic television more than outweigh the differences. As noted earlier, themes of rescue from the ravages of World War II provided the basic plot material for multiple productions. Both East and West mistrusted unfettered capitalism, associating it with the failed Weimar Republic and, in a cultural sense, with Jewishness.[25] Indeed, the tragedy of the Weimar Republic and the creation of the Nazi state, despite the East German insistence on assigning special importance to the left's resistance, followed much the same historiographical pattern in the two states. At first, television plays designated ordinary, non-Nazi Germans as witnesses to the hostile overthrow of an otherwise democratic society; later, they introduced more complicated figures who straddled the line between victim and perpetrator. In sum, the two nations' shared history seems to have left a deeper impression on the type and tenor of the histories presented in dramatic television programs than Cold War ideological differences.

* * *

It is not surprising that writers and producers in the FRG gravitated toward exceptional resistance and rescue stories in television's early years. The resistance trope had been an important pillar of West German collective memory since the war's end. Easy to identify, appropriate, and shape, such stories helped legitimize a wide range of institutions, including the non-Nazi military hierarchy (through the Stauffenberg conspiracy), the churches (both Catholic and Protestant), the Social Democrats (many of whom experienced internment during the war years), and others. Taken cumulatively, resistance narratives also functioned as a way to compartmentalize National Socialism. If legitimate political and social institutions during the Third Reich (such as the churches) had fought against Nazi hegemony, it would appear as though the regime's actions, in particular its excesses, were the work of a small group of hardcore devotees.[26]

Resistance and rescue narratives were just as popular on East German television, though they did not always serve the same purpose. The communist regime did not rely on the state's various corporate institutions (the Protestant churches or the "block" parties, for example) expressing their retrospective distance from and disapproval of National Socialism.[27] Instead, they claimed to have expunged said elements from their state. In this strategy, they only needed to demonstrate that communists and socialists had been the primary resistors during the Third Reich. One of the most prominent examples of this narrative in action was the 1960 DFF adaptation of Bruno Apitz's novel *Nackt unter Wölfen* (Naked among wolves).[28] The novel had its roots in the real-life communist resistance movement at Buchenwald. Until 1942, the camp consisted primarily of German political prisoners.[29] As such, conditions in the camp were far less desperate than at death camps or concentration camps outside Germany. To save resources, the camp hierarchy tolerated and even, to some extent, promoted internal organization among the prisoners. As the camp's international population grew in 1943, the communist International Camp Committee (ILK) became by far the most widely recognized leadership group. In much the same way the SED constantly touted its "anti-fascist" credentials after the war as the basis of its legitimacy, former leaders of the ILK such as Walter Bartel leveraged their situation at Buchenwald to political advantage in the postwar years. Bruno Apitz was part of this cohort. His novel, about how the secret communist resistance movement found, concealed, and ultimately rescued a lone Jewish child, is in many ways the perfect composite of the ILK's postwar memory strategy.

The organization and its members improvise a leadership structure, rescue helpless victims, fight a small cadre of truly maniacal Nazi officers, and even initiate an armed uprising. It also features an unscrupulous turncoat who tries to reveal the existence of the child in exchange for freedom. Given the structural harmony between this narrative and the SED's, it is not surprising DFF adapted Apitz's successful novel for television.

In another sense, however, *Nackt unter Wölfen* was a highly unusual program for its era. Though later celebrated as a hero, Apitz at first struggled to find a publisher to carry his story.[30] The Buchenwald communists, so universally celebrated in the late 1940s, found themselves pushed to the margins in the 1950s. The prisoner's postwar organization was dissolved in 1952, and Bartel was forced out of his position in the SED's inner circle in 1953. Ulbricht and his colleagues had spent the war in exile; the notion that a communist leadership structure had existed within the fascist state proved most inconvenient in their efforts to establish hegemony in the Soviet Zone. Fortunately for Ulbricht and his colleagues, the Buchenwald communists' claims to valor and courage appeared somewhat dubious in light of evidence that they had actually collaborated with the fascist guards as much as they had offered any sort of resistance. The SED thus felt enabled to appropriate Buchenwald's memory for its own purposes, commissioning a museum and (falsely) inserting the Communist Party itself as the source of all resistance inside the camp.[31] Apitz's story had unquestionable appeal for a broader audience, but the SED's disapproving stance made the specifics of his story unpalatable for prospective publishers.[32] Apitz had never seen the real-life Buchenwald child; he had only heard about it from other prisoners. Apitz did eventually find a publisher and significant success for his story, but only after it had been summarily rejected as unsuitable at Deutsche Film Aktiengesellschaft ([East] German Film Company—DEFA).[33]

After the bitterness of his rejection at DEFA, and before his rise to fame with the Nationalpreis der DDR for literature in 1958, Apitz had already turned to DFF in an attempt to secure a film version of his work. Television authorities proved more receptive than their cinema counterparts, but here, too, he found his story would be a tough sell. In this case, it wasn't the intra-Communist memory struggle that hindered production; rather, some censors questioned whether television ought to so frankly depict the harsh realities of a Nazi concentration camp on the small screen.[34] In terms of historical representation, it seems, *Nackt unter Wölfen* touched a raw nerve in the GDR's cultural-political apparatus. In the end, though, Heinz Adameck, intendant at DFF, reasoned that because the novel had proved sensationally popular and because his bosses in the SED had promoted the Buchenwald resistance myth so heavily since the mid-1950s (sans the ILK), a relatively faithful representation would prove equally popular in a television format.

The production, which actually became (ironically) a co-venture with DEFA, did run into serious casting problems and was pushed back more than six months.[35] However, once completed, Adameck spoke of the "general and all around approval" of the production.[36] He was right in his assessments on all counts. Viewers loved the program, and the state awarded the producers, executives, and actors a series of prestigious awards.[37] DEFA eventually decided to refilm *Nackt unter Wölfen* and give it a run in the movie theaters in 1963. This larger-budget production, which starred such famous actors as Armin Müller-Stahl and Erik S. Klein, is better remembered today, but the DFF version was one of the greatest early successes of the television genre and generated a wide echo, both in political circles, as demonstrated by the aforementioned prizes, and in the press. This, then, was an important milestone in television fiction about historical topics in the GDR. Direct references to the Nazis' murderous policies concerning Jews and the visual representation of a concentration camp became acceptable, and even encouraged, in this new climate. Programs and scenes promoting historical consciousness, carefully curated by the station executives and censors, became common occurrences on DFF.

Nackt unter Wölfen interweaves this new imperative for historical programming with a celebration of communism's courageous past and its potential to unify the public in the present. The program essentially begins with the discovery of a young, unnamed Jewish child in the laundry room. The inmates know the Nazis will simply kill the boy and, over the dissent of a few individuals who want to inform the authorities, they decide to smuggle him out of the camp. Eventually, the SS guards begin to suspect the child's existence but are unable to locate it. In retribution, they brutally interrogate suspect prisoners. Meanwhile, the camp's underground communist network (probably the ILK, but unnamed in the broadcast) organizes a resistance effort to coincide with the American advance in the hope that they can escape the impending Nazi evacuation. The plan works, and the prisoners, along with the Jewish boy, celebrate their freedom as American troops enter the base. Unlike in the later DEFA film, the prisoners do not arm themselves with guns to drive out the SS guards in advance of the camp's liberation.

Hildegard Tetzlaff helped Apitz adapt *Nackt unter Wölfen* for television well before the Eichmann media coverage of 1960/1961. It is not hard to see why it fits so neatly within the historical consciousness of the late 1950s: viewers could easily identify with the simple story of German resistance without calling up or bringing to light painful memories from the past. Despite the anonymous censor's objections, *Nackt unter Wölfen* does not show gas chambers, cremation facilities, or, as would have been more common in Buchenwald, starving prisoners and desperate circumstances. The prisoners seem well fed (in one scene, for instance, a prisoner removes his shirt and displays a relatively plump physique) and are even able to gather in secret at night. The program also attracted some attention from West German viewers, in the form of congratulatory letters.[38] It is unclear exactly how many tuned in to *Nackt unter Wölfen* in the West, but there can be no question that East German press outlets hoped their counterparts in the FRG would be watching. Katja Stern at the *Neues Deutschland* wrote, "We are sure: also in West Germany one heard the call from Buchenwald."[39] Klaus Rümmler echoed this hope that West Germans had "learned" from the show, adding that he hoped the "international working class" would draw on history to "overcome fascism."[40]

In part, *Nackt unter Wölfen* generated an echo among West Germans because it presents the decision to save the child as a universal moral imperative. However, the program also couches the decision itself within a specific, Marxist rhetoric. They first contemplate the rescue, and the means by which the prisoners will follow through on it, during secret committee meetings, held every night in a deserted basement. Those who break with the unified communist front, as, for instance, one "cowardly" prisoner who reveals the existence of the child, are eventually murdered by the Nazi guards. In contrast, only one major communist figure dies during the rescue attempt, demarcating the committee's position as the "right" one. The international makeup of the committee reinforces the Marxist flavor of the whole rescue process. Germans, Poles, and Russians communicate in German. The committee members treat the Russian delegate with great reverence, and he seems to act as the "patriarch" of the group, dispensing authoritative wisdom whenever the members disagree about strategy. The universal moral imperative of saving the Jewish child from certain death coincides with an orthodox approach to Marxist-Leninism, even incorporating a condensed version of the Warsaw Pact in the equation, via the Eastern European composition of the committee. These scenes presage the growing importance of the idea of international cooperation in defeating National Socialism.

Some early West German television plays likewise strove to direct viewers' attention toward the crimes of the past and, more specifically, to a simple story of rescue and resistance. For instance, the Nord- und Westdeutscher Rundfunkverband (NWRV, precursor to the West German station NDR) in Hamburg broadcast *Waldhausstraße 20* (20 Waldhaus Street) in October 1960.[41] In this program, the newly installed pastor of a Swedish Protestant church in wartime Berlin inherits a group of refugees, mostly theologians and friends of his predecessor who had resisted the Nazi regime. Heeding the pleas of the victims and with encouragement from the church's employees and volunteers, the pastor, Axel Tornqvist, reluctantly agrees to continue the rescue work. He bribes a Nazi official for fake documents and, when this attempt to smuggle the victims into neutral Sweden fails, personally escorts them to a ship waiting on the Baltic Sea. Ultimately, the "religious" refugees escape, but the pastor, smiling for joy despite his predicament, stays behind, to be captured by the German border patrol. The viewer never witnesses this final, undoubtedly brutal scene. In fact, the film contains almost no violence and very few glimpses of Nazi perpetrators. These characters seem more part of the background than participants in the teleplay, allowing the pastor and the refugees to occupy the spotlight. Perhaps the most prominent role, aside from Tornqvist, is that of Margot Lösser, a German woman more completely committed to the resistance and rescue causes than any of the Swedish characters. She often commands the attention of the camera, and large sections of the film involve a subtle romance between her and the pastor. In this way, *Waldhausstraße 20* shields German viewers from direct and inescapable culpability, allowing them to instead fixate on the attractive feminine (and German) resistance figure.

Another visible subtheme in *Waldhausstraße 20* is the role of the church in the rescue efforts. The connection between a Christian church and the rescue of persecuted groups had powerful predecessors and formed an integral part of early West German collective memories, in both the Protestant and the Catholic context.[42] The allied occupiers, and later much of the German population, saw the churches as the one major untainted organization in Germany. Elements of this collective memory have persisted even into the present day, but Rolf Hochhuth's 1963 stage play *Der Stellvertreter* (*The Representative*) shattered the public's near-universal acceptance of the churches as one of the few clear examples of moral steadfastness during the war. Nonetheless, in *Waldhausstraße 20*, Christianity itself offers a powerful moral context for the fictional rescue. First, Tornqvist decides to disregard his superior's order to stop helping the refugees (because of the possibility of soured diplomatic relations) in the context of his "Christian" conscience, which will not permit him to do otherwise. Second, Tornqvist's initial wrath at discovering the group abates when he learns they consist largely of theologians and church dissenters. No surviving production document indicates the play's authors, Maria Matray and Answald Krüger, considered using Jews, Gypsies, or other more well-known victims of ethnic persecution; rather, the program accords with the norms of the pre-Eichmann FRG in that it does *not* raise the question of the German persecution of Jews (though it does forward the persecution and deportation of non-Jewish or unidentified victims as a theme). Finally, the protagonists accomplish the pivotal action of the program, the smuggling of the refugees out of the church, during a Sunday worship service, where Tornqvist provides an extra-long prayer. The visual association between freedom and a Christian religious service gives the program its particular moral flavor. This is not merely about helping refugees for their own sake (although, then as now, such an enterprise seems unassailable from almost any moral foundation); *Waldhausstraße 20* depicts the rescues as an explicitly Christian act.

Interestingly, the press reviews were divided in their reception of the piece. The Catholic publication *Funk-Korrespondenz* praised the film for its depiction of the past, particularly lauding the emphasis on Christian mores, and called for more films along the same lines.[43] In contrast, the reviewers at the Protestant *epd—Kirche und Fernsehen* criticized the program for its "depoliticized" SS figures. They went even further, claiming, "A film does not become . . . spiritual, just because it shows a pastor in his robes."[44] Regardless of the piece's reception (it is now difficult to reconstruct because all the viewer responses have been discarded), *Waldhausstraße 20* drew heavily on the popular understanding that the churches aided the victims of Nazi repression, except where explicitly blocked or prevented.[45] Criticism against the churches on precisely this point had begun even during the war, but between the Western Allies' desire to use existing church institutions in the reeducation and rebuilding of the country, the churches' increased political power in the immediate postwar years (and extending through the 1950s with the Adenauer regime), the associated privilege of controlling radio and television media through direct influence on the stations' oversight boards, and the public's willingness, even desire, to accept the church as the representative of the "good" Germany that had survived the Nazi catastrophe, these criticisms were not widely circulated or perceived until the late 1950s, and even then most commonly in the print media.[46] In this case, television sustained rather than created a powerful, existing historical narrative. Matray and Krüger educated viewers about the nation's troubled past and prescribed correct behavior in such a situation. But they did not probe the depths of guilt or offer the sort of redemption narrative that would become more common in the second half of the decade.

SDR's *Sansibar* (*Flight to Afar,* literally Zanzibar, 1962), based on a well-known novel by Alfred Andersch and brought to the small screen by screenplay writer Leopold Ahlsen and director Rainer Wolffhardt, is a second example of the way West German television producers in the early 1960s understood their task in representing history as one of education and historical consciousness.[47] As with *Waldhausstraße 20* and *Nackt unter Wölfen*, the piece focuses primarily on a simple, easily relatable resistance story. Touted by SDR as one of the "biggest" dramas produced in 1961, *Sansibar*, like the novel before it, depicts the intersection of three different stories: a pastor's attempts to keep his parish's priceless works of art away from the local Gestapo, a Communist Party cell's ongoing struggles against the Nazis, and a Jewish woman's bid to escape to safety in Scandinavia.[48] Upon introduction, each of the three threads seems opaque from the viewer's perspective; referents such as why the preacher's art collection is so valuable, the Communists' real motives in coveting the art figure (it is later revealed to be an extremely valuable Ernst Barlach sculpture), and the woman's Jewish identity are explained only later in the film. This technique encourages viewers to focus on the characters' personal interactions with the Nazi regime, separate from the specific context of their situations.

The broader history of these victims' circumstances, which in a later program might be tied together by the Holocaust or the injustices of the Nazi regime, remains largely concealed. For example, when the Jewish woman first arrives in Rerik (the small village on the Baltic Sea where the story unfolds), the camera lingers on a newspaper with the simple headline "Jewishness is a danger." But Ahlsen and Wolffhardt never explain the nature of this danger or of the woman's reason for emigrating. The preacher and Communist Party sympathizer likewise appear as simple, unproblematic victims; the play does not attempt to duplicate Andersch's exploration of each character's internal motivations and fears. Similarly, the anonymous reviewer for *Funk-Korrespondenz* praised the piece because "the theme is still a hot iron," in terms of both Jewish *and* clerical persecution. But the same reviewer also felt compelled to explain that *Sansibar* "touched on euthanasia, but only tangentially."[49] In truth, euthanasia had almost nothing to do with any of the program's interconnected story lines. The reviewer, it seems, wanted to clarify that *Sansibar*'s invocation of National Socialism did not make it controversial.

Sansibar's use of the recent past to convey didactic messages fits into a larger pattern of literature and film in the late 1950s and early 1960s. As the novel before it, *Sansibar* clearly reflects and appeals to an ideal type of historical consciousness common in the 1950s: it uses the nation's totalitarian past as a dualistic vehicle to teach moral lessons best suited to present concerns. Unlike the *Heimatfilm* genre so popular in the 1950s, this strain invites a more critical type of historical consciousness. It simultaneously limits the scope of that consciousness by working with standard conventions such as resistance, escape, and rescue, established in the immediate postwar rebuilding years. In other words, this genre lacked the hallmark of future televisual representations in the 1970s and 1980s: what Nietzsche would have called the "critical" use of history. Instead, critics of the piece gravitated toward one of their favorite terms when referencing the oversimplification of the past: colportage.[50]

Finally, the television adaptation of *Sansibar* can also be said to create subtle new collective memories, at the "moment of historical consciousness" or reception.[51] *Sansibar* contains relatively few reformulations of "accepted" or epistemologically motivated types of history. In this sense, the historical-didactic purpose of the film has little to do with education or information, except at the most indirect level. But precisely this indirect reformulation or education acts as a potentially powerful type of memory. Members of the older generations who clearly remember the war period can reformulate or "tweak" their own individual memories, attaching greater importance to one personal act of resistance by dramatic amplification. All viewers, witnesses to the events in question or not, can selectively appropriate certain memory strategies employed by the actors (contingent on the believability of the piece in front of them, of course). The memory is "as much a result of conscious manipulation as unconscious absorption," both of which seem to take place via dramatic television.[52] The combination of reformulated historical consciousness and new collective memories (whether consciously or unconsciously perceived) carries significant moral implications.

The international composition of the Buchenwald Communist organization in *Nackt unter Wölfen* and the cooperation between the Swedish pastor and his German associates in *Waldhausstraße 20* marked the beginning of a long-standing trope in German television fiction: the united front between Germans and non-Germans in resisting fascism. Indeed, these early programs accorded neatly with the "reliable nation" narrative, in which German elites strove to prove many of their number had joined the broader international effort to defeat the Nazis during the war, an opportune trope in a period of European integration (the EEC, NATO, the Warsaw Pact).[53] Olick coined the phrase to describe the FRG, but, as *Nackt unter Wölfen* has demonstrated, similar narratives surfaced in the East. Another DFF production, the docudrama *Der Schwur des Soldaten Pooley* (*The Survivor*, 1961), foregrounds the idea of German participation in the international struggle against Nazism even more explicitly. Written by Kurt Jung-Ahlsen and Franz Führmann, and based somewhat loosely on a 1956 POW survivor memoir, the film depicts the massacre of a brigade of British soldiers at Le Paradis (outside Dunkirk), the escape and subsequent capture of the only two surviving witnesses from the brigade, the Pooley brothers, and the attempts of the surviving brother, Albert, to bring the man who gave the execution order to justice.[54] The teleplay was largely funded by DFF, but the station worked with an English film company, the Contemporary Society, and many of the scenes were filmed in England.

Like other simplistic versions of the Nazi past, *Der Schwur* does not touch on the more troubling aspects of the Third Reich, for instance, the Holocaust or the callousness of wide swaths of the population toward National Socialist war crimes. Instead, it focuses on a single instance of injustice and provides "good" Germans to counter the "bad" ones on several occasions. So, for example, the soldiers who initially capture Pooley's English brigade in France remark, "You fought well . . . but the war is over for you," and light Pooley's cigarette with a smile. There is no indication these soldiers are socialist or communist; Jung-Ahlsen and Führmann thus invite the viewer to consider a broader range of protagonists than is often the case in DFF historical plays.

In sharp contrast to these benign Wehrmacht privates, the British POWs shortly after their capture encounter a very different type of German soldier: the deranged SS officer. The main officer (and later the man charged with the massacre) shouts his commands and seems to revel in the machine gunfire. To mark these soldiers as dedicated Nazis, later that evening (when the two Pooleys emerge from the mass of bodies and try to escape), these same men can be seen singing "Horst Wessel Song," an unofficial anthem for SA (and later SS) storm troopers. This contrast between the Wehrmacht and the SS mirrored popular attitudes of the era; only the latter group's actions could be considered criminal or deviant.

Another instance of the "good" German occurs when a low-ranking POW camp official corroborates Albert Pooley's story about the older brother's murder because he was a witness to the massacre. Again, this "good" officer is not denoted as a socialist. He has no real motivation for helping Albert, other than his conviction to do the right thing. At the end of the program, Albert and the unnamed camp official walk away from a courtroom, and a voice-over proclaims: "They brought a wolf to justice. And now they returned to their everyday lives, to the countries from which they came." That this trial took place after the war reinforces the "reliable nation" narrative, proclaiming to the world (and, most especially, to the German viewers watching the program) that most Germans were not involved in the Nazis' heinous crimes. In this way, the audience, including viewers and critics (the latter awarded it with a prize at the television festival in Cairo), is allowed to revel in the triumph of justice while acknowledging the clear line of separation between the murderous SS major and these more positive historical German role models.

It is no coincidence this program occurred in the wake of the Adolf Eichmann trial. Eichmann, a high-ranking Nazi fugitive living under a pseudonym in Argentina, had been captured and extracted by an Israeli agent in 1960. His subsequent trial captivated the German public, particularly in the West. The East German authorities answered this surge in historical consciousness regarding the Holocaust and the crimes of the past by appealing to an international front against the fascists and pointing the finger at the FRG, which ostensibly still harbored such criminals. Nonetheless, the program does not serve the SED cause directly. The American officer charged with adjudicating in the matter is depicted as fair, and the British soldiers are not given any political context, for example, as left-leaning or "enlightened" exemplars. In fact, the show's major message seems to be a combination of international cooperation against the remaining fascist criminals and the simple moral imperative to find those responsible, wherever they might be.[55] While DFF television authorities clearly approved *Der Schwur des Soldaten Pooley* based on its indirect implication of West German society (which is where the mass murderer lived), the Cold War tit-for-tat plays only a very implicit, and secondary, role in the actual broadcast.[56] Jung-Ahlsen and Fühmann encouraged anti-fascists of all stripes and nationalities to join in the hunt for undiscovered war criminals. Many East German viewers responded positively to this representation, showering the station with celebratory letters.[57] In March 1963, DFF also recorded and trumpeted positive English-language responses, a result of its screening in Cairo.[58] These reviews in particular noted the East German station's decision to employ native English speakers, an unusual (and expensive) decision in the industry at that time.

Protagonists in DFF epic dramas before 1965 had no need for vindication. They only wanted in education and experience before they could become perfectly calibrated spokesmen for the GDR's political ideals. For example, Joachim Ebershagen, the hero of the East German *Gewissen in Aufruhr*, serves honorably in the German army during World War II but deeply dislikes his National Socialist superiors.[59] He hands over the city of Greifswald to the Red Army without offering any resistance. When he is imprisoned in West Germany, the show makes it clear he has done nothing wrong, except in the minds of the misguided West German authorities who see his decision at Greifswald as treason. The plot trajectory in *Gewissen in Aufruhr* is comic; in other words, the protagonist does not possess any telling flaws. He must simply overcome the set of circumstances placed in front of him. Similarly, Hans Röder, a humble auto mechanic working in Frankfurt (am Main) in an October 1960 multipart epic *Die Flucht aus der Hölle* (Flight out of hell), is tricked into serving in the French Foreign Legion.[60] But he does not have a dark past, and he does not require a great deal of redemption. He quickly comes to understand the French occupation of Algeria as illegitimate (thus aligning himself with the SED's own position on the matter). He deserts from the legion and undertakes a long, difficult journey to freedom in the GDR. While this journey might seem to connote redemption, *Die Flucht* characterizes its protagonist as more a victim than a complicit party.

In contrast, the protagonist in *Dr. Schlüter*, Martin Schlüter, is a complicated figure, at times allying himself with fascist or reactionary forces to further his own scientific ambitions, at other times embracing socialism. The series' chronological format, each segment in turn depicting scenes from the 1930s, World War II, the immediate postwar period, and the present day, further underscores the complexity of Martin's character. Episode 1 introduces Martin as a normal, well-adjusted chemist. He works on a team for a major chemical company in the mid-1930s. Quickly, however, the audience learns his best friend, Ernst, is committing espionage for the Soviet Union. Martin hides him in his apartment and eventually helps him flee the country. Whatever his sympathy for the communist cause, however, Martin has an ulterior motive: he has fallen in love with Ernst's girlfriend,

Eva. To complicate matters further, the daughter of the chemical factory owner, Fey, is infatuated with Martin. He rejects her advances at first, despite her wealth and connections. When the owner offers Martin a much more prestigious position at the factory, however, the situation changes. Martin's great tragic weakness, it turns out, is his love for work. He knows that the chemical company is closely tied to the military and that his projects will be incorporated into the Nazi war machine. This weighs on his conscience, but the allure of scientific discovery wins out. Furthermore, the owner insists, as part of the agreement, that Martin must marry his daughter. He initially hesitates, but, after discussing the situation with a Mephisto-like friend who insists "exceptional people need to make exceptions," he relents and accepts the promotion. In a symbolic scene, he drops his strictures about Fey's loud mannerisms and decadent lifestyle, joining her and her friends on an alcohol-heavy riverboat excursion. Martin has moved up the social ladder and greatly accelerated his career. But, in entering in this Faust-like pact (the episode's title, "The Pact," is a fairly explicit reference to the Faust legend), he loses Eva, who slips away soon after he signs the deal. His heretofore stoic moral character also vanishes, swallowed by brief scenes of drunken revelry and in his decision to tacitly support fascism.

Episode 2 further highlights Martin's tragic flaws. Taking place some ten years later, toward the end of World War II, the audience finds Martin working as the head of chemical operations—and as an SS officer—at Auschwitz. During the episode's first twenty minutes, he lashes out at his interns and clearly abuses his authority. This unsympathetic picture is complicated, however, when Martin praises the Polish and Russian prisoners who are forced to help him industrialize his chemical experiments. He speaks to them as equals, even partners, in his quest for a perfect formula. He then admits to one of the prisoners, a Russian woman with advanced training in chemistry, that he still "leans" toward socialism. The prisoners glance curiously at one another in the wake of these encounters, and the other SS officers are later furious to hear that Martin had paid them so much respect. Later in the episode, Martin is shocked to learn his closest associate at the camp, a Jewish doctor, has been exterminated. When Martin asks the camp guards where his Jewish associate has gone, one replies, "Well, in the air!" referring to the cremation process. The remarkably overt references to the Holocaust in the second installment serve as an effective turning point in Martin's ideological conversion away from fascism. He subsequently complains to the camp commander, to no avail, and later uses these "betrayals" as justification for helping a group of Russian partisans who have infiltrated the camp.

Collectively, these scenes amplify the redemption narrative's explanatory power by tapping into East German characterizations of and collective memories about World War II. For one, they perpetuate the myth of the non-fascist German officer. Martin, it turns out, was still a communist at heart and had been forced into the SS. By depicting this situation, Egel invites East German viewers to reconcile the fact that so many of their associates had made the jump from card-carrying National Socialists to SED party members.[61] Though perhaps not always blameless, television characters such as Martin Schlüter suggested otherwise "good" Germans had been coerced into service for the Nazi regime. This all-too-common narrative is reinforced by Martin's self-justification for his complicity: "I don't want us to lose; I just don't want us to win." He understands the Nazi regime is evil, but he maintains a sense of German nationalism and pride. For another, by presenting the title character simultaneously as a Nazi and a socialist, the producers demonstrated that even complicated figures like Martin could have redeeming qualities. After the Berlin Wall, SED and Stasi authorities usually avoided encouraging reactionaries or fascists to emigrate for fear that this would spark an intellectual or artistic exodus (they certainly deported some dissidents, as Wolf Biermann's situation demonstrates); by the same token, authorities could not easily claim fascists now existed only in the FRG. *Dr. Schlüter* thus functions as a corrective, allowing East German citizens to embrace those with complicated, unflattering pasts.

Episodes 3 and 4 depict Schlüter's imprisonment in Siberia, his return to Germany, and his gradual transformation from a flawed character with socialist "leanings" to a wholehearted advocate for communism. Much the same as other East German television productions from the 1960s, *Dr. Schlüter* portrays Russian internment as relatively benign. When Martin finally "chooses" to return, he first goes to the West. As he explains to his Russian companions, he needs to help make a "new Germany," and he is better placed to do that in the West than in the Russian zone. As the heir to the chemical factory, he is now a millionaire and can use his money to promote socialist causes. When he tries to bring a legal case against some of his fellow SS officers, however, he discovers a maze of blackmail and corrupt judges. His estranged wife, Fey, dies from a morphine overdose. At her funeral, a particularly emotional scene, he accuses the West German system of being fundamentally flawed. He immediately seeks refuge in the GDR (this scene takes place in the 1950s, well before the Berlin Wall). Martin's journey toward socialism does not end here, however. He takes up a job as a chemistry professor but has trouble adapting to the idea of socialist collectives and class equality. He still claims millions in a West German bank, and he sometimes treats the other faculty as his inferiors. The directors issue him with a warning. In despair, Martin returns to his friend Ernst, who is now an SED functionary. In a visual symbol of their complicated, fiery relationship, the two play chess as they discuss Martin's options. By the end of episode 4, Martin accepts a position at a new academic institute, where he can choose his own associates.

As a justification for Martin's journey, Ernst declares, "If we could rip up the roofs of all the houses in the GDR and look into the people's hearts, how many would actually be completely pure?" Martin replies, smiling, "Yes, I'm an average German." The implication here is that Egel believed his redemption story would resonate with many viewers, even on the other side of the border. For this reason, perhaps, earlier versions of the screenplay included an expanded title, *Dr. Schlüter findet Deutschland* (Dr. Schlüter finds Germany).

And resonate it did, as numerous viewer letters attest. One correspondent, for example, saw his own problems and concerns reflected in Martin's character: "I found in this film many questions that I've also asked myself. Some were answered, a much greater number provoked further reflection." Another letter echoed this "average German" sentiment: "Out of the doubter Schlüter . . . a good German was born."[62] The authorities' hope that the show would compare favorably with West German productions also seems to have been repaid. One East German exclaimed, for instance, "Millions of viewers in our Republic and surely also in West Germany are excited!"[63] West Germans, too, sent letters to the station. One viewer from West Berlin explained he found the story and dialogue "compelling." A more pointed response from the West noted, "The film was good because it forces us to think carefully about Germany's future."[64] As with so many other German television plays of the era, then, viewers contextualized *Dr. Schlüter* as something Germans on both sides of the border could watch. Egel thought so too, as his comments at a discussion panel at the Sporthalle Karl-Marx-Allee make clear: "It is our national mission to show the tens of thousands of viewers—also in West Germany—how to find the way to socialism."[65] Television dramas provided a broadly popular, increasingly subtle arena for Germans to examine political concerns and questions common to East and West alike. In this case, the examination was couched in a fictionalized biography that charted the historical development of a single individual.

Epics in the mold of *Dr. Schlüter* were not as popular among the West German stations, but redemption narratives still found a voice in many teleplays. Consider, for example, ZDF's *Menschen helfen Menschen: Zwei Tage von Vielen* (People help people: Two days among many, 1964).[66] The piece examines two days in the lives of workers in the Aid Society of the Berlin Episcopacy. Secretly tasked with harboring the city's Jews, who in 1942 were actively being deported to death camps, the workers risk their lives to help their charges. One German woman, a peripheral character in the show, admits she had long supported the National Socialists and their cause. As she explains to the group's leader, however, the deportations have made her question her political allegiances, and she has now resolved to take a more active role in helping the church groups shield her Jewish neighbors from deportation.

Redemption also functions as a major theme in Matray and Krüger's NDR play *Standgericht* (Court martial, 1966).[67] Three inhabitants of a village in southern Germany—the mayor, the teacher, and a farmer—were executed by SS officers in 1945, after they disarmed a group of Hitler Youth who were preparing to offer combat to the advancing American soldiers. The program cuts between the trial (which takes place in the present) and the events of 1945, as they are described by court witnesses. What emerges is the picture of respectable, right-leaning members of the community (and Nazi sympathizers) who, when faced with the prospect of twelve-year-old soldiers, end their allegiance to the established military order and take the children's weapons. The three victims were subsequently executed for treason by the local SS authorities. In writing *Standgericht*, Matray and Krüger intended to call attention to the fact that though many Nazi perpetrators and war criminals faced belated indictment and prosecution in the 1960s, they often escaped with little or no prison time. They make this clear in their official request for approval to air the piece, but the point is reinforced in the broadcast itself, which ends with a commenter reading a stark summary of the trial's verdict: two of the men are found not guilty, and one is found guilty and sentenced to prison for three and a half years.[68] While these are read, the bodies of the three men are shown hanging from a tree in the distance. The village's actual name is also revealed at the end of the production: Brettheim, in northern Württemberg. By withholding this information until the end of the piece (and, indeed, by not revealing whether the dramatization is based on actual historical events until the end), the director, Rolf Busch, universalizes the incident, implying this might have occurred anywhere in the Third Reich, not just in this particular, perhaps exceptional location. The play's dramatization of past events thus functions as a means of highlighting the true failures of the justice system in the present (1966). *Standgericht* visually represents the mayor, teacher, and farmer as men of conscience and sobriety, whereas the military leaders acted impulsively, becoming irate at the perceived contradiction of their authority. Moreover, by choosing to focus on naïve adolescent soldiers as the "resistance" to the regime, Matray and Krüger reinforce the immorality of the commanding officers' choices at the end of the war.[69]

While the play's main purpose was to highlight the failures of the FRG's justice system in prosecuting former war criminals, a major secondary purpose was to valorize those Germans who, when confronted with a specific moral dilemma, found a measure of redemption by choosing to turn against the Nazi regime. This point is expressed in a variety of ways. For one, a large number of the mayor's political opponents supported his actions, or at least said as much at the trial twenty years later. For example, one left-leaning inhabitant, a Social Democrat, stands as a witness at the trial and describes the mayor's actions as one of "reason" and "redemption." Another witness relates the teacher had always supported the regime's nationalism and pedagogical methods but had also recently lost a child to the war. This, combined with the sight of children girding for a fight with American soldiers, must have changed his mindset to one of "pity." The local pastor's actions also suggest a kind of redemption for the three victims. He mentions to the court that his relationship with the teacher had been full of friction, but he tried to give all three of the murdered men a Christian burial (the SS commanders prevented this). In sum, *Standgericht* spends as much time exploring their redemption as it does demonizing the SS soldiers.

By far the most widely discussed West German program touching on the theme of redemption and the Nazi past was Hädrich's WDR piece *Mord in Frankfurt* (Murder in Frankfurt, 1968).[70] This complex, cerebral program weaves together several narrative threads concerning the same two-day period in 1965 Frankfurt (am Main). Two of these threads directly involve German attempts to "come to terms" with the Nazi past. First, Andrej, a (non-Jewish) Polish witness to mass murder at Auschwitz, flies into the city as the prosecution's star witness. The city's politicians go to great lengths to demonstrate that Germany has turned over a new leaf. The Frankfurt City Commission sends two young women to greet Andrej at the airport, with instructions to make him feel welcome and comfortable. Andrej's initial impression seems positive enough. At the airport and on the street outside, the camera tracks Andrej's facial expressions as he takes in classic travel posters to Mediterranean destinations, a group of squabbling taxi drivers, and several long-haired young people (ostensibly students). He visibly smiles as he gets in his taxi. At the hotel, the maid turns on classical music and asks him, in English, if he would like her to draw his bathwater. His two female greeters then reappear to give Andrej some well-rehearsed information about the city's rich tradition of democracy, its old churches, and even a fine collection of palm trees at the arboretum. The mayor also greets him, hoping the guest will "take home a good impression of Frankfurt and of Germany." Another politician eats lunch with Andrej and tells him Germans are "generous," an obvious reference to the lavish hotel and hospitality vis-à-vis distinguished guests.

From this point forward, barely fifteen minutes into the broadcast, Andrej seems unsettled and disturbed. He asks the politician if he is old enough to remember the Germans' "generosity" twenty years ago, an ironic reference to his time in a German work brigade retreating from Auschwitz to Germany. When a waitress asks Andrej if Frankfurt has given a good impression, he responds by cutting right to the point: "It's very different than I imagined. Sometimes you have to forget, though, and not always hate." The waitress quickly picks up on his meaning and adds, "The Germans have learned a lot since then." Andrej's response is cryptic: "Maybe." At the trial, Andrej is grilled by the defense team, who in particular note he is an active member of the Communist Party in Poland. They also try to convince the judges that his memory is bad, that he didn't give testimony on a particular guard at similar trials in Vienna and Warsaw, and that his testimony here should therefore be invalid. The camera starts to swirl around the witness, creating a sense of disorientation. The prosecutors' voices become indistinct. At the end of the scene, Andrej walks out of the courtroom, goes back to his hotel, and declares to the two (now distraught) young greeters that he wants to catch the first train back to Warsaw.

The second thread in *Mord in Frankfurt* follows a frustrated acting troop's halting attempts to learn Peter Weiss's 1965 play *Die Ermittlung* (*The Investigation*), which itself depicts themes from the Frankfurt Auschwitz trials. In Hädrich's rendering, the actors and the director disagree over how to represent the various groupings: indicted perpetrators, judges, witnesses, and victims. The director tells the actors portraying SS officers they must play their roles straight, as he doesn't want the audience to sympathize too much with mass murderers. The actors object, partly because they want to give their characters more nuance and partly because, as they explain, many of their friends had been National Socialists and they aren't so bad. Some of the younger members of the troop then voice their disgust at this sentiment. As one young actor, Hans, puts it, "These people are all still here, and they are evil." He fears if the experienced actors get their way, the play will mimic the actual trials, where the perpetrators are paraded on stage and made to seem exceptional and nonrepresentative. Hädrich never reveals the outcome of this give-and-take, but the scenes serve to throw the philosophical and moral questions surrounding the actual trial into sharp relief. It also reveals a stark contrast between the intellectual world occupied by drama students like Hans and the film's third story line, which follows the city at a more quotidian level.

This third thread, which depicts a tabloid-driven uproar about a taxi driver's murder, grounds the other two plotlines within the city's current atmosphere. Andrej learns firsthand about the murder, as he spends hours shuttling back and forth in taxis between the courthouse and the hotel. His initial reaction is one of benign interest. When he sees how the entire city is immersed in the search for the murderer, his reaction becomes much more cynical. He looks out from his cab at signs such as "We demand the death penalty" and "No mercy for murderers!" When he vocally relates his displeasure, the driver responds, "Don't you have the death penalty in Poland?" Andrej says they do, and the driver notes, "If you were in our shoes, you'd feel the same way. You'd want justice!" In another cab scene, Andrej hears a radio announcer declaring, "It's as if everyone in this city wants to forget the Trial. Instead they're all crazy about a taxi murder." The driver turns it off, muttering,

"Such nonsense." Again, the camera lingers on Andrej's face, capturing his hardening facial features and increasing disgust. More than the trial itself, these scenes demonstrate the disconnect between the German elites who want to rehabilitate their nation's image and the German public, which is inexplicably more fascinated with a recent unsolved murder than with a trial involving the killers of hundreds of thousands of people.

The murder craze thread also intersects with the *Ermittlung* production. The passionate young actor, Hans, personally knows the only witness to the crime, a young woman named Franziska. As Franziska excitedly relates her newfound fame and interviews with the tabloids (one assumes she has given *Bild-Zeitung* a full rundown of her story), Hans looks disgusted. Franziska, annoyed that her story isn't making more of an impression, tells Hans she is sick of his plays: "Always Jews! Always concentration camps! It's no excuse for boring plays!" The actors' inability to understand the material, combined with the city's indifference toward the past, is manifest in the taxi murder thread and stands in ironic opposition to the actual court proceedings in the main story, featuring Andrej. *Mord in Frankfurt* implies not only that West Germans did not show remorse or shock about the trial but also that the Nazi past had ceased to play a prominent role in shaping the present. The elites who pamper Andrej desperately want to hear Germany has been redeemed, but, from the Pole's perspective, this is just a facade. The German people, embodied by the taxi drivers and the tabloid-mad girl, are unable to grasp the significance of the Auschwitz trials. Hädrich cleverly reinforces the citizens' inability to grasp the trial's significance by giving the scenes featuring *Die Ermittlung* and the taxi drivers' riot a choppy, amateur feel. The camera jerks and frequently comes out of focus during these narrative threads' climactic scenes. The same is true in the courtroom, which features the defense attorneys' arguments on behalf of the accused perpetrators. In most scenes involving the Polish witness, however, the camera remains still and focused, almost suggesting his viewpoint is both more mature and more real. The actor, Václav Voska, augments this with pained facial expressions.

Viewers disliked *Mord in Frankfurt*, thereby adding another level of self-reflexivity. Well-received by critics and station executives, as evidenced by its being selected for competition at the 1968 International Television Festival in Prague, viewers rated the program "0" in the qualitative index, an extremely low figure compared to most other dramatic programs.[71] Many appear not to have understood the purpose of including three simultaneous narratives, indicating both an inability to grasp the significance of the Auschwitz trials and the expectation of television programs to primarily center on entertainment.[72] One viewer's response encapsulated the lack of understanding by saying almost exactly the opposite of what the producers wanted the public to learn: "The concentration camp history didn't fit in here, no connection."[73]

In essence, at least some of the public reaction to *Mord in Frankfurt* demonstrated in practice precisely the negative message the program's producers wanted to convey: the Nazi trials belonged to "history" in West Germany, and the murder of millions twenty years prior was not nearly as important as the death of a single (German) individual in 1965. The disconnect that existed between West German politicians and the public *in* the film was mirrored by the same parties in their reactions *to* the film. The ARD rebroadcast the show numerous times, despite the initially negative viewer responses. Günter Rohrbach, head of WDR's *Fernsehspiel* department, noted the Hädrich film was superior aesthetically and educationally, claiming: "One 'Mord in Frankfurt' is better than two [of] *Der König stirbt* [a 1965 adaptation of Eugène Ionesco's avant-garde chamber piece] or *Romeo und Jeanette* [a 1958 rendering of a lesser-known Jean Anouilh play]."[74] Rohrbach compares *Mord in Frankfurt* to these two pieces because they are examples of more popular avant-garde adaptations, free from the burden of the German past and of the painful self-criticism expressed in Hädrich's work. And Rohrbach wasn't the only television authority who commented on the disconnect between program makers and viewers. For example, in response to a scathing viewer letter about the avant-garde *In der Strafkolonie* (*In the Penal Colony*, 1963), based on a short story by Franz Kafka, one SFB executive, Dagmar Fambach, wrote back to the viewer, "We are convinced that it is also television's mission to dare experiments, even when they say things that are uncomfortable."[75] Television authorities such as Fambach thus envisioned entertainment existing side by side with more difficult pieces.

Like *Standgericht*, *Mord in Frankfurt* criticizes postwar politics and culture in the FRG, bemoaning the fact that war criminals can escape punishment. It differs from the former (and from most other teleplays on the topic), however, in that it does not attempt to redeem any particular character. There are no moral victories for the German characters in *Mord in Frankfurt*; the taxi drivers fail to see the irony of their actions, the actors do not appreciate the significance of what they are performing, and the city's hosts, so keen to demonstrate Frankfurt's progressive nature, do not recognize the anguish experienced by their Polish guest. Hädrich thus dangles but ultimately rejects Germany's redemption. While they are very different in terms of trajectory and outcome, all of these redemption narratives demonstrate the nation's continued fascination with the question of crimes, guilt, and recovery. The disease metaphor runs like a red thread through this genre. As Andrej watches a group of German taxi drivers pummel one of their colleagues in *Mord in Frankfurt*, for instance, he quietly observes, "These people are sick." In an immediate sense, he means the drivers. But as his disgust with the city and the trial grows, this statement comes to stand for German culture in general. In *Dr. Schlüter*, Martin's socialist friends often refer to his time in the concentration camp as his "sickness." And as his time in Siberia draws to a close, one of his Russian guards asks Martin whether he has fully "recovered." Whether at a societal or individual level (or both), Germans in these programs are guilty of heinous crimes and/or misguided ideological allegiances. They are sick and diseased. But redemption is possible, and it comes in many forms. For East German protagonists, it comes in a recognition that socialism is the righteous antidote to fascism (and, as noted earlier, to criminality itself). West German characters can likewise earn redemption, but the cure always involves turning away from and rejecting the past as completely evil. Even the somewhat satirical *Mord in Frankfurt*, a grating experience for many viewers, offers the implicit chance of redemption, given a change of heart in the public mood and a hoped-for willingness to collectively confront the illness and its continued dangers.

The 1968 student movements, which gathered much of their momentum after Hädrich had written and filmed his piece, represent a new, much more pointed chapter in German attempts to grapple with the past. A handful of television dramas touch on these movements and protests directly, including, most famously, Dieter Meischner's *Alma Mater* (1969).[76] But television plays were expensive, time-consuming propositions. It might take two years or more to secure approval, allocate funding, secure the necessary staff, shoot on location, and find a suitable broadcast slot for a program. By 1970, West German television stations had shifted their focus to documentaries and news magazine programs. It is in nonfictional programming that much (though certainly not all) of the discussion about the Holocaust and other dark aspects of Germany's past took place in the 1970s and 1980s. For its part, the GDR never experienced anything like the moral reckoning of a student revolt and generational tensions. The redemption narrative continued in epics such as *Wege übers Land* (Ways across the country, 1968; see chap. 5) and *Krupp und Krause* (Krupp and Krause, 1969), but these involved little self-criticism.[77]

Conclusion

Television fiction during the medium's infancy and adolescence almost never depicted death camps or gas chambers. But popular plays did follow a clear trajectory. As early as the late 1950s, they represented protagonists and antagonists from the Third Reich, in stark contrast to most *Kino* films of the same era. Simple rescue and resistance stories were most common. After the Eichmann trial, producers in both East and West began to highlight the international nature of the fight against Nazi perpetrators. This trend emerged as a counterpoint to the pattern of representing only German suffering, common in films from the 1950s.[78] In this sense, early television plays might be seen as a predecessor to the New German Cinema movement, stylistically resembling the older films but politically quite forward-looking. Finally, as television became more firmly established by the mid-1960s, and as the Frankfurt Auschwitz trials began to gain a place in the public eye, TV produced more complex, sometimes self-critical appraisals of how contemporary Germans remembered their past. The redemption narrative replaced resistance and rescue as the dominant story type. None of these narratives, not even the unpopular and iconoclastic *Mord in Frankfurt*, would approach the deeper *Vergangenheitsbewältigung* of the late 1970s and 1980s. But they do demonstrate that television authorities had already begun to privilege moral engagements with the past, a kind of rudimentary medicine for the still-sick German nation.

Notes

1. Karl-Georg Egel, *Dr. Schlüter*, dir. Achim Hübner (DFF, 4, 5, 7, 8 December 1965; 27 March 1966).
2. Quoted in Heather Gumbert, *Envisioning Socialism: Television and the Cold War in the German Democratic Republic* (Ann Arbor: The University of Michigan Press, 2014), 116.
3. Ibid., 153.
4. Ibid., 12.
5. Peter Hoff, "Das 11. Plenum und der Deutsche Fernsehfunk," in *Kahlschlag: Das 11. Plenum des ZK der SED 1965, Studien und Dokumente*, ed. Günter Agle (Berlin: Aufbau Taschenbuch, 1991), 105–116.
6. Bundesarchiv (BArch), DR 8 548, Letter from Heinz Adameck to Kurt Hager (Politbüro), 25 October 1963.
7. *Allgemeine Deutsche Nachrichtendienst*, "Schlueter 1," 3 December 1965.
8. *Allgemeine Deutsche Nachrichtendienst*, "Meldung, Resonanz" 5 December 1965.
9. *Der Fernsehzuschauer* 10, no. 1 (1965): 4.
10. K. St., "Die Entscheidung des Wissenschaftlers," *Neues Deutschland*, 6 December 1965.
11. Lothar Schmidt-Renny, "Der Teufelspakt des Dr. Schlüter," *National-Zeitung*, 7 December 1965.
12. As evidenced by the regime's about-face in depicting previously discredited historical figures such as Klaus von Stauffenberg and Martin Luther. See Bill Niven, "The Sideways Gaze: The Cold War and Memory of the Nazi Past, 1949–1970," in *Divided but Not Disconnected: German Experiences of the Cold War*, ed. Tobias Hochscherf, Christoph Laucht, and Andrew Plowman (New York: Berghahn Books, 2013), 58.
13. For example, during an August 1965 meeting, station director Heinz Adameck noted his superiors were unhappy at what they perceived as a lack of "quality." While acknowledging that many programs, including *Dr. Schlüter*, appropriately reflected the imperative to expose West Germany's "political corruption," he worried other factors such as camerawork and dialogue would prevent West German viewers from taking it seriously. BArch, DR 8 42, Vorlage 79/65, 12 August 1965. Similarly, Edward von Schnitzler argued in

a December 1965 board meeting that the fight against West German stations would be better accomplished with higher-quality productions than by jamming television signals. BArch, DR 8 4912, "Protokoll der Beratung des Intendanten mit den Stellvertretern des Intendanten," 7 December 1965.

14. The shift toward nuance and redemption was not universally welcomed, however. In an internal review of *Dr. Schlüter*, for example, Dieter W. Angrick noted he was pleased to see the production "does not rely on clichés and black-and-white depictions. Even the Nazi officers are differentiated, which makes the whole piece more convincing." In a counterargument, however, Heinz-Victor Ivan notes, "the viewers can only handle so much nuance—they need simple answers to understand why the GDR is so important." Deutsches Rundfunkarchiv-Babelsberg (Dra-B), "Methodisches Kabinett Analysen," 3, 1966, 2–13.

15. Jeffrey K. Olick, *The Sins of the Fathers: Germany, Memory, Method* (Chicago: University of Chicago Press, 2016), 98–99; Jeffrey Herf, *Divided Memory: The Nazi Past in the Two Germanys* (Cambridge: Harvard University Press, 1997), 163.

16. Olick, *Sins of the Fathers*, 328.

17. Mark A. Wolfgram, *"Getting History Right": East and West German Collective Memories of the Holocaust and War* (Lewisburg, PA: Bucknell University Press, 2011), 37–40, 75–82; Robert G. Moeller, "Remembering the Past in a Nation of Victims: West German Pasts in the 1950s," in *The Miracle Years: A Cultural History of West Germany, 1949–1968*, ed. Hanna Schissler (Princeton, NJ: Princeton University Press, 2000), 83–109. Some scholars have challenged the notion that the 1950s were truly a period of silence about the Third Reich and its crimes. For example, Walter Uka has argued German films represented the war years far more often than historians usually realize. But he also admits such films almost always approach the subject in an ironic or satirical manner, and that the public was not ready for a realistic depiction of the past. Walter Uka, "Modernisierung im Wiederaufbau oder Restauration? Der bundesdeutsche Film der 50er Jahre," in *Die Kultur der 50er Jahre*, ed. Werner Faulstich (Munich: Wilhelm Fink Verlag, 2002), 86. See also Christoph Classen, *Bilder der Vergangenheit: die Zeit des Nationalsozialismus im Fernsehen der Bundesrepublik, 1955–1965* (Cologne: Böhlau, 1999), 8–10.

18. Television's self-critical turn, and the ongoing, uneven process of normalization, is exhaustively catalogued in Wulf Kansteiner, *In Pursuit of German Memory: History, Television, and Politics after Auschwitz* (Athens: Ohio University Press, 2006).

19. Neil Gregor, *Haunted City: Nuremberg and the Nazi Past* (New Haven, CT: Yale University Press, 2008), 301.

20. A West Berlin exhibit, *Die Vergangenheit mahnt*, described the demise of Europe's Jews as an international tragedy and may have played a role in shaping new teleplays of the early 1960s. Also, as Robert Sackett has noted, the public's broadly positive response to Gerhard Schoenberner's *Der gelbe Stern*, a photo documentation of the Holocaust released in 1960, also suggests a shift in German attitudes about the representation of the Third Reich's crimes. Robert Sackett, "Pictures of Atrocity: Public Discussion of *Der gelbe Stern* in Early 1960s West Germany," *German History* 24, no. 4 (2006): 528.

21. The prevalence of these story arcs in the late 1960s suggests the political emotion that Dirk Moses terms the "non-German German," or, the "redemptive republicans," experienced a period of ascendency at this time, even touching discourses in the East. Dirk Moses, *German Intellectuals and the Nazi Past* (New York: Cambridge University Press, 2007), 5.

22. With the possible exception of *Mord in Frankfurt* (1968), no television play during this era promoted the theory that the nation itself could be held guilty for Nazi-era

crimes. However, as Annette Weinke has pointed out, the GDR successfully injected itself into the West German discourse of guilt during the Frankfurt Auschwitz trials, promoting the notion that there were far more perpetrators in the FRG. These political machinations indirectly spilled over into East German dramas, as evidenced by *Dr. Schlüter* and *Schatten über Notre Dame*. See Annette Weinke, *Die Verfolgung von NS-Tätern im geteilten Deutschland: Vergangenheitsbewältigungen 1949–1969, oder: Eine deutsch-deutsche Beziehungsgeschichte im Kalten Krieg* (Paderborn: Ferdinand Schöningh, 2002), 236.

23. Olick, *Sins of the Fathers*, 244–250.
24. Ulrike Schwab, *Fiktionale Geschichtssendungen im DDR Fernsehen (II): Analyse und Dokumentation* (Leipzig: Leipziger Universitätsverlag, 2008), 7–8.
25. Jonathan R. Zatlin, *The Currency of Socialism: Money and Political Culture in East Germany* (New York: Cambridge University Press, 2007), 7; Frank Stern, *The Whitewashing of the Yellow Badge: Antisemitism and Philosemitism in Postwar Germany* (New York: Pergamon, 1992), 94–105.
26. This narrative of course ignored the astounding continuity of many German institutions from the 1930s to the 1950s and beyond. See Simon Reich, *The Fruits of Fascism: Postwar Prosperity in Historical Perspective* (Ithaca, NY: Cornell University Press, 1990), 2–3.
27. Of course, many of the same institutional continuities between the Third Reich and the FRG also existed in the GDR. See Delores Augustine, Heinrich Best, Axel Salheiser, Rüdiger Stutz, and Georg-Wagner Kyora, "Nazi Continuities in Easy Germany," special section, *German Studies Review* 29, no. 3 (2006).
28. Bruno Apitz and Hildegard Tetzlaff, *Nackt unter Wölfen*, dir. Georg Leopold (DFF, 10 April 1960); Bruno Apitz, *Nackt unter Wölfen* (Berlin: Mitteldeutscher Verlag, 1958).
29. Bill Niven, *The Buchenwald Child: Truth, Fiction, and Propaganda* (Rochester, NY: Camden House, 2007), 16.
30. Ibid., 93.
31. Ibid., 54–55.
32. See Peter Reichel, *Erfundene Erinnerung: Weltkrieg und Judenmord in Film und Theater* (Munich: Carl Hanser Verlag, 2004), 194. Catherine Epstein has investigated the regime's accelerating tendency to tightly regulate heterogeneous communist memories of the Weimar Republic and war years. Catherine Epstein, "The Production of 'Official Memory' in East Germany: Old Communists and the Dilemmas of Memoir-Writing," *Central European History* 32, no. 2 (1999).
33. Niven, *Buchenwald Child*, 92. The novel proved a huge success on publication, perhaps in part because the SED had, in 1955, decided to make Buchenwald a focal point of their "founding myth."
34. BArch, DR 8 487, untitled document, 11 May 1959.
35. BArch, DR 8 280, Problemskizze, 23 November 1959. A memo in BArch DR 8 487 even suggested the program might never come to fruition.
36. BArch, DR 8 280, Intendanz des Deutschen Fernsehzentrums, open letter to the producers of "Wolf unter Wölfen," 19 April 1960.
37. BArch, DR 8 27, Vorlagen Nr. 36/62 bis 53/62, 31 July 1962. See also Thomas Heimann, *Bilder von Buchenwald: Die Visualisierung des Antifaschismus in der DDR (1945–1990)* (Cologne: Böhlau Verlag, 2005), 71–97.
38. BArch, DR 8 280, Bericht des Dramatischen Kunstes, 3 August 1960. The letters are mentioned, but unfortunately, none are preserved at either the Bundesarchiv or the Rundfunkarchiv.

39. Katja Stern, *Neues Deutschland*, "Ihre Mordtaten verjähren niemals," 12 April 1960.
40. Klaus Rümmler, *Sächsische Zeitung*, "Mahnung und Verpflichtung," 16 April 1960.
41. Maria Matray and Answald Krüger, *Waldhausstraße 20*, dir. John Olden (NWRV Hamburg, 23 October 1960).
42. Matthew D. Hockenos, *A Church Divided: German Protestants Confront the Nazi Past* (Bloomington: Indiana University Press, 2004), 47–49.
43. *Funk-Korrespondenz* 45, 2 November 1960, 6.
44. *epd—Kirche und Fernsehen* 34, 31 October 1960.
45. Hockenos, *Church Divided*, 12.
46. On the privileged place of the two major churches in the immediate postwar era, see Maria Mitchell, "Materialism and Secularism: CDU Politicians and National Socialism, 1945–1949," *Journal of Modern History* 67, no. 2 (1995). On the erosion of the churches' moral authority vis-à-vis the Nazi past, see Nicolai Hannig, *Die Religion der Öffentlichkeit: Kirche, Religion und Medien in der Bundesrepublik, 1945–1980* (Göttingen: Wallstein, 2010), 103–148.
47. Leopold Ahlsen, *Sansibar*, dir. Rainer Wolffhardt (SDR, 28 December 1961). *Sansibar* aired after the Eichmann trial ended, but the novel on which it is based predates his capture, and the screenplay was written between his capture and most of the trial proceedings. It may therefore be considered a "pre-Eichmann" piece.
48. See *SDR Geschäftsbericht 1961* (Stuttgart: Süddeutscher Rundfunk, 1961).
49. *Funk-Korrespondenz* 1, 4 January 1962.
50. The term found broad usage among television critics of the era. Though the inherent reference to morality contained in "colportage" suggests *Sansibar* might also have been dismissed as such, neither the *Funk-Korrespondenz* nor the *epd*—two publications that gave extensive reviews—chose to use that term.
51. Kansteiner, *In Pursuit of German Memory*, 27.
52. Ibid., 12.
53. Olick, *Sins of the Fathers*, 63.
54. Kurt Jung-Ahlsen and Franz Fühmann, *Der Schwur des Soldaten Pooley*, dir. Jung-Ahlsen (DFF, 17 December 1961); Cyril Jolly, *The Vengeance of Private Pooley* (London: Heinemann, 1956).
55. This despite the claim that the program brought a case against the "Bonner Republik." *Neues Deutschland*, 30 August 1962. The simplicity of the appeal can be perceived in the narrator's final comment in the film: "They brought a wolf to justice. And now they returned to the everyday, to the midst of the societies from which they came."
56. Few insights into the producers' intentions have survived in the archive at Babelsberg, but the East German press certainly took the opportunity to denounce Western imperialism in their reviews. See, e.g., Myrian Selle-Christian, *Berliner Zeitung*, 14 December1961.
57. *FF Dabei*, 24 December 1961.
58. *Fernsehdienst*, 17 March 1963, 25.
59. Hans Oliva, *Gewissen in Aufruhr*, dir. Günter Reisch (DFF, 5, 7, 10, 12, 14 September 1961).
60. Rolf Gruddat, Gottfried Grohmann, and Hans-Erich Korbschmitt, *Die Flucht aus der Hölle*, dir. Korbschmitt (DFF, 11, 18, 25 October 1960; 1 November 1960).
61. Frank Biess, *Homecomings: Returning POWs and the Legacies of Defeat in Postwar Germany* (Princeton, NJ: Princeton University Press, 2006), 129–130.
62. DRA-B, "Methodisches Kabinett Analysen 3," 1966, 13.
63. Ibid., 14.

64. Ibid., 17.
65. This statement was more than mere lip service: Egel had worked as a radio dramatist for Radio Munich until 1947, only to leave for the East because American authorities thought he was a Soviet spy. See Peter Hoff's obituary, *Neues Deutschland*, 16 February 1995.
66. Paul H. Rameau, *Menschen helfen Menschen: Zwei Tage von Vielen*, dir. Ralph Lothar (ZDF, 11 March 1963).
67. Maria Matray and Answald Krüger, *Standgericht*, dir. Rolf Busch (NDR, 10 October 1966).
68. Staatsarchiv Hamburg, NDR 621-1 144 1091, *Standgericht*.
69. Not all viewers agreed with this assessment. While Infratest notes the piece received mostly positive qualitative reviews, around 18 percent of the viewers expressed their dismay that the Nazi past was being brought up yet again. One comment sums up this position: "After 20 years, they should just stop. We need to move beyond the past." *Infratest Wochenbericht*, October 1966, 33.
70. Rolf Hädrich, *Mord in Frankfurt*, dir. Rolf Hädrich (WDR, 30 January 1968).
71. *Mord in Frankfurt* was nominated for a prize at the International Television Festival in Prague. The viewer ratings can be found in *Infratest Wochenbericht*, January 1968, 29. Negative scores (-1, -2, etc.) were also possible.
72. More than 23 percent of viewers, only a portion of those who gave the film a poor rating, called the film "incoherent."
73. *Infratest Wochenbericht*, January 1968, 31.
74. Historisches Archiv des Westdeutschen Rundfunks, 13469, letter from Günter Rohrbach to Hans Joachim Lange, 17 September 1968, 7.
75. DRA-B, SFB 1531, *In der Strafkolonie*, letter from Dagmar Fambach to viewer, 13 March 1963, response to a postcard dated 11 March 1963.
76. Dieter Meischner, *Alma Mater*, dir. Rolf Hädrich (NDR, 5 February 1969).
77. Gerhard Bengsch, *Krupp und Krause*, dir. Horst E. Brandt (DFF, 5, 7, 9, 12, 14 January 1969).
78. Elizabeth Snyder Hook, "Awakening from War: History, Trauma, and Testimony in Heinrich Böll," in *The Work of Memory: New Directions in the Study of German Society and Culture*, ed. Alon Confino and Peter Fritzsche (Urbana: University of Illinois Press, 2002), 149.

Chapter 2

CRAFTING POLITICAL ROLE MODELS

The Righteous Fugitive and the Man (or Woman) of Conscience

While properly representing historical figures, events, and themes from the Third Reich loomed large in the minds of television authorities, as encapsulated by Klaus von Bismarck's statement that viewers needed to see elements of the difficult German past represented in "unabridged" form on the small screen, it by no means comprised the totality of their efforts to reestablish and reinvent Germany's moral universe.[1] Indeed, in the face of viewer resistance to depictions of the Third Reich, encapsulated in one viewer's insistence that "the whole business with the Jews during the war" was tiresome and unnecessary, stations could hardly expect even the most explicit depictions of National Socialism's moral failures to always achieve the desired resonance or lead to any significant soul-searching among certain segments of the population.[2] In response to this perceived indifference, program makers elected to weave stories from the war with important considerations in the present.[3] Writers and producers sought ways to make the past relevant before they unfolded lessons and morals from the Nazi catastrophe. For this reason, even television plays that focused on events from the Weimar Republic or World War II often also referenced the Cold War.

One of the most popular combinations of history and politics in this vein was the multipart September 1961 play *Gewissen in Aufruhr* (Conscience up in arms).[4] Based on a real-life memoir written by the commanding officer of Greifswald, a city north of Berlin, *Gewissen in Aufruhr* is a classic example of how East German authorities wanted the public to remember the war and its consequences. Hans Oliva and Günter Reisch's program begins with a sense of deep foreboding on the part of its protagonist, a Wehrmacht captain named Joachim Ebershagen.[5] He writes a troubled letter to his wife, explaining that despite the long run of German successes on the Eastern front, winter is setting in and he may not return. Through Ebershagen's eyes, viewers witness the death and starvation of most of the men in his company, and their shallow burial in the drifting snow. They also see how many of the generals and high-ranking officers, terrified at the prospect of their own demise, demand they be airlifted away from the now-doomed 6th Army at Stalingrad in the winter of 1942/1943. Because of a serious leg wound, Ebershagen is one of the last to be transported out (despite his protests that he should stay). He returns to his home in Greifswald, where he later commands a reserve garrison.

In 1945, Ebershagen receives an order to conscript the few remaining able-bodied men and boys in the city, and to fight to the death against the imminent Russian invasion. He refuses the order, instead surrendering the city to the Red Army without resistance. Remarkably, Ebershagen willingly goes to a POW camp in the Soviet Union, as a kind of penance for what he considers his bloodthirsty actions earlier in the war. Upon return, the Communist Party leaders fete Ebershagen as a "true man of conscience," despite his refusal to join the SED. Because of his strong pacifist credentials, Ebershagen often receives invitations to speak at conferences in the FRG. At one of these events, in Munich, Ebershagen is the victim of a plot to frame him as an East German operative. When he confides to a seemingly conflicted young German working for the CIA that he would be better off in the GDR, West German authorities arrest him on espionage charges. The prosecutors successfully insert his "treasonous" decision at Greifswald as evidence of his untrustworthy character, and he is sentenced to six years in prison. At the end of this term, and disillusioned with the West, Ebershagen returns to the East, dramatically walking through Brandenburg Gate and into the arms of his waiting wife (the Berlin Wall had not yet been established when the show was filmed). A voice-over declares the hero had chosen to live in the only "true Germany."

Gewissen in Aufruhr intersects with contemporary political imperatives in numerous ways. For example, when the Russians capture Greifswald and subsequently meet with Ebershagen, the commanding general presents the impending change from fascism to socialism as a victory for democracy. He implores Ebershagen, "The 'struggle-less' handing over of the city proves that you think about the future. Offer your services for the configuration of democracy." The Russian leader here connects the future with a democratic "configuration." The GDR did not, of course, adopt particularly democratic institutions in practice, but it frequently countenanced the term in justifying its own existence, with the regime even referring to itself as a "People's

Democracy." East German citizens, the SED proclaimed, had chosen socialism as an alternative to fascism, and out of disdain for what propagandists labeled the sham liberal democracy in the FRG. Democracy thus became a contested term.

In a later installment, in fact, Ebershagen tries to convince the aforementioned potential defector that he should join with the "democratic" forces in the East (opposed to the "fascist" forces still in control of the West). When this seemingly innocuous suggestion lands Ebershagen in prison, held for months without a trial, the program invites the viewer to consider whether the West is truly as liberal and democratic as it purports to be. Moreover, the West German police subject Ebershagen to booming loudspeakers and other deprivations. Ebershagen experiences flashbacks of men in SS uniforms, hitting and shooting civilians in Eastern Europe. By invoking torture and signaling continuity between these tactics and the Nazi state, Oliva and Reisch here refer to Nazi practices, which likewise included immoral "reeducation" techniques with communist and socialist prisoners. In the early Cold War, the combatants often framed political decisions as a continuation of the choices faced by the German public during the Third Reich.

Other, subtler cues in the broadcast reinforce the notion of continuity. For example, while serving time at Landsberg Prison, Ebershagen witnesses the visit of a Christlich Demokratische Union (Christian Democratic Union of Germany—CDU) functionary, who, with animated language, explains to former SS officers that Munich is once again "defensible" and that the Americans have already given permission for the restoration of the German Armed Forces (Bundeswehr). The former Nazis heartily cheer these announcements, while Ebershagen looks on with seeming disgust. The assembled group then sings "Deutschland, Deutschland über alles," which, as the tune progresses, is superseded by a minor rendition of the same piece.[6] In a subsequent scene at the same facility, a guard hands out gifts from Konrad Adenauer to the prisoners; Ebershagen, widely perceived as a traitor, does not receive one. Oliva and Reisch thus use visual markers and music to reinforce the sense that the FRG is the natural successor to the Nazi state.

Gewissen in Aufruhr also neatly demonstrates the relational nature of television fiction in the two German states. Authorities intended Oliva's piece, along with an earlier escape story, *Die Flucht aus der Hölle* (Flight out of hell, 1960), as a response to the 1959 WDR adaptation of *So weit die Füße tragen* (As far as your feet can carry you), an adventure story that features a German POW escaping a Siberian gulag and making his way across the steppe to Iran and, eventually, freedom.[7] The functional similarities between this piece and *Gewissen in Aufruhr* are striking. For instance, Ebershagen's tired expression when he staggers toward the waiting arms of his wife at the end of the East German production closely mirrors the reaction of *So weit die Füße tragen*'s protagonist, Clemens Forell, when he finally realizes he will get to return home. All three pieces also feature squalid prisons, panoramic shots of a barren landscape, and false friends who offer help to the protagonist only to subsequently betray him. The image of the unjustly imprisoned POW looms large on both sides in postwar German television. The returning prisoner represented a reestablishment of the masculine order.[8] In a sense, the prisoner's return contributed to the nation's rebirth and redemption.[9]

As one scene in *Gewissen in Aufruhr* demonstrates, however, a POW's homecoming was not merely about the righting of past wrongs or injustices. When Soviet troops advance on the emaciated 6th Army at Stalingrad, they are accompanied by a handful of German soldiers, ostensibly communist refugees. One of these soldiers explains to his comrades, "Now we have to create a new world with these people."[10] In other words, those Germans who saw through and rejected Nazism from the start are now tasked with converting, reeducating, and rehabilitating those who stayed. This theme is repeatedly expressed for the duration of the series. For example, the same German "defectors" are stationed as guards at Ebershagen's POW camp. They explain to Ebershagen (whom they trust, on account of his actions at Greifswald) that some prisoners have joined the communist resistance group Antifa and appear to be on the road to penance and rehabilitation. Other POWs, however, try to frame their own "conversions" in a different way, by becoming active in the camp's Catholic and Lutheran church groups and by regularly attending sermons. As the guards note, these perpetrators have become *scheinheilig* (hypocritical), in that they are not true believers.

The imperative to strengthen and heal the German nation after its long National Socialist interlude often found expression in Cold War political terms. Indeed, the corpus of 1950s and 1960s television fiction is teeming with examples of interstate rivalry and animosity. But while the battle to win Germans' hearts and minds originated in large measure from the escalating standoff between the Soviet Union and the West, political themes—particularly ones that conveyed moral lessons—also derived from a widespread desire to remake German political consciousness and awareness at a fundamental level. Political reeducation began as soon as the war ended in 1945, featuring Allied-influenced print media, radio, and even the infamous questionnaires handed out by American occupiers.[11] To be sure, the Cold War accelerated the process of international political reintegration, but many German observers in the 1950s and 1960s continued to harbor doubts about the sincerity and depth of citizens' political transformation. The publicist (and former concentration camp prisoner) Kurt Hirsch wrote in 1967, "Evading World War II's political realities might seem comprehensible as an election tactic, but it makes it easier . . . for right-wing extremists to infiltrate the Federal Republic's shaky buttresses."[12] The political scientists Carter Kniffler and Hanna Schlette, writing the same year, expressed similar—albeit veiled—doubts: "*Bild-Zeitung* readers, to put it succinctly, don't want a dictatorship, but they are going along with one."[13] On top of all this, authorities in the FRG were keenly aware that while democracy had become a popular watchword, public opinion surveys suggested authoritarian values such as obedience and conformity persisted throughout the 1950s and 1960s.[14]

While they never openly acknowledged any fascist movements or tendencies within their state, East German authorities were privately just as concerned as their Western counterparts about the possible failings of political reeducation. Soviet zone administrators, for example, explicitly aimed to prevent a resurgence of Nazism when they reformed the education system in the East, according to what they understood as an "anti-fascist" ideology.[15] And this imperative did not begin and end with schools. The anti-fascist memory regime created by the SED broadly memorialized former concentration camps in the hopes of expunging Nazi ideology from the nation. For instance, President Otto Grotewohl wrote that planned memorials at Buchenwald and Sachsenhausen were to "place the shame and disgrace of the past before the young generation so that they can draw lessons from it."[16] Authorities therefore perceived the persistence of fascist attitudes as a real danger and the source of reeducation efforts. Moreover, these same leaders understood artists as possessing a pivotal role in overcoming twelve years of National Socialism.[17]

Few dramatic programs included classroom-style lessons in democracy, socialism, or voting rights, of course. Instead, producers and writers embedded correct (or deviant) political behavior into their pieces. East German politicians at first did not fully appreciate the value of television as anything more than an extension of radio propaganda. They considered it a space to be conquered and occupied, reflecting little on the medium's potential for visually complex messages.[18] As they learned the medium's value in the context of the Cold War struggle, they hired writers and producers who bluntly valorized protagonists as well-adjusted communists or socialists. Over time, these representations became both more refined and more visually appealing, and they came to see TV as the ideal tool for disseminating correct thinking about politics.[19] In contrast, their West German counterparts appreciated television's potential to shape post-Nazi political sensibilities from the start. Here, too, however, dramatic lessons underwent a transformation between 1956 and the late 1960s, as depictions gradually became more nuanced and less concerned with countering a specific, communist threat.

There is no shortage of secondary material on the intersection between politics and television, of course. Older sources focused heavily on the connections between politics and television viewing.[20] More recent works, which largely focus on "programming history," begin and end with a politics-first model of television: producers and propagandists created representations of political values in a never-ending Cold War battle for viewers.[21] Recent adaptations of this model recognize some interaction involving viewers and/or critics, instead of the simple unidirectional dynamic favored by studies in the 1960s and 1970s.[22] But, almost without exception, when the histories of East and West German television have been presented together, the political and competitive aspects of the medium have been placed at the forefront. In many ways, this school of thought merely reflects the realities of competition. The political dimensions of German television persistently took center stage. Politics has provided an easily accessible common denominator for comparison, and a rich source of material. Any study of German-German television that leaves politics out of the equation has overlooked the eight-hundred-pound gorilla in the room.

Heretofore, then, most scholars have focused on either the intentions of producers or politics at the macro level. My examination of moral themes suggests an alternate approach: television fiction depicted individual strategies for managing and implementing political ideologies. These strategies drew on a palette of possibilities and techniques, presenting the viewer with choices, role models, and a concrete set of ethical guidelines. The contents of this palette derived from the Cold War struggle between East and West, but it also had firm roots in the postwar rebuilding project. Moral political lessons, though often couched in Cold War terms, were a vehicle for overcoming Germans' perceived political miseducation.[23] In contrast to many news programs, teleplays stressed the virtues of democracy and political participation by modeling such behavior in a dramatic context.[24] And because of television's increasingly prominent position in living rooms across Germany, producers expected these lessons to be internalized and individualized.

Plays on both sides thus gravitated toward the valorization of a political role model. More often than not, the protagonist in such productions did not appear as the ideal representative of any political ideology. They often followed a similar (though perhaps not so turbulent) path as Martin Schlüter: they are simple, even innocent, men and women at the start of a program or series, then experience the injustices of the "other" Germany, and eventually throw their lot in with the "correct" side. Two story types in this vein emerged as dominant in the late 1950s and 1960s. First, some role models experienced their conversion to the "correct" political orientation by undertaking a daring escape from oppression. *So weit die Füße tragen* acted as the genesis of such narratives, but East German writers and producers quickly became the chief practitioners of the escape story. The "righteous fugitive" trajectory was particularly relevant in the years and months leading up to the erection of the Berlin Wall in 1961, when millions of East Germans fled to the West. By highlighting fugitive stories in which left-leaning or socialist sympathizers are forced to flee some politically rooted, systemic threat in the West, East German authorities tried to push back against the narrative that the GDR oppressed its citizens and therefore lacked legitimacy. When the Wall appeared, however, these fugitive tales fell out of favor (though it took more than a year for this new position to be reflected on the small screen, given the time it took to plan, write, produce, and broadcast a television drama). Television fiction in the GDR would continue to fete defectors from the West, but the notion of an adventure-filled escape seemed inadvisable given the SED's decision to seal off the border.

The second story type to emerge, the man or woman of conscience, had a more lasting appeal, on both sides of the divide. This type of representation began with *Gewissen in Aufruhr*. Unlike in the escape narrative, the protagonist here wrestles with difficult ideological and philosophical choices. They will be torn by identification with more than one point of view, as, for example, Ebershagen struggles to reconcile his growing affinity to socialism (which was nonexistent during the war) with a sense of duty to his former commanding officers, now residing in the West. Similarly, West German plays depicted how East Germans with a seemingly strong sense of loyalty to their country experience some moment of epiphany and disillusionment. Notably, this type of narrative emerged as a vehicle for self-criticism in the West. For many producers, the development of a self-sufficient moral compass, irrespective of political ideology, was one of the most important safeguards against a return of National Socialism. The democratic consensus style of government in the FRG, so important in the wake of National Socialism, thus began to erode under the skeptical eye of the generation that came of age during and after the war (and which favored a more liberalized public sphere).[25]

* * *

The righteous fugitive trope has exercised a powerful pull on the human imagination since ancient times. A hero, unjustly held captive, makes a daring escape and defeats all odds to return home. Given such universal popularity, it is no surprise Josef Martin Bauer's 1955 novel *So weit die Füße tragen* quickly became a bestseller. The novel's protagonist, the former Wehrmacht soldier Clemens Forell, attempts an almost unthinkable escape after four years of coerced labor in a Siberian lead mine. He treks across the vast Asian continent, eluding the Soviet authorities and finding help from Russian and non-Russian natives alike. Three years later, he stumbles into the West German embassy in Iran. Despite the protagonist's agonizingly slow progress, the novel moves at a brisk pace and is written with a broad, popular audience in mind. The book's commercial success, however, also derives from its choice of setting. The question of German prisoners of war remained fixed in the public eye. One of the most widely accepted West German narratives about the war's end was that the German people had likewise been victims of Hitler's crimes. Hundreds of thousands of POWs had been interned in the Soviet Union, and even more ethnic Germans flowed into the two German states as part of a massive program of forced displacement. Catholic and Protestant bishops, with conservative politicians at their side, protested vigorously against the POW and refugee situation. Newspapers in the FRG constantly ran stories and editorials about the injustices, particularly regarding the Soviet POW camps. Historians now understand the fixation with POWs and refugees not only as a means for deflecting guilt (though this was doubtless true in many cases) but also as an expression of dissatisfaction with the state of German masculinity. The hypermasculine world of the Third Reich had been turned upside down, as POWs found themselves stripped of their dignity and virility. Some physicians even diagnosed returning soldiers with female pubic hair.[26] Bauer's book taps into this vein of uncertainty. At least one soldier does not have to wait for release, and, as far as the reader knows, he was not a war criminal. He is a victim who seizes the initiative and somehow defeats an uncaring, bleak natural world (represented by Siberia and Eastern Russia).

Fritz Umgelter's 1959 television adaptation of this popular novel, then, was bound to attract significant attention.[27] For one, it closely followed the novel in terms of its representation of a revitalized masculine figure. For example, the situation as conveyed at the beginning of the miniseries makes it clear Forell had not been a war criminal at all. Neither the novel nor the TV version depicts the events in Moscow, but the German prisoners discuss how the mass trial had been a sham. His experience thus mirrored that of many postwar Germans: Forell, like others, was duped into serving in the Wehrmacht and had been unjustly held guilty for crimes he did not commit. He therefore became a righteous fugitive, who in his adventurous escape regained the status of a noble warrior. As an extension of this new masculine model, Forell avoided killing bystanders and enemies, even, as in one scene, when in possession of a gun and under fire. He maintains his moral compass throughout. The broadcast also appeared at precisely the right moment. The development of television in Germany had been consciously delayed compared to the United States and Great Britain. Regular broadcasting began only in 1956, and few Germans owned a set until 1959. Programming on the new medium largely consisted of inexpensive chamber pieces. *So weit die Füße tragen* was one of the first real hits, airing at exactly the same time as television set purchases started to explode. Some executives even attributed this expansion to the success of Umgelter's broadcast. The combination of the medium's rise and the continued popularity of "homecoming" stories featuring POWs proved a recipe for success.

In a Cold War atmosphere, however, what might seem a simple narrative of heroic escape, interspersed with a measure of masculine redemption, became a political statement. The Russian soldiers stationed at Forell's lead mine, for instance, appear as inhuman monsters. They indiscriminately shoot at the train convoy as it pulls into the mine station, and they set their dogs on the weak or straggling prisoners. One German POW mentions to his comrade, "Christmas doesn't matter for the Russians anymore . . . nothing is holy for them anymore," a reference to the decline of religion in the Soviet Union. The passing reference to the lack of religiosity in Russia may seem trivial, but Umgelter lingers on the theme by using a church choir, complete with an organ as accompaniment, as background music to the first leg of Forell's escape, across northeast Siberia. Forell even says, to himself, that the white, snowy landscape reminds him of a quiet church, "maybe even a Roman cathedral," and the scene fades into a slowly spinning shot of a ceiling fresco. To religious West German viewers, this statement indicted the Soviets' official policy of atheism by bemoaning heartless, cruel atheism in such a beautiful location.

The criticism of Soviet policies continues as Forell makes his way across Asia. He meets native reindeer herdsmen, for instance, who help the curious German refugee not only out of pity and compassion but also because they find the Soviet gulag system repellent. One native, in a lengthy conversation with Forell, explains he once provided reindeer meat and milk to a gulag camp. But when he one day saw how the camp operated, and how many bodies the guards threw into shallow graves every day, he took his herd and moved away from the gulag, in disgust. When Forell asks him why he wasn't caught, the herdsman says the Red Army does not understand anything about the landscape more than a few kilometers from their railways and mining centers. They are ignorant of how the natives live in the far north. In another encounter, Forell travels with three other refugees, all from Western Russia. Two of the men claim to be communists but also explain that the country is disintegrating. The three men, it turns out, had been sent to a gulag because they allegedly stole from the collective. Forell's first encounter with the local Russian authorities in Siberia likewise reflects poorly on the Communist Party in the Soviet Union. When confronted by the townspeople in one village, the three prisoners (and Forell) find it easy to bribe the local mayor, even though they are known criminals. In the wake of this scene, Forell tells his dog, "You're the only honest creature in Russia."

SED elites perceived *So weit die Füße tragen* as an attack on communism itself, by association. Over the next several years, they accordingly pressured East German television producers to respond.[28] They already recognized television as an important battleground, as it could reach viewers in both states. Albert Norden, a member of the *Zentralkomitee* responsible for DFF, noted in 1960: "The 'artistic' programs of the [DFF] influence millions of people in both German states and in West Berlin. Therefore it must be the most politically and artistically able cadre which design them."[29] Accordingly, the television industry received many of the best dramatic talents of the era. The station executives then instructed these creators and actors to devote their skills to negative depictions of the West.

The first response came in the form of another fugitive tale, *Die Flucht aus der Hölle* in 1960. The multiauthored film follows the adventures of Hans Röder, an auto mechanic from Frankfurt (am Main). After he allegedly makes a faulty auto repair that leads to a driver's death, he enlists in the French Foreign Legion to escape legal punishment. While in Algeria, he refuses to participate in the execution of *fellaghas* (partisans) and subsequently escapes back to West Germany. There, an international fascist group called the Red Hand threatens and persecutes him for taking his story of the massacre to the press. Finally, arrested on trumped-up charges in West Berlin, Hans eludes his police escort and jumps out of a train onto East German soil and freedom. The program constantly explains Hans's motivations within a Cold War political context. For example, his troubles in Germany essentially mirror the ones he had in Africa: a nongovernmental fascist organization infiltrates both the French foreign legion in Algeria and the police force in Hamburg. In both Algeria and Germany, he uncovers criminal actions perpetrated by the Red Hand, only to see his co-accusers murdered by agents. Even the atmosphere of the fascist hideouts in both countries is similar, populated by scantily clad foreign women, neon lights, and well-dressed mobsters. *Die Flucht* thus attempts to implicate West Germany in a supranational fascist ring, drawing connections between the FRG police and a broader capitalist conspiracy. Hans's "faulty" auto repair, for instance, was nothing of the sort; the local police station had agreed to help obtain recruiters for the Legion as part of a covert anticolonial operation in North Africa.

The series' climactic scenes occur in the fourth and final installment, when Hans finally begins to realize he cannot trust the West German police. After his return from Tunis (where he had been a refugee), he tries to settle in Hamburg with his fiancée, Ilse. But the Red Hand seems to be conspiring with the authorities here, too. The customs officer refuses to register Hans as a German citizen without a birth certificate and adds, for good measure, he believes him to be an illegal refugee from the East. Hours later, Red Hand agents try to murder Hans and Ilse with a car bomb, only to mistakenly kill a journalist with whom the couple had been corresponding about events in Algeria. He goes to the police department, only to be informed the car bomb is none of their concern and that the Red Hand does not exist. A trip to the Interpol office similarly bears no fruit, as they consider the Red Hand a "political organization" and thus outside their purview. After yet another near escape from operatives, Hans declares to Ilse, "I just want to live in peace. Like a human being." Together, they decide to emigrate to the GDR. Even this action is difficult, as French agents, again with the help of West German police detectives, remove Hans from his airplane and try to deport him to France. Only by jumping off a moving train while traveling through East Berlin does Hans finally escape to freedom. Improbably, Hans immediately encounters an East German police officer on patrol, who accepts his story without question and takes him to see a relieved Ilse and several sympathetic police inspectors.

Another, somewhat belated DFF response to *So weit die Füße tragen* appeared in 1962, with Herbert Freyer and Rudi Kurz's rollicking *Das grüne Ungeheuer* (literally the green monster, but translations often reference a figure called the green pope), based on a 1959 Wolfgang Schreyer novel of the same name.[30] The German-born protagonist, Morena, works as a pilot at a private airfield in the United States (Georgia) in the late 1950s. The airfield owner, a flamboyant American businessman named Steve, uses intermediaries to frame Morena for murder. Steve then appears with a solution: he can procure a passport to Honduras, where he will be relatively safe from extradition. Morena flies with a small group of other refugees to a mysterious island in the Caribbean. Here, he meets a socialist journalist, Dr. Guerra, and his daughter, Isabel. All three find themselves in the custody of a Guatemalan general who has come to recruit officers for his ongoing war against communist guerilla fighters. The "reactionary" army receives significant backing from the United Fruit Company, famous for its role in funding private wars and enabling US-backed coups in Central America. Dr. Guerra disappears. Morena, fearing for his life, becomes a pilot. Isabel overhears the officers' plot to use chemical weapons against the insurgents and is nearly executed. Morena intervenes, however, and the two eventually flee into the jungle. This section of the film, the fourth installment, closely resembles similar scenes from *Die Flucht aus der Hölle* and *So weit die Füße tragen*. Panoramic shots of the wilderness, action sequences involving narrow escapes from wild animals, and the pair's interactions with Guatemalan natives—some sympathetic, others hostile—add a sense of adventure to the escape. In the final installment, Morena and Isabel reach Guatemala City, find Isabel's father (who, it turns out, had been captured and released by communist spies), evade the advancing United Fruit army, and find refuge in Cuba.

The program's creators clearly intended the piece as a criticism of American imperialism first and as an adventure story second. Schreyer's now-obscure novel relied loosely on former US Marine Corps Major General Smedley D. Butler's inflammatory piece *War Is a Racket* and on eyewitnesses who subsequently fled to Cuba as refugees. In an interview for DFF's promotional materials, Schreyer refers to himself above all as a journalist and historian.[31]

His invented characters found themselves trapped in a swirl of imperialist and guerilla forces, and slowly realized the United Fruit Company had sinister intentions in Guatemala, as elsewhere in Central America. In a 2008 memoir, Rudi Kurz explained his involvement with the production began when he met Janos Székely, a Hungarian immigrant living in Los Angeles who, because his left-leaning Hollywood screenplays were deemed unacceptable during the era of McCarthyism, moved to Berlin. Székely's daughter, Kati, was cast as Isabel.[32] Contemporary critics almost universally reviewed *Das grüne Ungeheuer* as a political commentary on American imperialism, with a neutral, "undecided individual" forced to pick a side.[33] Most viewer letters on the piece, such as those carefully selected and reprinted in the *Bauernecho*, a weekly magazine for rural areas, likewise painted Morena and Isabel as models of "political sincerity."[34] Even several decades later, in honor of a rebroadcast, the famous East German television historian and erstwhile critic Peter Hoff noted the center of the film was the "refugees" making resolute "political" decisions.[35]

In much the same way *So weit die Füße tragen*, in details and in circumstances, reveals the injustices and moral deficiencies of the Soviet Union through a nonpartisan German fugitive's eyes, *Das grüne Ungeheuer* bluntly casts the struggle between American capitalism and native-run resistance groups in stark Manichean terms. The screenplay makes it clear that Morena, played by the well-known actor Jürgen Frohriep, comes from Bavaria. He has no previous connections with the GDR or with any socialist entity. And he lives happily in Georgia. Thrust into the civil war in Honduras and Guatemala, however, Morena becomes disillusioned with the Americans and their conspirators. For example, in the third installment, he encounters another German, a man named Hardenberg. At first, they share a beer and reminisce about their home country. The mood changes, however, when Morena learns his companion once served as a Nazi *Gauleiter* (regional leader). He fled in 1944 to escape imprisonment (or execution), and he now works as a consultant for United Fruit. Freyer and Kurz paint Hardenberg's immorality in definite terms. After a few drinks, he tells Morena the US-backed juntas and dictatorships in Latin American are "exactly the right method" and that the Guatemalans are like petulant children who need a firm hand. By explicitly referencing National Socialism, Freyer and Kurz inserted a signal their audience would immediately grasp, and left no doubt as to which side the protagonist should choose. As in *Die Flucht aus der Hölle*, fascism, capitalism, and imperialism are closely linked.

Das grüne Ungeheuer also reinvents German masculinity. Morena, like his predecessor Forell, seizes the initiative and attempts a daring escape. Most remarkable, though, is how the program positions Morena as a virile but gentle figure. During the second installment, Isabel eavesdrops on a staff meeting while imprisoned at the United Fruit Company's villa in Honduras. When she is discovered and taken back to her room, the general asks for a volunteer among his staff members to rape the girl, both as punishment and to keep her "quiet." The camera pans the room, showing how each (male) staff member seems terrified by this prospect. Finally, the German-born hero Morena, pressed into service against his will but considered a valuable soldier because of his advanced training, agrees to do it (although he has no intention of raping Isabel, his close friend). Thus, the film shows the capitalist staff members, stereotyped as aristocratic European officers with military decorations and monocles, as impotent and emasculated. The lone outsider, Morena, is presented as the only virile soldier in the room. The reactions of these characters, representatives of their specific ideologies (Morena later joins a communist resistance movement), genders the Cold War political struggle, making the capitalist side seem full of bluster but unable to fulfill its promises. The socialist side, on the other hand, comes across as simultaneously fertile, reliable, and controlled.

Das grüne Ungeheuer proved wildly popular among viewers and, as indicated by how often it reappeared on Saturday afternoons for the next few decades, among television authorities. Indeed, it in many ways followed the 14th SED Party Plenum's directive in 1961 about television, that it was "in all areas to prove the superiority of our socialist societal order in contrast to that of capitalism in West Germany . . . the overcoming of imperialism and militarism in West Germany is the life question of the German people."[36] It is noteworthy, however, that the story of a righteous German fugitive moved from an inter-German affair in the last two installments of *Die Flucht aus der Hölle* to the Central American jungle in *Das grüne Ungeheuer*. On its face, the change in location seems relatively benign. In fact, though, East German television would fund very few pieces with the same "adventurous escape from capitalism" trope after *Das grüne Ungeheuer*. The Berlin Wall, erected in the summer of 1961, had drastically altered the political narrative. With the construction of an "anti-fascist" barrier, explicitly presented as a way to keep right-wing forces out of the country, the idea of West Germans "escaping" to the GDR was not one the SED wanted to trumpet. Moreover, as Heather Gumbert has demonstrated, in the wake of political backlash against the operatic television opera *Fetzers Flucht*, television writers could no longer depict the choice between East and West as one of simply crossing the border.[37] West German defectors still found their way into teleplays throughout the 1960s, but they came to the GDR with a legal visa and through border control. Subsequent West German stories with a fugitive motif likewise took on a very different flavor as a result of the Wall. For example, Herbert Reinecker's *Nachtzug D 106* (Night train D 106, 1964) similarly depicts an attempted escape, in this case from East to West.[38] An

East German youth jumps aboard a temporarily stopped "interzone" train, prompting an angry, protracted debate among the (West German) passengers about whether it is their moral duty to try to harbor the boy from the patrolling soldiers. In the end, an opportunity presents itself and even those who had argued against aid decide to participate in helping the boy. But when the guard sees the passport they had planned to present twice, in different parts of the train, the youth realizes he has no chance and that his hope for freedom had been unfounded all along. He jumps off the train, into the night.

In a sense, *Nachtzug D 106* looks at the question of border jumping and political refugees from the perspective of the bystanders. The East German youth speaks very little; indeed, it seems Reinecker chose this character precisely because his situation seems so uncomplicated from the viewer's perspective. The play's real moral discussion occurs as the other passengers discuss the situation. What had been a comfortable journey inside the compartment, with one couple flirting, two men sharing a laugh over cigarettes, and another passenger's nose buried deep in a novel, turns suddenly uncomfortable. As the youth then watches (with a look of terror on his face), the conversation turns to the ethical merits of helping a refugee in the first place. One passenger, a cynical businessman named Schäkel, compares the situation to a game of chess. The youth is merely a pawn, he says, and not worth risking trouble with the East German border guards who are checking tickets. Two of the younger passengers, Billy and Vera, declare it is their moral duty to help anyone in need, just as Christ taught. This sort of abstract conversation dominates the play. Reinecker, as indicated in production documents about the piece, clearly intended *Nachtzug D106* as a criticism against what he perceived as the increasingly complacent West German press.[39] The abstract comments about chess and religion contrast sharply, and visually, with the disheveled youth asking simply and politely for help. In other words, Reinecker intended to shame viewers into action. Some television critics saw this as a welcome gesture. The left-leaning *Kieler Nachrichten*, for instance, saw *Nachtzug D106* as a good choice as it held up a mirror to the "pathetic West."[40] W. P. at the regional daily newspaper *Kölnischer Rundschau* agreed, noting the "bitter" piece had fulfilled its purpose in destroying the myth that brothers will help brothers in Germany.[41] Inasmuch as Reinecker chose a specifically German-German setting, and as critics seemed to zero in on the question of charity and integrity in the FRG, *Nachtzug D106* saw West German apathy as part of the border problem.

By the late 1960s, East German programs could no longer visualize fugitives in such a blatant manner, and West German shows used the motif to express dissatisfaction with the state of divided Germany or with FRG citizens' moral shortcomings. A January 1968 SWF broadcast, *Die Einladung* (*The Invitation*), acts as a kind of coda on the whole fugitive genre.[42] The program centers on a family divided by the German-German border: a nearly retired East German engineer (Franz), his wife (Hilde), their disgruntled son (Achim, married to a still-communist wife, Lisa), and their daughter (Hanna, who lives in Düsseldorf with her West German husband, Karl). One weekend, Franz and Hilde entertain both children in their apartment near the border in Berlin. The program begins with the customary pleasantries inherent to a family reunion of this kind, but, after settling in and consuming a fair amount of alcohol, Hanna and Karl reveal a plan to smuggle the entire family across the border into the FRG. At first, Franz seems pleased with the idea. Although he is an SED member, he has long been disillusioned with the regime and wants to move his restless son, Achim, to relative safety in the West. Lisa, though, reminds him of the dangers involved in border crossing. If they fail, she wonders, what will happen with her young child? The local police have long seen Achim as a potential risk; he might well have to endure a lengthy prison sentence if they can't get across. Each of the six adult family members weighs in, and an increasingly heated ideological argument breaks out. Is socialism really so bad, they wonder, that they need to carry out such a desperate plan? Are the amenities and comforts of the West worth giving up Franz's forthcoming pension? The son, disillusioned by the family's bickering, storms out, leaving the remaining five to wonder whether he tried to navigate the border defenses on his own.

Originally conceived as a 1966 radio play and converted into a 1967 play at the Schlosspark Theater in West Berlin, the television version of *Die Einladung* in many ways typifies the nature of moral lessons about politics on the small screen. The original author, Jochen Ziem, wrote Franz as an *interzonal* pensioner who could have lived just as well in the West as in the East. This was in many ways a self-portrait. Ziem had lived in Leipzig and studied under the world-famous playwright Bertolt Brecht. He became disillusioned with the Ulbricht regime in the wake of the 1953 uprisings and resettled to the West in 1956. Franz thus loosely reflects Ziem's personal experiences. One of Ziem's main objectives in creating *Die Einladung* was to highlight and reinforce the significant commonalities underlying German culture on both sides of the divide. Helmut Griem noted in *Der Spiegel* that the family members, though long divided, still "adhere to the same petite bourgeois mentality" and possess the same "hopes, prejudices, and complaints."[43] The radio play pits Franz, Lisa, and Achim against one another in a complex assessment of East German Communism's strengths and weaknesses. Lisa and Franz, in particular, position the discussion about whether to escape within a highly abstract set of observations. The stage play recasts these questions and themes within a more specific dramatic context; the characters are given complex backgrounds and personalities. Franz spends five years in an East German prison, for example, and it is revealed Achim and Lisa have a young son. The piece's director, Heinz Schimmelpfennig, carries this even further. Viewers catch several glimpses of Achim and Lisa's son, reminding them of the significant risks involved in attempting a border crossing. Schimmelpfennig also decides to include references to Hanna and Karl's West German lifestyle; the program features shots of their Mercedes and close-ups of the Rhenish wine they bring as presents to their family in the East.[44] Such references necessarily remained oral in the stage play and were thus not as evocative for the audience. Television thus added new dimensions to Germans' ongoing discussions about politics, including the enduring notion, explicitly endorsed by Ziem, that the two German states shared fundamental cultural touchstones.

Escape scenes and fugitive tropes are inherently exciting, and viewers no doubt watched such programs primarily for entertainment purposes. But as the evidence shows, viewers also received what producers saw as a lesson in political morality. Without exception, these tropes centered on the Cold War, but they also extended to the question of political reeducation in the wake of Nazism. The specter of fascism lurked in the background in every political jab about communism or capitalism. Fugitives in DFF broadcasts encountered antagonists that might best be described as the heirs to National Socialism, be they German or not. Their counterparts in ARD or ZDF pieces saw in the GDR the same type of authoritarian figures that filled the ranks of the SS and Gestapo. The escape genre proved quite popular and therefore persisted as a political device throughout the 1960s. But as the German-German border hardened, both in a physical and a cultural sense, such situations (at least those that took place in Germany) seemed far-fetched. A new type of program, centered on the righteous person of conscience and stability, superseded the escape trope.

The first East German program to offer a response to *So weit die Füße tragen* mirrored the West German production in that it featured a hero's epic journey across a barren wasteland. However, the accusatory politics in this piece, *Die Flucht aus der Hölle*, must have seemed a bit forced. In practice, very few West Germans involved themselves in the Algerian War of Independence. But the secondary response, the aforementioned *Gewissen in Aufruhr*, paints its enemy as an integral part of the West German state. The protagonist's dilemma would have appeared much more believable, given the well-documented presence of former Nazi officials in the West German government, particularly the 1950 revelation that Hans Globke had played a major role in drafting anti-Semitic legislation during the Third Reich. In fact, the station's decision makers chose to push back the broadcast date to September to coincide with federal elections in the West.[45] The program was clearly aimed at West German viewers. *Gewissen in Aufruhr* turned out to be more than another answer to *So weit die Füße tragen*, however. The enormous number of positive viewer responses convinced Heinz Adameck, intendant of DFF, and Günter Kaltofen, head of the television play working collective, that the series should act as a kind of blueprint for future productions. This included a wide range of characteristics, from the six-part format (which became standard in DFF's subsequent "event" dramas) to the continued emphasis on the FRG. For Adameck, though, the play also modeled the notion of the new man: intelligent, loyal to the working class, and cognizant of what he perceived as West Germany's accelerating decadence. He instructed Kaltofen to focus less on adventure films (though these would continue to be useful in indoctrinating youth) and more on visualizing what he termed a "man of conscience," patterned after Ebershagen.[46]

The "man of conscience" narrative proved a durable one in the 1960s. East German productions, for example, the 1962 programs *Tempel des Satans* (Satan's temple) and *Geboren unter schwarzen Himmeln* (Born under black skies) duplicated the Ebershagen character by representing an ostensibly neutral character and his budding realization of capitalism's moral deficiencies.[47] West German stations, too, adopted this approach in the years following *Gewissen in Aufruhr*. For instance, one of ZDF's first teleplays, Gerd Oelschlegel's 1963 *Sonderurlaub* (Special leave), features an eighteen-year-old East German border guard, Rolf, and his moral qualms about shooting and killing a would-be escapee.[48] Rolf follows protocol to the letter, shouting, "Stop!" three times. But he immediately expresses regret, asking his partner, "Why wouldn't he stop?" His discomfort increases significantly when he sees the escapee had been driving a cement mixer to get past the initial barriers. "He was a worker," bemoans Rolf, a reference to the GDR's self-image as a workers' state. The commanding officer notices Rolf's despair and tries to comfort him with cigarettes and the unfounded assurance that this fugitive had likely stolen the truck. When this does not seem to have any effect, the officer authorizes two weeks' paid home vacation ("special leave").

But Rolf's experiences at home do not set his mind at ease. First, Rolf's father complains about his collectivized farm, noting their potato harvest is spoiling because party officials demand the collective "follow the plan." Moreover, he bemoans the village's lack of milk, despite the fact that it has hundreds of dairy cows. Rolf, still trying to come to terms with his traumatic experiences in Berlin, takes issue with these descriptions and defends the Communist Party. In the subsequent shouting match, Rolf accuses his father of opportunistically switching his allegiance from the Nazis to the Communists after the war. The father counters that his son is guilty too: "Or isn't it a crime to shoot refugees at the border, simply because they want to cross?" At this point, Rolf's father actually does not know his son's vacation is related to a shooting, and the conversation makes Rolf even more uncomfortable. Seeking justification, he finds his former high school teacher Herr

Zinner and confides in him about the shooting. Zinner tells Rolf the state is always right but also adds, "Couldn't you have missed on purpose?" Zinner later tells the mayor about the incident, who in turn tries to tell Rolf he did the right thing: "The party has a broader view than you; don't second-guess your actions as a soldier." Soon, however, the whole village knows Rolf has shot a refugee and, because of an obviously propagandist newspaper article about the man in question being an American spy, that the escapee was probably a common worker. A stony-faced crowd confronts Rolf at the local tavern. At last disillusioned with the GDR and paranoid he will meet an "accidental" demise on account of his divulging a military secret, Rolf returns to Berlin and plots an escape to the West. The play ends with yet another young man shooting at Rolf, and the camera fades out while focused on a piece of barbed wire swaying in the wind.

While the circumstances facing each protagonist are very different, *Sonderurlaub* structurally resembles *Gewissen in Aufruhr* in two ways. First, the pieces' original authors, Gerd Oelschlegel and Rudolf Petershagen, focused on the GDR's legitimacy as a central plot point. Both men, in fact, had significant experience with the two German states and their differences. Petershagen, under much the same circumstances as explained in the film, spent four years in prison and under house arrest in the FRG. Oelschlegel resided in the GDR in 1945 and at first sympathized with the socialist project. In the wake of the 1953 worker uprisings, however, he sought an opportunity to move to the West. He succeeded and by 1955 had already begun producing radio plays about the GDR for West German stations. *Sonderurlaub* followed in that tradition. Second, both pieces feature protagonists who wrestle with the moral justifiability of a difficult decision. In each case, moreover, the authors superimpose individual struggles on a larger battle between two contrasting ideological systems. The war for Germans' allegiance in the Cold War is fought, at least in television dramas, at an individual level, but the stakes are far greater than the fate of a single, conflicted man or woman. In the case of *Sonderurlaub*, ZDF Intendant Karl Holzamer contextualized this situation rather directly by addressing viewers in a two-minute speech before the broadcast began (such a gesture does not seem to have been all that common, in either the West or the East). Holzamer tells the audience, "We cannot be silent about what is happening in the 'Ulbricht state.'" Moreover, he continues, some may find the theme disturbing, but television must also "show the darker sides of humanity."[49] Critics agreed with this position, with *Christ und Welt* noting Oelschlegel knows the GDR well, as he once lived there, and that the piece had presented a nuanced representation of life in the troubled East.[50] This nuance and believability, argued Egon Netanjakob at the Catholic *Funk-Korrespondenz*, allowed the audience to make their own determination as to the morality of Rolf's actions.[51]

Nuance might not have been the word of choice for viewers of NDR's *Die Kette an deinem Hals* (The chain around your neck, 1965), which features a cynical, acerbic East German teenager named Ute Erb.[52] Nonetheless, under Claus Hubalek's screenplay writing and Claus Peter Witt's direction, Ute's adolescent disdain become but one part of a balanced, nuanced critique of society and culture in the two German states. The story itself is relatively simple: Ute, in an autobiography, recalls her experiences as a student and compulsory member of the FDJ. Her family has raised her as a communist, but she is repulsed by what she calls the formulaic, "pharisaical" party in practice. While the students around her conform to state pressure, for example, by agreeing to spy on their friends and parents, Ute verbally eviscerates what she sees as a hypocritical, uncaring system. Instead of passing out communist leaflets in her neighborhood, as she promises her FDJ youth leader, she and her friend Georg distribute self-printed criticisms of Walter Ulbricht. The FDJ does not discover this act, but her father, an SED member, does. After a heated discussion, she proclaims she would be better off living in West Germany.

But Ute does not seem to fit in the West, either. Viewers first get a sense of this when she tells one of her Christian friends, "I don't need God. He's either mean-spirited or incompetent." This might fit the communist worldview in which she had been reared, but few Westerners in the early Cold War (before 1961) so openly proclaimed their atheism. The show neatly encapsulates her predicament when she tells the same friend, "I'm as good a communist as I am a Christian." Later, she gets the chance to travel to the West on a temporary visa (the events take place before 1961). But when she arrives in West Berlin and meets Dr. Schalk, a longtime correspondent and dedicated member of the West German Free Democratic Party, she turns defensive. Schalk attacks socialism and declares, "If I had to live in the East, I'd kill myself." Ute counters that while Ulbricht may be a "swine," the state at least provides for the poor and hasn't teamed up with the American "dogs." The show ends on an ambivalent note. Ute tells her parents she doesn't want to defect to the West after all but that she also doesn't belong in the East. *Die Kette an deinem Hals* thus criticizes both states, the one for hypocritical socialism, the other for the unadulterated capitalism espoused by Dr. Schalk. Viewers from both states could identify with the protagonist. There is no data on how East Germans felt about Ute (or if they even watched in any great numbers), but West German comments suggest this aspect of the production indeed resonated with them. One remarked, for example, "An interesting dilemma, that young people in the zone have to confront."[53] The use of "dilemma" here suggests this viewer saw as much to criticize in the West's Cold War position as in the East's. Others suggested, however, that the production felt a bit too one-sided, that it was a "propaganda" program against the East.

Unlike most television plays of the era, the protagonist in *Die Kette an deinem Hals* narrates her story in the first person. Ute often speaks directly into the camera, providing commentary in monologues between dramatic scenes. Even the enacted sequences "feature" Ute by dimming the lighting around the characters in the scene not immediately within her field of perception. Moreover, the producers adopt Ute's literary devices, casting all monologues in the past tense, as if these events are set in stone and not to be changed. The same "dimming" effects create a sense of perpetual flashback, reinforcing the sense that Eastern oppression and manipulation inflicted the damage. Thus, the director's choices in framing the program justify Ute's choice to flee to the West. Perhaps for these reasons, *epd—Kirche und Fernsehen* echoed the aforementioned viewer comment in calling the piece "anti-East propaganda."[54] The *epd* editors wondered whether students could really be so passive (except Ute) in real life, in effect calling out the program for depicting the enemy in unrealistic tones. They also complained about Hubalek and Witt's depiction of a West German capitalist who wants to help the intelligent, headstrong Ute. This figure, they argue, is presented, "much as East German television imagines capitalists!" If the West Germans receive the same critical treatment, it may be that the piece's peculiar narrative strategy tends to paint everyone but Ute in stereotypical stripes, or that it has been emplotted as a satire (a reading reinforced by the heavily sarcastic and universally cynical tone of the original literary work). Indeed, Erb's original story follows the same strategies as the teleplay (albeit in literary fashion), featuring a first-person narrative and frequently breaking the unity of place (depicted in the television production through lighting effects and changes). Moreover, the piece's criticism of the FRG is also a recurrent theme in the book, as Ute says, for example, "The Church is just like the FDJ. If an institution wants to control a lot of people, it can only do so by oppressing the individual."[55] Both memoir and television reveal why the political situation in the East, embodied by the manipulative and dogmatic youth in charge of her FDJ committee, is untenable. Erb is thus a woman of conscience, driven away from self-serving political ideologies and simplistic justifications. The East may well be worse, as the *epd* seems to gather in its critique, but for a truly self-conscious individual, the Cold War struggle is not merely a one-sided affair.

West German television authors' determination to represent self-criticism and skepticism as healthy finds an extreme manifestation in Christian Geißler's controversial 1963 *Schlachtvieh* (*Lambs to the Slaughter*).[56] The basic plot involves a series of strange, unexplained occurrences on board a passenger train. The telegraph system goes out, the train misses stops, and the passengers suddenly find the doors to adjacent cars locked. Some of the passengers, including an East German man and a left-leaning woman, fear some foreign agent or entity has captured the train and think they have the responsibility to find out what has happened. Others, including a priest and several businessmen, seem unperturbed by the incidents, even dismissing the failure of the emergency brakes as chance. Eventually, the latter group convinces the majority that nothing is wrong, and the train hurtles on into the unknown. The East German concedes that democracy must take precedence. The woman, however, grows increasingly hysterical. She is arrested and taken to a mental facility at the next station. The woman of conscience in this case faces punishment for daring to question the group. *Schlachtvieh* must have been difficult for the average viewer to grasp. While it was clearly an intellectual critique, Geißler gives the main characters almost no background and does not refer to them by name. As a result, the play relies on visual images and loosely connected scenes to convey its message. The piece begins and ends, for example, with video footage of a group of cattle being led onto and off a train. A voice-over recites lines such as "Safety and security. This is the true meaning of human progress!" In another scene, almost surrealist in nature, two passengers simultaneously tell the unconvinced woman, "Tradition builds trust," as if their saying this together settles the matter. Later, some of the passengers play "slaughter cattle," a charade game in which the passengers must guess which animal is being "slaughtered." Moments later, a man simulates a nuclear explosion with his hands, to wild applause.

As this description reveals, *Schlachtvieh* views untempered democracy with a skeptical eye. The purpose of the avant-garde, sometimes surrealist interruptions is to demonstrate the power of group behavior and peer pressure. The voice of the majority might not be right, and the impulse to fall in line, like a herd of sheep, or, in this case, beef cattle, must therefore be repressed. *Schlachtvieh* makes a strong case against authoritarian rule and thus argues for a critical, educated citizenship. The Nazis, after all, initially came to power within an existing system of democracy. In fact, NDR's program description, sent out to press agencies and newspapers in advance of each major production, directly references National Socialism as one of Geißler's inspirations: "The show is above all directed . . . at those who proved guilty during the Third Reich, knowingly or unknowingly."[57] More broadly, Geißler shows the dangers of blindly following orders, in any political system, and warns against a democracy devoid of examination and scrutiny on the part of voters. In other words, the ideal government system will be democratic only inasmuch as this form will allow voters and citizens access to decision-making and policies. *Schlachtvieh* thus portends post-1968 generational tension and antiauthoritarianism. Perhaps because of this, Geißler's piece received extremely negative feedback from viewers and critics alike. For instance, *epd—Kirche und Fernsehen* accused Geißler of waging a war on order, and the *Funk-Korrespondenz* declared the play "insulting," not least because it depicted the priest figure in such an unsympathetic light.⁵⁸ Viewer responses were almost uniformly negative, with many calling it "incomprehensible."⁵⁹ In sum, most viewers did not understand the piece as the analogy Geißler intended, and critics decried the situation described as a gross oversimplification. The self-critical person of conscience narrative had definite limits in the FRG.

Early East German representations of the political man or woman of conscience tended to emphasize external factors as the reason for the protagonist's agony. Joachim Ebershagen, for instance, never really wavers in his moral decisions; he only lacks information before he emerges a true socialist. By the mid-1960s, perhaps in response to the more complex characters highlighted in West German depictions of the same topic, writers at DFF began to create more nuanced heroes. Gertrud Kalluweit of the miniseries *Wege übers Land* (Ways across the country, 1968, see chap. 5), for example, makes some very poor decisions in her youth and actively resists collectivization in her village, only to find enlightenment and redemption with the help of her more stalwart friends. Similarly, Klara Baumann in *Die Mutter und das Schweigen* (The mother and the silence, 1965) faces a deep internal struggle before she decides to join a communist resistance movement during the World War II.⁶⁰

One of the most popular programs in this vein was the 1966 piece *Ohne Kampf kein Sieg* (Without struggle, no victory), based on the auto racer Manfred von Brauchitsch's autobiography of the same name.⁶¹ Like so many other East German miniseries, *Ohne Kampf kein Sieg* starts in the Weimar Republic. Brauchitsch serves as a cavalry officer in the German army, at his aristocratic father's insistence. But Brauchitsch dislikes this career, and the film depicts the harsh conditions he must endure. His Sunday motorcycle rides offer something of an escape for him, though, and he dreams of driving professionally. With the help of his close friend Claus von Stauffenberg (famous for his role in the 1944 Hitler assassination attempt), Brauchitsch secures a medical release and finds work as a mechanic. Here he learns, for the first time, how the working classes in Germany live and why so many (including his boss, Theo) find themselves attracted to socialism. Over time, Brauchitsch proves himself an excellent driver and lands a contract from Mercedes. With the onset of the Great Depression, however, Mercedes cannot afford to pay his team. Desperate to keep racing, he joins the Nazi Party and personally meets with Hitler to arrange government funding for his races, which now include international events such as at Le Mans and Monte Carlo. Theo is crushed at his friend's decision, but Brauchitsch never truly embraces Nazism. In 1938, in fact, he provides money and assistance for one of his fellow drivers (a Jew) to covertly escape to New York. And in one particularly poignant scene, he refuses to continue a race that has been appropriated by the Third Reich and used to demonstrate Germans' alleged superiority to other drivers (recalling the 1936 Olympics). During the war, his old friend Stauffenberg arranges for Brauchitsch and Theo to work on tanks. He thus avoids the horrors of war, but his disillusionment with the Third Reich persists throughout the early 1940s.

After the war, he is relieved to start racing again but quickly loses enthusiasm for the budding West German state when he and his fiancée are robbed and molested by American officers, and he receives no help from the provisional government in Bavaria. He decides to emigrate to Argentina, where he has been offered an extremely lucrative contract, but he sours on this situation, too, when he discovers former Nazi war criminals run the track circuit. On his return to the newly created Federal Republic, he is welcomed as a minor celebrity and offered a position as the president of the Automobile Club of Germany. When he demonstrates sympathy for communism at a German-German sporting conference in East Berlin, however, West German government officials charge him with high treason. He decides to move to the GDR permanently. The show ends on this note; the real-life Brauchitsch later became a member of East Germany's Olympic Committee, and one of the state's most decorated sporting figures.

Like *Dr. Schlüter*, which doubtless served as an inspiration for Kurz and other producers at DFF, *Ohne Kampf kein Sieg* characterizes Germany during the Third Reich as sick. At times, Kurz writes this metaphor into the dialogue directly. In the third installment, for instance, the drivers on the 1938 circuit frequently tell each other (and Brauchitsch) something is amiss in Germany. At an unnamed race in France, one French driver, in response to the German fans shouting "Heil Hitler" at Brauchitsch's victory, remarks, "We [France] are healthy. Germany is sick." At Monte Carlo, a prominent Italian driver notes to the German contingent, "I can see what's wrong with your country: you're allowing Hitler to do what he wants, and now Germany is sick." The refrain becomes even more poignant when Brauchitsch is first assigned as a tank driver during the war. He never sees any action (Stauffenberg makes sure he remains in Germany as a mechanic), but he becomes emotional upon seeing his conscription letter. Kurz here intersperses scenes from Brauchitsch's past, including the foreign drivers' comments about Germany's sickness. He resolves, in an internal monologue, that he will never shoot the enemy, as the Hitler government does not deserve his allegiance.

Kurz also expresses the notion of a sick or fevered Germany in indirect ways. The war scenes, for example, heavily feature archival footage of tank divisions firing on infantry and air strikes on now-destroyed villages, with typical military march music as an accompaniment. But Kurz also peppers the old film reels with close-ups of the soldiers' deranged faces as they carry out their tasks. These close-ups were clearly shot in the 1960s, as the film quality differs significantly. Perhaps most importantly, at the end of this montage, the viewers see footage of emaciated Jewish prisoners and even, in a highly unusual scene for East German television in the 1960s, still images from the cremation pits at Nazi death camps in Poland.⁶² This remarkable montage, which has little to do with Brauchitsch himself, characterizes the war as abnormal and immoral. The soldiers' faces imply that Germany had gone insane, driven by an unhealthy bloodlust. One character in the fourth installment (after the war) reinforces this interpretation. Hans, an American officer who had grown up in Germany but moved to California as a teenager, becomes friends with Brauchitsch and his fiancée. He tells the protagonists he is happy to be back in his mother country, and to enjoy German beer once again, but that he doesn't really recognize the nation. The people are cold and cynical, and he can hardly believe what he saw at Dachau. "It's as if Hitler has wiped [Germany] off the map," he says. Brauchitsch replies with a question, "Hans, where is Germany now?" Hans does not answer, but the remainder of the series suggests the only true Germany is in the East.

This process of discovery, which begins in the first installment when Brauchitsch meets Theo, but picks up in earnest after the war, dominates the program's narrative. Like Petershagen and Erb, Brauchitsch must decide between East and West, as a matter of conscience. As in *Gewissen in Aufruhr*, the protagonist here is not at first interested in politics, as evidenced by Brauchitsch's friendship with a staunchly communist mechanic and his simultaneous fraternization with Nazi officers (through his connections at Mercedes). In the end, Brauchitsch is forced to choose between one polar opposite and the other: East Germany (the "true" Germany) and the FRG (heir to the Nazi regime). On the one hand, his racing career and relative fame bring Brauchitsch face to face with the crimes of the Nazis and the decadence of the West German state; Kurz presents the state as an omnipresent problem in the West, in both the past and the present. During the war, for example, Brauchitsch sees firsthand the brutality of the Gestapo when they beat him for insubordination. Even Hitler's would-be assassin, Stauffenberg, appears to disparage the regime; when he catches Brauchitsch and his mechanic sabotaging a tank, he encourages them to sabotage additional vehicles. Later in the program, Brauchitsch notices many of his old Nazi friends have positions in the new West German regime, and after his speech to reporters in favor of sporting cooperation between the East and the West, the journalists accuse him of being a communist. As a result of these experiences, which are presented as epiphanies, Brauchitsch chooses to struggle against his oppression—hence the title *Ohne Kampf kein Sieg* (Without struggle, no victory), which refers to both his auto racing career and to his fight against the Nazi/FRG political constellations.

On the other hand, however, at no point does Brauchitsch specifically come to understand Marxism and choose the associated ideology as superior.⁶³ Rather, subtle cues and markers along the way inform his decision. For example, Theo gives him cryptic pieces of "socialist" advice and gradually steers him away from the "right[ist] extremists." The closest Brauchitsch comes to being presented, forcefully, with Marxist ideology is at a youth sporting conference in the GDR, where he hears East and West German youth arguing about the role of the church in government (in which the East German position comes off very favorably). Overall, the drama's rhetorical strategy for forming political identity and morality is summed up by Theo's advice to Brauchitsch when he is in deepest despair and legal trouble with the West for his support of East German athletes: "There's only one way," to which Brauchitsch replies, "Yes, I know." *Ohne Kampf kein Sieg* presents the hero's decision as a matter of conscience and ethics, not merely a simple matter of preference or whim.

As with other highlight programs, authorities obsessed over whether viewers from the other Germany watched and appreciated *Ohne Kampf kein Sieg*. Unfortunately, the archives contain no trace of West German opinion. A letter from Hellingen (in the GDR), however, demonstrates at least some viewers saw the production as more than an exciting story about a famous race driver: "Manfred von Brauchitsch, despite all the stops and pains of Bonn's justice [system] persevered and came to the GDR . . . Hopefully many viewers in West Germany also saw this film."⁶⁴ Brauchitsch fought against "Bonn's justice" but was, in the end, forced to flee to the GDR. The letter's reference to other West Germans shows how viewers clearly perceived the programs as able to cross the border. What they were supposed to do (struggle against Bonn or flee to the East) is less clear. Also unclear is how much weight to assign individual letters kept and preserved by East German authorities. The archive reveals almost nothing about this writer's identity, even failing to mention their gender. As critical readings also appear in both the archival record and in letters to newspapers, however, one can reasonably assume these are genuine viewer letters. One viewer, H. Rostek from Wernigerode, wrote to the *Volksstimme* (a Magdeburg daily newspaper), for example, that the scene depicting an international sporting conference between East and West German youth comes across as unrealistic. The viewer explains such a conference would likely be less amiable and much more cynical.⁶⁵

Most of the programs in this chapter deal with weighty political choices. Even the "righteous refugees" come to an epiphany about the virtues of one state and the ills of the other. A very different type of program—one that often achieved high viewer figures in both states because of the genre's unparalleled popularity—also deserves mention: the famous criminal thrillers, or *Krimis*. In many ways, however, *Krimis* offered little in terms of the reinvention or reformulation of morality. The genre, by definition, entailed the representation of criminality, deviance, and, ultimately, justice.

At the heart of each program in this genre lay the depiction of hardened criminals brought to justice by stalwart police detectives or, sometimes, heroic vigilantes. Most early *Krimis*, particularly before 1961, never seriously engaged with the question of how or why the criminals turned away from the law in the first place.

After the Berlin Wall went up in 1961, however, some *Krimis* began to circumscribe the question of the "other" Germany, including its political circumstances, into these more general moral representations of criminality.[66] By introducing a political element into the programs, the question of political morality became embedded in the more banal types of criminality described earlier, drastically changing the nature of the moral discourse surrounding the television events in question. One set of programs stands out in this regard: the long-running serials *Blaulicht* (Bluelight; DFF) and *Stahlnetz* (lit. Steel net but perhaps better translated as Dragnet; ARD). As Nora Hilgert has argued, these two series often included political commentaries about the dangerous criminals found in the other state. In much the same way scholars have treated the more modern West German series *Tatort* (Crime scene), Hilgert sees the two competing *Krimi* series as a barometer of current events.[67] And, if the barometer established by these two shows is to be trusted, no event was more "current" in 1960s Cold War Germany than the German-German divide. The East German *Krimis* studied here, which were largely non-serial (in other words, they are not recurring programs), follow this pattern of grafting political statements onto generalized representations of justice and criminality. The most visible exceptions to the "politicization" pattern occurred before 1961 and were part of the non-serial *Weimar Fernsehpitaval* set of programs, which effectively removed criminality from socialist society by historicizing the events in a prerevolutionary era. In DFF-produced *Krimis* of the 1960s, forces located in the West posed a real and present threat, and the guardians of justice (police/authorities/vigilantes) needed to fight that threat for the sake of security.

Walter Baumert's *Die Nacht an der Autobahn* (Night on the Autobahn, 1962), for instance, portrays an East German woman, Frau Kramer, who has been blackmailed and drawn into complicity with a West German crime ring. The villains, led by her abusive husband, smuggle illegal drugs across the border into the GDR, using the couple's house, conveniently situated along the border, as a waypoint. When an agent in this secretive network accidentally passes a note to the wrong person, the recipient, a young communist doctor named Eberhardt, tracks the crooks to the Kramers' house and discovers a stash of drugs and West German money. He learns the full truth from Frau Kramer, confronts the husband, and calls the local police.[68] The crime ring is thus uncovered and brought to justice. *Die Nacht an der Autobahn*, while closely following the usual *Krimi* genre, locates the source of criminality and deviance on the *other* side of the Wall. Bystanders like Frau Kramer represent the public, who might all too easily be caught up in a similar ring of oppression and blackmail without the constant vigilance of the border guards and police agencies. To SED Politburo members such as Albert Norden, teleplays could blaze far more believable inroads into the public's consciousness than standard, abstract pieces of propaganda. Moreover, the dramatic lesson here is made more potent in that it focuses on a family torn apart by the East/West divide, a common occurrence in Cold War Germany.

The notion that *Krimis* functioned as a "barometer" of current events also included dominant notions of gender. The West German *Krimi* series *Stahlnetz*, for instance, almost always emphasized obvious moral lessons about criminality: hardened criminals will be caught, they have no scruples over what they are doing, and the public should thus feel no remorse for bringing such characters to justice. Some notable exceptions to this pattern, however, were the few installments featuring female perpetrators. Rather than depicting them as equally unrepentant criminals, producers took pains to provide them with extenuating circumstances, specifically psychological, and thus somewhat "excusable" motives for their crimes.[69] In at least one such case, the woman involved was blackmailed because she had a child out of wedlock. The *Stahlnetz* series thus included female perpetrators, even murderers, under the umbrella of potential victims, shielding them from the harsher criticisms implicitly leveled against the unscrupulous male criminals. The gendering of culpability is no accident. Women, protectors and mothers of the nation themselves, were afforded special status, both because the producers refused them agency and because the notion that German wives and mothers, who were seen as protectors and keepers of a sanctified private sphere, could commit unspeakable acts of greed and purposeful malice, did not accord with dominant gender conceptions of the era.

During the 1960s, a second phenomenon swept West German television stations: imported and translated criminal thrillers from England. These programs, among the most popular events in the history of German television, did not speak to political circumstances in Germany in the same way *Stahlnetz* did, though they did implicitly make abstract arguments for security as an end unto itself. Interestingly, the gender dynamic in *Stahlnetz* also appears in the Francis Durbridge thriller *Melissa* (1966). The female character Melissa, assumed missing and victimized throughout the program, turns out to be a coconspirator and perpetrator herself.[70] However, she remains a sympathetic character in that she tries to the end to shield her relentless brother, Guy, from the other members of her gang, thus acting as a protector despite her transgressions. Domestic, nonpolitical moral lessons aside, the non-serial West German *Krimis* rarely, if ever, spoke to the topic of the border. Perhaps because the genre had proved so wildly popular, non-serial West German *Krimis* between the early 1960s and 1971, with a few notable exceptions such as ZDF's *Die fünfte Kolonne* (The fifth column), avoided overt politicization. In contrast to other genres, *Krimi* producers in the ARD and ZDF did not react to East German vitriol and appropriation with counterprograms of their own. As in the East, West German *Krimis* after 1971 became simultaneously more closely connected with societal concerns and overtly political in respect to the "other" Germany; in many ways, *Tatort* replaced ZDF's *Das Fernsehspiel der Gegenwart* series as the barometer of contemporary social issues and concerns. Nonetheless, much of the focus on "protecting" West German citizens gradually turned to other potential threats such as terrorism.

Conclusion

In the German context, terms such as denazification and political reeducation most often refer to overt efforts, for example political purges in each of the zones of occupation and cultural initiatives like the Amerika Haus. Television, which came to prominence years after such programs' zenith, seems at first glance to offer little in terms of a post-fascist political education. On closer inspection, however, television fiction proved an important arena in shaping what it meant to be a citizen of Germany after the Nazi catastrophe. On the one hand, viewers adored stories about fugitives and daring escapes. Many of these programs were crafted with the Cold War struggle for supremacy in mind. But behind the contemporary issues stood a deeper imperative to escape National Socialism itself. A German-born pilot living in the Americas, for instance, must resist and later flee a group of military officers who bear a strong affinity to the militarism and moral degeneracy of fascism. A Wehrmacht POW, in a very different example, escapes not only the unjust Soviet Union but also the senseless war of aggression the Nazis waged in the East.

On the other hand, and at a more incisive level in terms of reeducation, viewers witnessed strong-willed men and women standing their ground against a perilous enemy that often represented both the Cold War divide and the demons of the Nazi past. Manfred von Brauchitsch thus resists both fascists and West German intransigence, eventually learning (in his eyes) the affinity between the two. Ute Erb becomes disillusioned and cynical about the "totalitarian" FDJ and the shallow pleasures of the post-Economic Miracle FRG alike. In both types of narrative, the audience is invited to reconsider previous assumptions about politics and to learn the value of conscious choice, democracy, and, in some cases, pacifism.

Television plays with political themes thus had much in common, at least in a formal sense. DFF played a central role in reaffirming and bolstering the state's more official criticisms of the West, which blasted the FRG's decision to join NATO and Adenauer's desire to arm American troops during the Korean War as aiding and abetting blatant imperialism.[71] West German broadcasts depicted the East as a continuation of totalitarianism. They emphasized East Germans' lack of political and personal freedom, using visual and verbal cues to highlight similarities between the Third Reich and the GDR. In short, both sides tied the Cold War confrontation to the project of political reeducation in the wake of the Nazi catastrophe.

Notes

1. Klaus von Bismarck, "Die nationalen Aufgaben von Rundfunk und Fernsehen" (Cologne: Westdeutscher Rundfunk, 1967), 3.
2. The viewer quote is from the *Infratest Wochenbericht*, January 1968, 31, in relation to the WDR program *Mord in Frankfurt*. Wulf Kansteiner has demonstrated that viewers usually rejected films about the Third Reich in the 1960s, unless they followed the "predictable and schematic narrative universe" that sanitized the depiction of crimes and invited the viewers to identity with the German, anti-Nazi protagonist. See Wulf Kansteiner, *In Pursuit of German Memory: History, Television, and Politics after Auschwitz* (Athens: University of Ohio Press, 2006), 140.
3. As one example of this, WDR Intendant Klaus von Bismarck says as much in 1967 speech, speaking about the upcoming play, *Mord in Frankfurt*. See Klaus von Bismarck, "Der Rundfunk und sein Publikum" (Cologne: Westdeutscher Rundfunk, 1967), 29.
4. Hans Oliva, *Gewissen in Aufruhr*, dir. Günter Reisch (DFF, 5, 7, 10, 12, 14 September 1961).
5. The actual commander's name was Rudolph Petershagen. The production documents do not explain why Oliva changed this.
6. East German writers and authorities were not alone in their criticism of this song's rehabilitation in the FRG, which accelerated after 1949. The SPD and a large number of Liberal Democrats, led by Theodor Heuss, vehemently opposed the anthem's reintroduction. See Margarete Feinstein, "Deutschland über alles? The National Anthem Debate in the Federal Republic of Germany," *Central European History* 33, no. 4 (2000).
7. Knut Hickethier and Peter Hoff, *Geschichte des deutschen Fernsehens* (Stuttgart: Metzler, 1998), 197.
8. Frank Biess, *Homecomings: Returning POWs and the Legacies of Defeat in Postwar Germany* (Princeton, NJ: Princeton University Press, 2006), 4, 97.
9. Christina Morina, "Instructed Silence, Constructed Memory: The SED and the Return of German Prisoners of War as 'War Criminals' from the Soviet Union to East Germany, 1950–1956," *Contemporary European History* 13, no. 3 (2004): 325.
10. This world would be populated by the "new socialist person," a concept vividly described in David Tompkins, "Orchestrating Identity: Concerts for the Masses and the Shaping of East German Society," *German Studies Review* 30, no. 3 (2012).

11. David Welch, "Political Re-education and the use of Radio in Germany after 1945," *Historical Journal of Film, Radio, and Television* 13, no. 1 (1993): 75–77.
12. Kurt Hirsch, *Kommen die Nazis wieder?* (Munich: Verlag Kurt Desch, 1967), 100–101.
13. Carter Kniffler and Hanna Schlette, *Politische Bildung in der Bundesrepublik* (Neuwied am Rhein: Hermann Luchterhand Verlag, 1967), 17.
14. Moritz Scheibe, "Auf der Suche nach der demokratischen Gesellschaft," in *Wandlungsprozesse in Deutschland: Belastung, Integration, Liberalisierung 1945–1980*, ed. Ulrich Herbert (Göttingen: Wallstein, 2002), 246.
15. Benita Blessing, *The Antifascist Classroom: Denazification in Soviet-Occupied Germany, 1945–1949* (New York: Palgrave, 2006), 15.
16. Otto Grothewohl, "Mahn- und Gedenkstätte Buchenwald" (13 January 1958), Otto Grothewohl NL 90/553: Bundesarchiv—Stiftung Archiv der Arbeiterparteien und Massenorganisationen (BArch-SAPMO), ZPA, 95.
17. Joshua Feinstein, *The Triumph of the Ordinary: Depictions of Daily Life in the East German Cinema, 1949–1989* (Chapel Hill: University of North Carolina Press, 2002), 12.
18. Heather Gumbert, *Envisioning Socialism: Television and the Cold War in the German Democratic Republic* (Ann Arbor: University of Michigan Press, 2014), 30.
19. Ibid., 11–13.
20. Christian Longolius, ed., *Fernsehen in Deutschland: Gesellschaftspolitische Aufgaben und Wirkungen eines Mediums* (Mainz: Hase & Koehler Verlag, 1967); Clemens Burrichter, *Fernsehen und Demokratie* (Bielefeld: Bertelsmann Universitätsverlag, 1970).
21. Thomas Beutelschmidt, "Von West nach Ost—von Ost nach West: Irrlicht und Feuer," in *Alltag: Zur Dramaturgie des Normalen im DDR-Fernsehen*, ed. Henning Wrage (Leipzig: Leipziger Universitätsverlag, 2006).
22. Heather Gumbert, "Split Screens? Television in East Germany, 1952–89," in *Mass Media, Culture and Society in Twentieth-Century Germany*, ed. Karl Christian Führer and Ross (Basingstoke: Palgrave, 2006), 147.
23. As Nicholas Schlosser has recently demonstrated, many West German broadcasting authorities in the late 1950s understood the broadcasting war with the East as a war of news, information, and propaganda, in much the same way as the Allies understood their own information war against National Socialism. In this sense, one of the most important values in radio broadcasting had been objectivity and the appearance of truthfulness. Entertaining television fiction emerged as an increasingly popular alternative to this model. Nicholas Schlosser, *Cold War on the Airwaves: The Radio Propaganda War against East Germany* (Urbana: University of Illinois Press, 2015), 3–7.
24. Sabine Hake, *Screen Nazis: Cinema, History, and Democracy* (Madison: University of Wisconsin Press, 2012), 24.
25. Nick Thomas, *Protest Movements in 1960s West Germany: A Social History of Dissent and Democracy* (New York: Berg, 2003), 7.
26. Frank Biess, "Men of Reconstruction—The Reconstruction of Men: Returning POWs in East and West Germany, 1945–1955," in *Home Front: The Military, War and Gender in Twentieth-Century Germany*, ed. Karen Hagemann and Stefanie Schüler-Springorum (New York: Berg, 2002), 340.
27. Fritz Umgelter, *So weit die Füße tragen*, dir. Fritz Umgelter (NWRV, 10, 24 February 1959; 10, 24 March 1959; 7, 21 April 1959).
28. Bundesarchiv (BArch), DR 8 19, Protokoll 12/61, 31.5.1961.
29. BArch-SAPMO DY 30/IV A 2/2.028 60, letter from Büro Prof. Albert Norden to Genosse Hager, 2 April 1960.

30. Herbert Freyer and Rudi Kurz, *Das grüne Ungeheuer*, dir. Rudi Kurz (DFF, 16, 18, 20, 22, 23 December 1962).
31. "Das grüne Ungeheuer," *Funk und Fernsehen der DDR*, 16–22 December 1962.
32. Rudi Kurz, *Das grüne und andere Ungeheuer: Theater, Fernseh- und Lebenszeit* (Berlin: Verlag Wiljo Heinen, 2008), 48–51.
33. E.g., in "Flucht aus teuflischen Fängen," *Schweriner Volkszeitung*, 29 December 1962; in Gerhard Dittmann, "Das grüne Ungeheuer," *Sächsische Zeitung*, 27 December 1962.
34. *Bauernecho*, 4 January 1963.
35. Peter Hoff, "Fernsehklassiker mit heutigen Augen gesehen," *Neues Deutschland*, 19 August 1980.
36. BArch, DR 8 23, Kollegiumsvorlage 62/61, 18 December 1961.
37. Gumbert, *Envisioning Socialism*, 124–125. The larger problem with *Fetzers Flucht*, as Gumbert meticulously argues, was its modernist style, which placed it at odds with the emerging consensus that television was best for providing light entertainment, not necessarily intellectual depth or innovative visual forms.
38. Herbert Reinecker, *Nachtzug D 106*, dir. Helmut Ashley (ZDF, 17 June 1964).
39. Historisches Archiv des Zweiten Deutschen Rundfunks, Nachtzug D 106 3/2/126, Berichtsnummer FT 1079 F.
40. *Kieler Nachrichten*, 19 June 1964.
41. W. P., *Kölnischer Rundschau*, 19 June 1964.
42. Jochen Ziem, *Die Einladung*, dir. Heinz Schimmelpfennig (SWF, 16 January 1961, 20:20).
43. Helmut Griem, "Dichter und Mauer," *Der Spiegel*, 22 May 1967.
44. Egon Netenjakob, "Verwischte Konturen," *Funk-Korrespondenz* 4–5, 25 January 1968, 15–16.
45. BArch, DR 8 22, Vorlage 39/61, 5 July 1961.
46. BArch, DR 8 19, Protokoll 12/61.
47. Wolfgang Schreyer, *Tempel des Satans*, dir. Georg Leopold (DFF, 1 March 1962).
48. Gerd Oelschlegel, *Sonderurlaub*, dir. Dieter Lemmel (ZDF, 17 June 1963).
49. R. H., "Gespräch," *Hannoversche Presse*, 19 June 1963.
50. "Sonderurlaub," *Christ und Welt*, 28 June 1963.
51. Egon Netanjakob, "Unsozialistischer Realismus," *Funk-Korrespondenz* 26, 26 June 1963, 15–16.
52. Claus Hubalek and Claus Peter Witt, *Die Kette an deinem Hals*, dir. Witt (NDR, 17 October 1965).
53. *Infratest Wochenbericht*, October 1965, 59–60.
54. *epd—Kirche und Fernsehen* 41, 23 October 1965.
55. Ute Erb, *Die Kette an deinem Hals: Aufzeichnungen eines zornigen jungen Mädchens aus Mitteldeutschland* (Frankfurt: Europäische Verlagsanstalt, 1960), 233.
56. Christian Geißler, *Schlachtvieh*, dir. Egon Monk (NDR, 14 February 1963).
57. "Schlachtvieh," *Deutsches Fernsehen Programm*, 7/63, February 1963.
58. "Schlachtvieh," *epd—Kirche und Fernsehen* 7, 16 February 1963, 7–8; "Auf der Strecke geblieben," *Funk-Korrespondenz* 8, 20 February 1963, 16–17.
59. *Infratest Wochenbericht*, February 1963, 29–30.
60. Michael and Ursula Tschesno-Hell, *Die Mutter und das Schweigen*, dir. Wolfgang Luderer (DFF, 21 November 1965).
61. Rudi Kurz, *Ohne Kampf kein Sieg*, dir. Rudi Kurz (DFF, 28, 30 August 1966; 2, 4, 6 September 1966). Kurz's film is based on the autobiography by Manfred von Brauchitsch *Ohne Kampf kein Sieg* (Berlin: Verlag der Nationen, 1964).

62. The blunt images were unusual, but inasmuch as Brauchitsch and his friends assign ultimate blame to Hitler, the scene does not deviate from the memory politics of the era—the German people were victims, too.
63. *Ohne Kamp kein Sieg* and *Dr. Schlüter* are precursors to what Rüdiger Steinmetz and Reinhold Viehoff have identified as the disappearance of the "impeccable socialist personality" in East German serials from the 1970s, especially noticeable in *Die lieben Mitmenschen*. See Rüdiger Steinmetz and Reinhold Viehoff, *Deutsches Fernsehen Ost: Eine Programmgeschichte des DDR-Fernsehens* (Berlin: Verlag für Berlin-Brandenburg, 2008), 326.
64. *Freies Wort*, 16 September 66, Leserin G. Werner aus Hellingen.
65. H. Rostek, "Ein weniger Pathos," *Volksstimme*, 14 September 1966.
66. Ingrid Brück, Andrea Guder, Reinhold Viehoff, and Karin Wehn, *Der deutsche Fernsehkrimi: Eine Programm- und Produktionsgeschichte von den Anfängen bis Heute* (Stuttgart: Metzler, 2003), 42.
67. Michelle Mattson, "Tatort: The Generation of Public Identity in German Crime Series," *New German Critique* 78 (1999); Nora Hilgert, *Unterhaltung, aber sicher! Populäre Repräsentationen von Recht und Ordnung in den Fernsehkrimis* Stahlnetz *und* Blaulicht, *1958/59–1968* (Bielefeld: Transcript, 2013), 7–10. See also Haydée Mareike Haass's forthcoming dissertation on Herbert Reinecker's *Krimis* from the 1970s and 1980s as a barometer for changing cultural-political language.
68. Walter Baumert, *Die Nacht an der Autobahn*, dir. Wilhelm Gröhl (DFF, 16 September 1962).
69. Brück et al, *Der deutsche Fernsehkrimi*, 119.
70. Francis Durbridge and Marianne de Barde, *Melissa*, dir. Paul May (WDR, 10, 12, 14 January 1966).
71. David Clay Large, *Germans to the Front: West German Rearmament in the Adenauer Era* (Chapel Hill: University of North Carolina Press, 1996), 65–69.

Chapter 3

MANAGING PROSPERITY

Moderation, Empathy, and Christianity

Few authors of television fiction worked harder to reanimate Germans' moral world after the Third Reich than the Baden native Karl Wittlinger. An advanced graduate of German and English studies at Freiburg im Breisgau, he had risen to prominence with a 1955 novel, *Kennen Sie die Milchstraße?* (Do You Know the Milky Way?), which he subsequently adapted as a theater piece with the Städtische Bühne Köln in 1956 and, with Wolfgang Neuss, as an SDR television play in 1958. The stage production won the Gerhard Hauptmann Prize in 1956 from the Freie Volksbühne in Berlin. This proved only the beginning for Wittlinger, who continued as a dramatist for theaters around the FRG and as a prolific contributor with WDR and SDR. He displayed remarkable versatility, writing criminal thrillers, children's tales, comedies, and even cerebral morality plays. The latter pieces, including the infamous program *Dr. Murkes gesammelte Nachrufe* (Dr. Murke's collected obituaries, 1965), proved controversial inasmuch as he favored complex, nuanced characters, which were difficult for the audience to categorize as antagonists or protagonists.[1] Viewers, however, adored Wittlinger's most direct moral intervention during these years, a 1962 piece entitled *Seelenwanderung* (Soul migration).[2] It achieved high viewership statistics and received almost no criticism in the qualitative ratings. It also won two international prizes, the Prix Italia and an honorable mention at the television festival at Monte Carlo. The plot for *Seelenwanderung* was simple and familiar. Bum, an unemployed manual laborer from Berlin, decides to sell his soul. In this case, he does not meet the devil; rather, he "thinks" his soul into a shoebox and sells it to a pawnshop for 5 DM. He subsequently becomes a rich and powerful man, despite his friend Axel's pleas to redeem his lost soul. In the end, Bum dies from a heart attack. But his spirit does not pass on, as it is bound to the soul in the now missing box. In desperation, he finds Axel (the only person who can see Bum), whom he despised during his "soul-less" years. Axel reluctantly agrees to find his soul in the city landfill and, upon opening the box, releases Bum.

Moral imperative or not, it should come as no surprise that a variation on the Faust story should emerge on German television. It was and is one of the most common plot trajectories in Western literature. Other pieces from the era employed the same themes, for example Adelbert von Chamisso's *Peter Schlemihls wundersame Geschichte* (*Peter Schlemihl's Miraculous Story*, 1967) and, as described in chapter 2, the East German epic *Dr. Schlüter* (1965).[3] Far more puzzling is the audience's overwhelmingly positive response to a show that was explicitly constructed as a criticism of West German society in the early 1960s. Wittlinger and the other dramatists who helped construct *Seelenwanderung* consciously intended Bum's fate as a warning about what they perceived as the economic miracle's negative influences: "The current importance of the theme corresponds to the necessity of the visual representation," where the "current" issue clearly refers to prosperity and emerging decadence in the FRG.[4] The writer at the Protestant trade publication *epd—Kirche und Fernsehen* understood the "parable" in the same terms: "The history of the German economic miracle runs through it." The anonymous critic especially associated Bum's character with the negative effects of the phenomenon.[5] These associations are not at all remarkable given the West German stations' crusade against Germany's moral illness and contemporary intellectuals' almost compulsive tendency to heap praise on pieces that criticize banalities and superficialities. But how did the public, which generally disliked other West German pieces that hit too close to home, come to like *Seelenwanderung* so much?

One possible answer is that Wittlinger and Rainer Erler, the director, wrote it as a comedy. Bum (played by Wolfgang Rauchmann) and Axel (Hanns Lothar) speak in exaggerated Berlin accents, signaling to the audience that the characters should not be taken too seriously. The scene in which Bum deposits his soul in a shoebox takes place in a bar, and the pair act like drunken simpletons. These are not great men wrestling with important questions, as is common in the Faust tale, but rather good-natured workers who struggle to keep a job and pay their bills. Bum's demeanor changes drastically after he ditches his soul, and the audience witnesses scenes of hard work and brusque, fact-of-the-matter television conversations, indicative of the character's ascension from self-employed man to delivery magnate to politician. Axel, however, continues to speak in a lilting, unsteady Berlinerisch, which the older Bum finds derisive and "childlike." Upon his death, however, Bum reverts to the simple, broadly comedic character seen at the start of the program. Rauchmann and Lothar's friendly, down-to-earth characters, then, must have appealed to the average TV viewer, in the grand tradition of other Berliner television personalities such as Herbert Köfer in *Da Lacht der Bär* (The laughing bear), a variety show featuring hosts from different German regions, including Berlin.

Also important was the fact that Wittlinger carefully disguised his criticism as a universal human tendency toward greed and avarice. In fact, before the "soul migration," Bum and Axel discuss the fact that Bum, a typical German worker of humble extraction, is simply not ruthless enough by nature to get ahead. His conscience is too strong, in other words. Some visual cues do ground the piece in West Germany, however. For example, Bum uses his 5 DM to purchase goods for his delivery business. With each return on his investment, viewers see additional 5 DM coins collecting on a table. This eventually becomes a pile of West German money, symbolizing, as it were, the FRG's miraculous recovery. In fact, Bum can be read as a symbol for Germany itself: he loses everything and despairs, just as the nation did in 1945. But through hard work, enterprise, and ruthlessness, both Bum and the nation regain their prestige and wealth. For Bum, this of course comes at a cost. He constantly writes down "redeem soul" in his weekly calendar but never finds the time for it. In the analogy, West Germany should be thankful for its new position, but it has perhaps likewise come with a steep price: the nation has lost its spiritual and moral footing. Wittlinger adds credence to this interpretation by inserting a discussion between Bum and a preacher (his denomination is unclear). Bum, now rich and powerful, asks the preacher metaphysical questions about the nature of the soul. In keeping with the tone of the piece, this discussion revolves around a comical misunderstanding about the terms *lösen* (release) and *einlösen* (redeem). The cleric explains a soul can be redeemed through Christ. Bum takes this to mean a soul can be *gelöst* (freed or disassociated) and repurchased. The preacher, unaware of Bum's detached soul, is bewildered by the whole discussion but advises Bum to "redeem" or reattach his soul as soon as possible. Astute viewers may have recognized the metaphorical meaning here, or they may have simply laughed about the bizarre exchange between a cleric and self-absorbed businessman with a unique understanding of his own soul. Regardless, Wittlinger avoids an overly direct approach to contemporary criticism.

Whatever the reason for *Seelenwanderung*'s popularity, it was certainly not the only piece of its kind, and it was not at all unique to the FRG. This chapter examines a particularly resonant issue of the 1950s and 1960s: the accelerating resurgence of a consumer culture and its accompanying challenges. Few issues united East and West German television authorities more than the firm belief that an unchecked lust for material possessions and wealth could quickly turn healthy prosperity into immoral decadence.[6] For the East, this meant explaining that the material comforts of the FRG were illusory and corrupting. In practice, this often led writers to depict a sharp contrast between West German consumers, who had become overly obsessed with their possessions and with American-style consumer culture, and East German consumer citizens, who likewise experienced the comforts of postwar prosperity but also owed allegiance to a higher cause: socialism, and the destruction of class inequalities.[7] Producers in the GDR faced a tremendous challenge in that the regime desperately wanted its citizens to believe affluence was possible in equal measure to that experienced in the West. In plans for state-approved television advertising, for example, station director Heinz Adameck noted: "Now it is important to demonstrate explicitly and convincingly to workers how the quality, beauty, and practicality of these [East German] articles quickly makes everyone's life . . . more pleasant. Herein lies the great field of advertising television." The DFF Executive Committee prefaced this promotion of *Werbefernsehen*, or television advertising, by quoting one of Walter Ulbricht's speeches: "Socialism means good work *and* good living."[8] Television thus created programs with an implicit version of "socialist" affluence in mind. At the same time, however, the two states were locked in a competition, and if the FRG was allowed to set the stakes (wealth and affluence), then the GDR was always likely to lose. Producers thus also felt compelled to denigrate West German society as decadent and short-sighted, even as Ulbricht, with his New Economic System in 1963, and Erich Honecker, who stressed consumer products when he took power in 1971, attempted to reform centralized planning with a hybrid consumerist model in mind.[9]

As for producers in the West, Cold War comparisons were only ever part of television's purpose. To be sure, some broadcasts in the FRG criticized the flagging living standards in the East, and implicitly celebrated the return of healthy consumer culture in the West. Erica Carter has observed many viewed housewives' consumption in the 1950s as a "public contribution to national regeneration."[10] This image of the consuming housewife, the master of domesticity, certainly played out in many West German dramas. These sorts of representations helped solidify liberal democracy's legitimacy among a population that so recently had greeted the new political system with skepticism and indifference. But the unforeseen speed with which economic recovery brought material prosperity and abundance caught West German elites off guard.[11] Not all shared equally in the abundance, of course, as the standard of living and consumption habits of many working families remained "limited and dull."[12] Nonetheless, television executives, more so than many in the CDU, wanted to check and circumscribe the perceived culture of abundance. Pious Christians who sat on the decision-making bodies at the regional stations favored programming that taught virtues such as moderation, frugality, empathy, and spirituality. They were joined by left-leaning board members—often members of the Sozialdemokratische Partei Deutschlands (Social Democratic Party of Germany—SPD)—who likewise felt a moral imperative to warn the population against decadence. This temporary alliance between clerical and Social Democratic elements at each station bore significant fruit, in the form of entertaining parables and lessons, like *Seelenwanderung*, but also in that they successfully warded off Adenauer's attempts in the late 1950s and early 1960s to establish a commercial television station, which would have opened the door to American-style advertisements and corporate influence. Though the television set itself emerged as one of the symbols of postwar economic prosperity and domesticity (*Häuslichkeit*), the makers of programming in Germany ironically envisioned the medium as a key element in checking the dangers of that success.

While the immediate purpose of these television plays, on both sides, was to counteract what authorities perceived as an infatuation with luxury, they also did so with an eye to avoiding a repeat of the catastrophe of 1933. Even before Hitler gained power, many Germans perceived the Weimar Republic as a cautionary tale about the dangers of Western capitalism and liberalism. For contemporaries such as Walter Benjamin, Bertolt Brecht, and Ernst Bloch, the Nazis were only possible because Germans had been so easily rattled by material concerns such as hyperinflation and the onset of the Great Depression. Historical research has tended to corroborate the link between material affluence and the legitimacy of the regime.[13] German citizens came to expect prosperity and comfort during Hitler's regime.

The end of the Third Reich brought a new wave of claims that Nazism was the natural outgrowth of an unhealthy obsession with consumption and material well-being. For example, the conservative historian Friedrich Meinecke returns again and again to these themes in his famous 1946 assessment of the Nazi catastrophe, sometimes chastising the German middle classes for their increasingly decadent lifestyle, sometimes claiming a causal link between the Jews' unnatural greed and their own destruction.[14] Karl Jaspers, too, felt genuine renewal and moral transformation could not occur within an American-imposed system of unfettered consumerism, for this was part of the reason German culture had failed so miserably before.[15] The struggle likewise filled the pages of the *Frankfurter Hefte*, a series of publications commissioned and edited by left-leaning Catholics.[16] A similar, though far less intellectual, Christian anti-materialist message pervaded the popular theater productions of Frank Buchman's Moral Re-Armament group.[17] Even towering intellectuals such as Max Horkheimer and Theodor Adorno turned their attention to the pernicious influences of standardization, consumerism, and popular culture in the late 1940s, especially in conjunction with their diatribe against mass media in the *Dialectic of Enlightenment*.[18] The Third Reich and the troubled times that followed gave rise to a "materialistic mentality of scarcity," which in turn fostered the economic miracle and the return of affluence. During the 1960s, West German observers began to question this mentality, and to link it to the National Socialist period before it.[19]

The breadth of consensus surrounding the dangers of consumer culture and materialistic mentalities, stretching even across the Cold War divide, is remarkable.[20] This raises an important question, especially regarding conservative voices in the FRG who might have easily embraced the Anglo-American model: Why did so many contemporaries put so much stock in this particular reason for the rise of National Socialism? There are doubtless many reasons, but one of the most important was the way the mainstream Christian churches, Catholic and Protestant, dominated the political and social landscape of the FRG in the late 1940s and early 1950s. The one long-standing public institution untouched by the Western Allied occupation, the churches envisioned a grand program of restoration and re-Christianization. Particularly among Catholic leaders, such a project necessarily included purging the German nation of the more decadent forms of consumerism. For a short period after the war, this dream must have seemed well within reach. Church attendance skyrocketed, lending the institutions greater legitimacy and political capital. Devout lay members formed the backbone of the newly organized CDU; even the SPD felt the gravitational pull of the churches. After the formation of the FRG, church voices helped form consensus regarding educational issues and family policy.[21] Even the SED embraced (or, to put it bluntly, instrumentalized) church leaders in the East, in particular the Protestant bishop Moritz Mitzenheim and superintendent Günter Jacob, who advocated a "church in socialism."

Bishops also exerted an oversized influence at the newly reformulated broadcasting stations in the FRG. With the blessing of the occupation authorities, and later the West German federal government, Catholic and Protestant leaders seeded the stations with church-appointed personnel. When television arrived, each constituent member of the ARD reserved places for representatives of the Catholic and Protestant churches on their councils. The situation was similar at ZDF when it was created in the early 1960s. In East Germany, where official persecution against the church often led to anti-Christian tracts and diatribes by Communist Party leaders such as Alexander Abusch, authorities similarly acknowledged a spiritual, anti-materialist atmosphere. Television programs often stressed the importance of spiritual rebuilding, sometimes explicitly appropriating Christian figures and messages to demonstrate proper behavior. Indeed, despite the Eastern churches' weaker political position vis-à-vis their Western counterparts, strong threads of continuity existed in the heavy anti-materialist bent of early postwar television (and radio) programming in the two German states. This can be seen in the abundance of children's programming based loosely on traditional anti-materialist parables and fables, but television fiction aimed at more mature audiences often also provided sharp warnings against worldliness and greed.

Above all, this discussion about the tension between consumer culture, materialism, and spirituality came to a head in the mid 1950s as West Germany's economy underwent a nearly unparalleled period of acceleration and expansion. Konrad Adenauer and the CDU did not hesitate to claim credit for the ever-accelerating windfalls, and the state received a sharp boost in legitimacy. In many ways, this newfound faith in the capitalist model gave rise to Adenauer's attempt to establish a private television station. But the concerns of intellectuals in the late 1940s persisted. In the wake of Adenauer's failure to establish a commercial station, television, itself a major symbol of American capitalism, ironically became a primary tool in the hands of social critics, especially clerics, who warned against the excesses of materialism. Appearing as a mass medium right amid the miracle years and capable of delivering messages in the comfort of the viewer's own home, television emerged as an alternative to travel offices, magazines, and department stores as an ideal platform for mediating the material concerns, desires, and expectations of German consumers in the late 1950s and 1960s.

* * *

Few television plays addressed the perceived worldliness unleashed by the miracle so bluntly as *Seelenwanderung*. Some adaptations of classic theater productions, such as a 1959 SWF version of Friedrich Schiller's *Die Räuber* (The robbers) and a 1966 WDR telling of August Strindberg's *Nach Damaskus* (*To Damascus*), made similar anti-materialist gestures but did not take place in a contemporary setting. East German television, which might be expected to advance didactic messages with the deficiencies of capitalism in mind, rarely tackled this particular theme head on.[22] In the 1960s, at least, teleplays instead tried to link the FRG with the Third Reich, and perhaps with the "corrupt" American system. Messages about individual decadence and greed appeared largely as byproducts of a wayward political system. The East Germans' reservations may perhaps be explained by Marxism's essentially materialist foundations. For Marx, all of human history amounted to a struggle for the means of production. Material goods thus stood at the center of the conflict; anti-materialist philosophies merely distracted from the core issue. Individual television writers and producers might blast the West for decadence and an obsession with its newfound prosperity, but they could hardly present communism as a diametric opposite. Instead, DFF indicted the West for excessive or deviant worldliness and an obsession with consumerism. Affluence and material well-being were not in and of themselves bad; indeed, the overarching Marxist message was (and is) that the working classes should also enjoy the fruits of their labor. The problem was that an individual might cross the line between successful and overindulgent. Functionally, this message resembled the cry for moderation found in *Seelenwanderung*.

One DFF production, Karl-Georg Külb and Rudi Kurz's thriller *Die Spur führt in den siebenten Himmel* (The tracks lead to the Seventh Heaven, 1963) strikes just such a balance between celebrating affluence and recognizing greed.[23] On the surface, *Die Spur* presents a standard criminal thriller plot, one that accords with the acceptable ideological parameters for the East German political system. The official press release (put out by the station itself) reads: "Although there is no recognizable connection between the various violent crimes, a particular circle of people who frequent the nightclub 'Siebenten Himmel,' persistently comes up. For all these people the same motive comes into question: they all need money!"[24] Indeed, the production itself gives visual and dramatic clues as to the "decadence" of the ring, including jazz music, neon lights, alluring female dancers, and reckless spending by the robber band's richer members. Moreover, the story takes place in Austria, putting distance between the events and the GDR.

Beneath these surface markers, however, Külb, the program's writer, presents a much more complex and ambivalent relationship between morality and money. The lack of a socialist hero, a figure so common to other East German productions, means there are no "correct" examples to follow. Thus, the neon lights and "fast" lifestyle appear more desirable. The bar itself is glamorized, with some of the scenes attempting to simultaneously advance the plot and entertain viewers (thus keeping them away from the West German channel). The film's location in Austria moreover provided an excellent opportunity to defame Western European wealth and affluence. As Renate Holland-Moritz puts it in the East German publication *Funk und Fernsehen*, a station-supported television guide magazine that rarely passed criticism on programs, "Because the bloody affair was located in Austria, one would have expected at least a small amount of social critique from author Karl-Georg Külb."[25] In the context of the Cold War, this seemed even to sympathetic journalists an obvious missed opportunity. But a critique of Austrian society is only to be found tangentially. The dramatic indication that the film takes place in Vienna comes not through the visualization of decadence and capitalism (which, during large stretches of the program, might just as well take place in Berlin) but through the characters' association with Catholicism. One of the members of the ring, Emmi, is a devout Catholic, and she justifies a brutal murder by claiming, "I admit it . . . and why? The Holy Virgin revealed to me that he was the murderer," referring to another murder that took place earlier in the program. The reference to the Virgin Mary locates the piece specifically in a Catholic area. But Emmi's motivation, at least in the case of this murder (one among many in *Siebenten Himmel*), does not teach moral lessons about the evils of money and decadence which, as Holland-Moritz puts it, would be expected of such a production. Instead, it remains at the level of a perversion of religion, which was indeed part of the Marxist repertoire of criticisms about capitalist society (i.e., that the clerics were in bed with the capitalists and fascists) but does not seem to have been a particularly biting critique. E. Schmidt Novotay's half-sarcastic comment in a September preview of the film best captures the tone of this piece: "Money is the key to pleasure."[26] Novotay clearly means the piece demonizes money, in other words, that it shows the opposite, but, as was abundantly clear based on evidence during and after the program's broadcast date in December 1963, this moral lesson came across as ambiguous at best. In the same preview, director Kurz foreshadows some of this ambiguity when he says to Novotay, who asks him what he's going to do after the film, "I'm going to buy a motorboat and take a vacation."

Indeed, several television programs during this era set the proper means for procuring and spending money within ethical boundaries. The prevailing boundary during this time frame, even in East Germany, was bourgeois: money provided comfort and social status, but it could also be "consumed" in excess. Within this framework, money became a secondary value, behind the things it could buy, like appliances, cars, works of art, fashionable clothing, and so on. It was these outward markings, the hallmarks of owning and having money, that television fiction presented as values, the end products of consumer culture. Such values accelerated during the 1960s because they were embedded in "waves" of consumption: manufacturers created products which were *meant* to be replaced, both as a marker of social inclusion and as a manifestation of progress and modernity.[27] Furthermore, both the post-Stalin Soviet Union and its satellite states pinned their hopes to rising consumption, whether of television sets or refrigerators (Appendix 3 demonstrates the meteoric rise of television viewership in Germany).[28] The rapid growth of such a stable, self-perpetuating system of consumerism, which took place in both East and West Germany and at least in part coincided with the rise of television, represented one of the most visible dynamics of cultural change during the 1960s, especially when viewed with the luxury of hindsight.

Perhaps no German program better encapsulated the German-German nature of these tensions and changes than the DFF adaptation of the West German author Max von der Grün's *Irrlicht und Feuer* (Ghost light and fire, 1966). Inasmuch as *Irrlicht und Feuer* was written by a West German with a West German audience in mind but was then adapted by one of the most prolific East German screenplay writers and filmed within an East German studio, the show can be said to truly speak to both sides. Both novel and broadcast portray a few months in the life of West German mine worker Jürgen Fohrmann, who oscillates between resignation to staying in his low-paying job and the quest for new employment. At times, he is satisfied with his hard work, but at other times, he is tempted by the promise of higher pay and more free time at an office job. Moreover, *how* he values his money, depicted visually and dramatically, also varies over the course of the program. For example, at one point, he and his wife, Inge, happily engage in a spending spree, cast in a positive light by carnival-like music, smiles on the faces of both partners, and outdoor walks bathed in sunshine. Later, however, when his wife celebrates winning a lottery prize (about 10,000 DM), he expresses displeasure at her shortsightedness and points out the money will not solve their financial problems. This climax, which seems to privilege the more austere option, is made ambivalent by the ending, however. Inge goes to find Jürgen after he stormed out of the fight. She seems repentant, and he too concedes he wants her to be happy and that their money is of course important.[29] The overall impression, then, reinforced by the closing scene, is that a middle way between spending and saving, in other words, between some form of materialism and one of its alternatives, is preferable. This middle way is made comprehensible to viewers via dramatic demonstration—in other words, in a normative fashion.

Unsurprisingly, much of the East German discourse about *Irrlicht und Feuer* that touched on money or materialism condemned the situation in the FRG as immoral. Following Marxist ideological lines, newspaper critics blasted capitalism, even as a refracted, fictional representation, for exploiting the miners of the Ruhrgebiet: "A physical . . . and psychological exploitation . . . the author has (fundamentally) seen behind the facade of the economic miracle."[30] One such critic, however, narrowed his focus on Jürgen's complicated actions, proclaiming, "The way of an unheroic hero resembles a staircase. The rhythm in which he moves is uneven. At times he pauses, discouraged and helpless, and then he storms up again, step by step."[31] In a Marxist interpretation, these "uneven" measures are the result of the imperfect system in which he lives. The notion that he might truly be torn between two ways of life did not accord with East German ideology. A viewer's letter to *Neues Deutschland* echoes such carefully measured praise for Jürgen: "Jürgen Fohrmann became a good friend to me, despite his behavior."[32] Other letters make similar points. For example, a section of letters to the *Lausitzer Rundschau* ask, "Is Fohrmann doing the right thing?" and one letter explains that the film is so good because Fohrmann exposes the contradictions in capitalist society *because* of the complexities of his own life.[33] In both article and letters, Fohrmann is described as confused and imperfect. The viewer even calls him "shaky," apparently in reference to his sometimes choosing "capitalism." The *Neues Deutschland* viewer subsequently justifies his hero: "How could he have found the right way from the outset, when the guides of his environment lead him into a dead end?" But the program does not visually bracket, justify, or marginalize these moments of sympathy for a materialist lifestyle. They seem to belong to Von der Grün's complex characterization. Televisual devices such as music and camera angles might have made Fohrmann more sympathetic and relatable from a Marxist perspective, but they could not completely remove the complexity and nuance created by a medium more suited to the task: literature. This is echoed in a *Neues Deutschland* article that admits Fohrmann is a many-sided and difficult character to come to terms with, especially in the original novel. The producers, hoping to capture West German viewers, refused to completely whitewash the program as a representation of simple exploitation.[34] While it is impossible to know exactly why *Neues Deutschland* chose to publish such letters, it seems East German authorities deemed it prudent to highlight Fohrmann's authenticity and complexity in order to avoid the charge of simple propaganda.

This ambiguity toward the economic miracle can also be demonstrated in SWF's decision to purchase and broadcast *Irrlicht und Feuer* in 1968. Like the East Germans critics, SWF and ARD officials attempted to smooth out the piece's rough edges, in this case by contextualizing both the East German production and Von der Grün's criticism of the West with the addition of an explanatory, more "factual" program after the end of the broadcast that examined the erosion of salaries in the mining industry.[35] Political posturing notwithstanding, *Irrlicht und Feuer* stirred up a discussion about the representation and correct measure of material wealth but tacitly criticized both materialism and some voices' ultimate opposition to it. West German newspaper reviews reflect this ongoing discussion. Eckart Kronenberg at *Die Zeit*, for instance, maintained, "*Irrlicht und Feuer* is an uncomfortable film . . . It is symptomatic of the problems of the working class."[36] In particular, Kronenberg noted that Fohrmann, more so in the film than in the book, seems simultaneously attracted and repulsed by his possessions.

Perhaps some of the discomfort Kronenberg associated with *Irrlicht und Feuer* derives from Jürgen's contentious relationship with Inge. Jürgen seems at times to genuinely love his wife (a symbol of his aspiration to live in material comfort) but also initiates an affair with another worker, named Irene (a symbol of his somewhat vague desire for freedom). More generally, Jürgen struggles in his interpersonal relationships. In one poignant scene, for example, he punches out his manager at the mine. He feels justified in doing so, as he has just witnessed a serious—and preventable—industrial accident. But the characters in *Irrlicht und Feuer* seem alienated and estranged from one another. And this situation in the Ruhrgebiet was not to be explained merely as a generalized byproduct of modern life or as a remnant of European industrialization; *Irrlicht und Feuer* frequently references the Third Reich as one of the causes. The unscrupulous mine boss, for example, is later revealed to have been a Nazi Party leader. When Jürgen's teenage neighbor asks about whether he knew, during his service in the Hitler Youth, the Nazis were rounding up their opponents and shipping them to concentration camps, he replies, "Oh, we knew. We knew." This same teenager's father cannot receive a pension because he wrote "Hitler is a filthy swine" on a train station platform. Von der Grün's novel thus fits into a broader worry about the long-term effects of the Third Reich on individual Germans and their relationships with each other. Had the Third Reich caused a lack of empathy among the population?

A lack of empathy certainly seems to be a root source of the problems seen in NDR's 1963 *Stadtpark* (City park). The program begins with idyllic shots of families enjoying a public park in Berlin on a summer afternoon.[37] In fact, *Stadtpark* at first seems like an advertisement for the economic miracle itself. For example, the program briefly visualizes one family, an attractive middle-aged couple and their equally attractive teenagers, enjoying a ride in a convertible. Another family enjoys ice cream from a freezer in their own home (a novelty at the time). In broader terms, this first part of the program features a seemingly endless amount of leisure time for suit-clad executives. Beneath these comfortable representations, however, lie two problems. First, the program's protagonist is not really a part of this happy group of people. Frau Thielecke is a single, elderly ice cream vendor at the park. Ice cream is her only source of income, and she therefore lives in a very small apartment. Hans Schubert, the program's writer, thus exposes class inequality, even in an egalitarian setting such as the city park. Second, and more importantly, even the bourgeois families who enjoy all the comforts afforded by the miracle are not what they seem. One mother, for example, tells an elderly man who is admiring her children, "Kids aren't a blessing; they're an anchor." This pronouncement sets the tone for the show, which above all promotes the ideal of a nuclear family.

The main plot revolves around a young boy (Peter) who runs away from his newly divorced parents. The parents meet at the park to exchange Peter (they have dual custody), but the father takes offense to his ex-wife and her decision to bring her new boyfriend. Shouting ensues, and Peter angrily storms off. He hides in the park until it gets dark. Thielecke finds him hiding behind her cart, and decides to take him home. The next morning, she brings Peter back to the park, intending to find his parents. The parents do come to the ice cream stand but immediately start fighting about whose turn it is to have Peter. Peter runs off, and Thielecke scolds them for putting their own concerns ahead of their child's. Eventually, Thielecke decides to take Peter, who refuses to go home, to the police. Before the police release the boy to his parents, however, the local judge (*Gerichtsamt*) chastises the parents for their behavior. He interviews the two parents separately, asking the father, "Where is the boy's mother?" and the mother, "Where is the boy's father?" He explains to each the importance of two parent figures in a child's life, one woman and one man. He then calls the two into his office, unequivocally denounces their decision to divorce, again explaining the developmental and emotional reasons for a child to grow up with a mother and a father in the home, united in their upbringing. He also notes the absurdity of their attempts to recapture the boy's affection with ice cream and gifts. The real purpose of the interview is to discuss not merely the welfare of the child but the welfare of the nuclear family in modern, divorce-ridden society. Both parents work long hours, which, as he puts it, lies at the heart of their problems. The lecture, reminiscent of a sermon and presented by a paternalistic, loving authority figure, echoes a common platform of both churches in the 1960s (and today): counteracting the disintegration of the family. Schubert thus appropriates religious imagery and vocabulary to teach a lesson to the two feuding, modernized parents (as well as the audience). The effect of the "sermon" here is enhanced by the eventual reconciliation of the two and the boy's return to his family. In this case, the viewers might also stand for the missing element important to most depictions of a sermon: the nodding and approving audience members. The purpose of the judge's interview with the parents is to remind the viewer of the ultimate reasons for those requirements.

At the end of the program, Thielecke resorts to seemingly extreme measures to uphold this same ideal. She learns the reason for the split was an extramarital affair (on the husband's part) and tries to tell them, "It was only one affair! Move on with your lives!" Amazingly, this ploy seems to work, but Peter, now attached to Frau Thielecke, runs away again. When she cannot successfully convince him to return to his family, she slaps him across the face, hoping physical abuse will turn him against her. She values the nuclear, unified family so strongly that she is willing to initiate violence against a child to defend it. Despite this sequence, and the blunt moralizing that takes place throughout, viewers universally adored *Stadtpark*. It was, qualitatively, the highest-rated television play of the era, with a +8 rating.[38] The only really negative comment Infratest recorded describes the characters as *too* good, claiming, "Such good people don't really exist." Clearly, the program's messages resonated with viewers across the nation. The parents lacked empathy and understanding, and once they reconciled, life returned to normal. Finally, in a remarkable final scene, Thielecke finds a piece of Nazi propaganda on a park bench and emphatically places it in the trash. In an indirect fashion, the reconciliation of the quarrelling parents reflects on the nation as a whole, and its return to health.

Despite its "sermon" and didactic plot, viewers could easily overlook the real message in *Stadtpark*, a lighthearted comedy with sympathetic characters and a joyful reconciliation. This would have been impossible for someone watching Christian Geißler's 1964 *Wilhelmsburger Freitag* (A Friday in Wilhelmsburg), which offers a more direct, and more negative, commentary on the perils of newfound economic wealth. In this case, the plot centers on a young, working-class married couple. The wife, Renate, in accordance with the prevailing bourgeois family values that pervaded the 1950s, stays at home, even though the couple does not yet have any children. The husband, Jan, a mid-level construction worker, makes enough money for a small apartment in the suburbs and an automobile, not at all a given, even in the miracle years.[39] Against this background, the program shows how the pair spend an ordinary workday, in an atmosphere that would seem, according to prevailing norms and standards, to make each partner happy (Jan has a stable job and the favor of his employer, Renate spends her day shopping and reading books). But based on the silent, morose way the two conduct themselves, in combination with the clearly false expressions of happiness with which they greet their acquaintances and co-workers (immediately followed again by scowls and apparent reflection), the viewer is invited to deduce the opposite: neither is genuinely happy, and the material world in which they are swallowed up is the root cause. When Renate reads glossy magazine articles about modern kitchens and housekeeping strategies, they seem, in this context, hollow, as do the stuffed animal and records she buys at a Karstadt department store. Jan's decision to rub elbows with his rich employer seems illusory, as the boss clearly "uses" him for the lack of other company, not as an equal or comrade. At the end, the pessimistic attitude prevalent throughout the program is brought to a boil, as Renate throws away the magazines, designs for her children's room (we gradually learn she is pregnant), and finally tells her disbelieving husband she does not want the child. All the major characters, then, display a lack of empathy: the husband who wants a child cannot understand why his wife is so unhappy; the wife cannot understand why the husband does not make more money; and the husband's employer cares little for his employee's real well-being, even in a casual setting after work hours.

More broadly, the visual association between these instances of extreme unhappiness and consumer culture and goods (the magazines, the books, the husband's automobile, Karstadt, etc.) signals an overt condemnation of consumer culture and material wealth. Viewers detested *Wilhelmsburger Freitag*, accustomed as they were (especially in the early 1960s) to more optimistic or relaxing fare on television, perhaps interspersed with veiled or partly hidden negative commentaries on the prevailing consumer milieu (as with *Stadtpark* or *Seelenwanderung*).[40] Critics, on the other hand, generally praised *Wilhelmsburger Freitag* for its educational elements and hoped it would spur the public to a better awareness of the darker sides of modern consumer culture (alienation and unhappiness).[41] For some producers and decision-makers, the mandate to instruct superseded the wishes and dislikes of viewers; the social scientific barometers, while apparently heeded in some contexts and by some executives, were shunned in other settings. In any case, television performed both, pandering to viewers while at the same time trying to shock and moralize using modernist dramatic techniques. This was rarely more apparent than in programs set against wealth and materialism as explicit moral values.

As noted earlier, one of the most durable voices against greed and materialism was that of the Christian churches. While Western Allied commanders and officials felt a great deal of ambivalence about the churches' role in denazification efforts, they ultimately agreed the churches had played a major part in the resistance movement and should be given autonomy to remove Nazi clerics themselves.[42] In this relatively open atmosphere, religious leaders and politicians formed the Christian Democratic Union, fusing the old Catholic Center Party, the great moderating force of the Weimar Republic, with Protestant political elements to capitalize on the postwar prominence and popularity of the Churches. Though Catholics set the political tone and ideology, the CDU quickly became the largest party in the FRG, with 31 percent of the vote in 1949. In the 1957 election, the CDU won with more than 50 percent.

Though it did not always act in accordance with the Churches' wishes, the CDU exemplified the power of Christian consensus during the postwar era. Forged in the spirit of compromise, party organizers such as Leo Schwering, Theodor Scharmitzel, and Hans Schlange-Schöningen promulgated the idea of a resurgent Christian culture on German soil. The party's most prominent member, Konrad Adenauer, famously underscored Germany's place within a Western European *Abendland*, a German term that could signify either the occident or Christendom. He accordingly forged relationships with French, Dutch, Belgian, and British conservative parties who leaned toward a Christian worldview. Clerics actively joined CDU politicians, unabashedly taking sides on political issues and throwing their weight around during the constitutional assembly in 1948/1949. This influence contributed to perhaps the strongest point of consensus, one that endured throughout the 1950s and most of the 1960s: a traditional conception of the family and women's role as mothers (see chap. 4).[43]

The CDU consensus was not comprehensive, of course. Wedges appeared between Catholics and Protestants over old, slow-burning issues such as confessional schools. Moreover, although CDU politicians in many ways relied on support from clerical authorities for their continued legitimacy, they quickly realized they were not ultimately beholden to the bishops' councils. Catholic politicians defied the bishops in allying with economic liberals (despite the resounding success of Ludwig Erhard's social market economy, based loosely on Catholic welfare principles). The disconnect between politics and church positions became even more visible in the late 1950s when Adenauer sought approval for his Deutsches Fernsehen GmbH. Leery of the current broadcasting system, which was decentralized in its structure (per the Allies' wishes) and often critical of his regime, Adenauer sought to introduce a second, semiprivate television station that would act as a mouthpiece for the federal government and simultaneously provide advertising revenue along the lines of the American system. Adenauer courted the churches' support but was unable to secure more than a few bishops' extremely hesitant cooperation. Nevertheless, he forged ahead with his radical plans.[44] A 1960 decision by the Constitutional Court put an end to the scheme, but the episode demonstrates the limits of consensus in the political arena.

Despite their inability to dictate federal policy, the churches enjoyed unquestioned hegemony and institutional power for years after the end of the war. In an effort to gain political capital, leaders from both confessions encouraged the public's perception of clerics as resistors and victims of Nazism.[45] Aid organizations such as the Catholic Caritas provided Germans in the rubble years with valuable access to international aid. While the vast majority of CDU politicians by the 1950s were lay Catholics or Protestants, clerics continued to use networks they had established as theology students to influence political culture throughout the FRG. Many religious minorities, meanwhile, found themselves legally immune from persecution but culturally and institutionally marginalized by a kind of mainstream Christian duopoly.[46] In this atmosphere, a broad culture of consensus emerged in West Germany, even at times including Social Democrats.

Media censorship and anti-materialism were major, interrelated components of this consensus. When morally objectionable films appeared in 1948—*Der Apfel ist ab* (*The Original Sin*)—and 1951—*Die Sünderin* (*The Sinner*)—authorities from both confessions organized a very public pushback against the American authorities' decision to allow screenings. When the West German theaters dug in their heels and refused to be coerced, the church representatives on the Freiwillige Selbstkontrolle, the censorship board, resigned in protest, one calling it "an ethical atomic bomb."[47] These attempts at shaping and controlling the cinema mirrored an ongoing consensus that Germans needed to be shielded from the moral shortcomings of unfettered capitalism. Early CDU politicians diverged somewhat in their vision of Germany's economic future. Some favored a kind of Christian socialism, while others demanded liberal reforms as a counterweight to the spread of communism; nonetheless, they all agreed, as did their religious leaders, on a platform of anti-materialism, bourgeois austerity, and nuclear families. Conservative, Christian values underpinned both film censorship and anti-materialist economic and family policy gestures.

In this atmosphere, then, it is unsurprising church leaders exerted influence, both direct and indirect, on decision-makers at West German television stations. Clerics sat on television boards (*Fernsehräte*) at both the national and regional level. Some, such as Karl Becker, head of the Katholischer Rundfunkarbeit (Catholic Broadcasting Committee), simultaneously represented one of the Churches and the station itself, as a member of the Rundfunkrat (an important decision-making body) at SWF. Despite Adenauer's attempted end around, CDU politicians enjoyed fixed representation in the political councils essential to the public television system and similarly exerted their power in the service of the churches' broad interests. Even Klaus von Bismarck, longtime head of WDR (the largest constituent member of the ARD), sat on the Protestant Kirchentag (Church Day) committee and shamelessly lobbied on behalf of the churches.[48] In sum, the churches exercised considerable institutional control at each of the West German stations. They did not organize boycotts or compose open political statements as they had done with objectionable films a decade earlier, but they heavily shaped the direction and tenor of Germany's new televisual moral education.

The indirect mechanisms of control operated by religious figures within the television industry are only one facet of the relationship between Christianity and postwar German television. Producers also regularly included religious motifs and themes in their programs, whether news magazine or television fiction.[49] For example, the Protestant churches largely funded a WDR television drama about Martin Luther's defense at the Diet of Worms called *Der arme Mann Luther* (The poor man Luther, 1965), and both Catholic and Protestant authorities wrote letters of support for *Seelenwanderung*.[50] The same authorities sometimes complained about certain plays in private correspondence, as when Karl Becker asked Gerhard Schröder, head of NDR, to refrain from representing religious figures in a negative light, as occurred (in his mind) in *Schlachtvieh* (1963).[51]

The notion that Christian mores and teachings could counter excess and decadence found expression in a wide variety of early West German teleplays. In general, these early programs relied on simple delivery mechanisms such as sermons and clerical role models. One such example is NDR's *Waldhausstraße 20* (see chap. 1). The main character, Swedish Lutheran Pastor Tornqvist, arrives in late 1930s Germany with little inkling there will be any trouble in his new parish. He drives an open-air Mercedes and shows up at the parish office dressed for tennis. Tornqvist clearly lives a life of affluence and privilege. German officers, including Gestapo agents, bring him gifts, invite him to the theater, and generally make him feel comfortable. But he quickly learns that his predecessor illegally harbored church dissidents in the parish's basement. He starts to don the mantle of protector. Finally convinced that his idleness has real consequences, he actively helps his secretary bring food and water to more than a dozen potential victims they harbor in the church basement. His newfound courage seems to be accompanied by a rediscovery of his calling as a representative of God. He lengthens and improves his Sunday sermon, distracting the guards that surround the chapel and allowing the refugees time and opportunity to enter the crowd undetected from the side doors. The hunted dissidents then disperse with the rest of the crowd. His willingness to sacrifice and put the welfare of others above his comfortable lifestyle demonstrates model behavior to contemporary Germans, even in the absence of an oppressive regime.

The 1963 WDR adaptation of nineteenth-century playwright Theodor Fontane's classic *Unterm Birnbaum* (*Under the Pear Tree*), in which a carpenter (Hradscheck) murders a debt collector to escape bankruptcy and debtor's prison, similarly casts a cleric as a positive role model.[52] True to Fontane's original story, each character in the WDR version contains both virtues and faults; in the pastor's case, however, Herbert Reinecker's version follows a less damning dichotomy, projecting outrage and forbearance at seemingly appropriate times. Moreover, in the television version, the pastor does not seem to be motivated by the prospect of material acquisitions. In the context of a story that centers on murder, revenge, and jealousy, he thus appears doubly exceptional. The lack of a "clerical" fault in a show filled with tragically flawed characters suggests respect toward religious authority figures. An anonymous reviewer at *epd—Kirche und Fernsehen* said, "It is good to finally experience a piece in which a pastor (Erwin Aderhol) does not have the slightest hint of comedy or embarrassment."[53] Presumably, the author took issue with stereotyped church figures from previous programs (which also, it must be added, demonstrate the limits of church influence on specific plays). In contrast, the more "serious" pastor in *Unterm Birnbaum* at once projects Christian charity, curbing the Prussian prosecutor's actions against the suspected murderer Hradscheck, and sternness, expressing outrage over Hradscheck's presumed complicity in the murder, discovered at the end of the play. Though some programs indeed portrayed what the reviewer at *epd* saw as comic and caricatured clerics, priests surfaced as strong-willed role models far more frequently in television's early years. They thus figured prominently in television's moral mandate of reeducation, providing positive role models, even in the degenerate episodes of Germany's troubled past. Priests and preachers appeared as the bearers of "good" German culture, which had been particularly repressed after 1933.

There was one notable exception to the trend of simple, heroic Christians in early West German television. In 1958, the SWF broadcast a decidedly modernist piece entitled *Ein gewisser Judas* (A certain Judas).[54] Originally a Claude André Puget play that was translated and adapted as a German television production by Oskar Werner, *Ein gewisser Judas* follows the story of Judas's betrayal of Christ from the former's perspective. After Jesus declares one of his followers will betray him, some of the apostles despair and want to ask him what he meant. Judas, in contrast, declares, "You have forgotten that he is first and foremost a God. You pull him down . . . that is the betrayal." More than the others, then, Judas has a transcendent faith in Christ's divinity. Thus, when he later surrenders Jesus to the Romans, his purpose is to make Him show His divinity, not because he (Judas) seeks money or because he lacks faith. After Jesus dies, however, Judas questions the basis of his acts of faith and hangs himself.

Ein gewisser Judas has obvious implications for how the Judas passages in the Bible should be interpreted. However, as the editors at *Funk-Korrespondenz* and *epd—Kirche und Fernsehen* understand it, the play's real purpose is to insert a modernized, proof-driven pattern of "believing" onto a past situation, asking, in essence, if modern believers might not also stumble into the same trap as Judas, forcing the divine to manifest itself as a means of bolstering their own faith, however strong it might already be.[55] At a simple level of analysis, this seems to merely reinforce a Christian message repeated in numerous permutations throughout the New Testament: "We walk by faith, not by sight."[56] At a deeper level, however, Judas acts on his convictions, visually "manifesting" a stronger faith than the other apostles. He always looks directly at the audience, speaking, until the last scenes, with a calm, serene, almost saintlike voice. To highlight Judas's almost saintlike faith, the camera is positioned below him while he recites his monologues. Furthermore, Werner's simple, modernist sets, combined with the black-and-white technology of the era, allowed for a stark contrast between light (Judas) and dark (Peter and James, whimpering in the dark corners of the stage). The television play, in contrast to Puget's original stage production, thus reinforces the radical paradox presented here: the apostle with the greatest faith was also the one who showed the least, looking for Jesus to demonstrate his divinity according to Judas's rational preconceptions. For modern believers, then, *Ein gewisser Judas*, a piece clearly designed to speak to a contemporary audience, demands a faith removed from mankind's imperfect rationality while simultaneously disparaging those with weak convictions. What this means in concrete terms, however, is not addressed. The protagonist, Judas, seems ill suited as a role model, but, as a tragic figure, has been constructed with viewer identification in mind. Most importantly, the Judas character is animated by real conviction, rather than by the thirty pieces of silver the New

Testament famously has him take in exchange for his betrayal. Werner's play thus forwards piety as an alternative to materialism.

Later West German productions visualized a more complex intersection between the Christian worldview and contemporary West German society. For example, in 1970, ZDF aired a controversial Oliver Storz production entitled *Die Beichte* (The confessional), which depicts a Catholic priest's quest to reveal a Nazi mass murderer who repeatedly comes to confession.[57] The perpetrator shows remorse and wants to obtain God's forgiveness but refuses to hand himself over to the police. The priest, increasingly frustrated with his clerical oath of secrecy, searches the congregation for the villain. In doing so, he alienates many in his flock and brings censure from his superiors. When he finally latches onto a real lead, the perpetrator deserts his wife and children and disappears into the night.

On the surface, *Die Beichte* urges viewers to consider the ongoing ethical dilemmas posed by the nation's recent past. Storz's work acts as a window on (West) Germany's un-confronted Nazi past. The Third Reich may have been defeated, he suggests, but echoes of the past endure and must be confronted. However, he seems less than optimistic that confronting the past will lead to healing and resolution. The play itself provides no simple moral answers, "no new '*Vergangenheitsbewältigungs*' history, no backward-looking analyses, no material . . . about the Third Reich itself."[58] In this sense, *Die Beichte* simultaneously reacts to the 1968 student uprisings, which in general criticized the older generation for ignoring the Nazi past, and portends the more nuanced and self-reflexive representations of the Holocaust that began in the 1980s. Storz, moreover, consciously perceived his work as a questioning, critical piece, indicative of the rising generation: "The history of *Die Beichte* is a history of today. It tells of the shock . . . of my generation."[59] He further explains that his generation—the *Hitler Jugend* cohort, which reached adulthood after the war had ended—did not have the appropriate tools to confront the evils of the Nazi regime until the late 1960s.

But the piece also addresses two less visible, though related, themes: a fundamental transformation in the role of religion in modern society and the dangers of an increasingly affluent (and therefore complacent) society. The program's central character, the Catholic priest Bernhard Weller, must decide how to deal with the confessing perpetrator in light of his responsibilities as a priest. Religious identity colors his choices throughout: in his initial decision not to report the ex-Nazi (because of his oath of confidentiality as a Catholic priest), in his change of heart and subsequently proactive response to the presence of evil in his congregation (a damning critique of Nazism and German nationalism in his sermons), and in his own despair (a loss of faith in God because he is personally confronted with the banality of genocide). These are not the isolated throes of a marginal member of society; the play locates the priest as an essential part of the community. The opening camera sequences catalog the priest's warm reception in the town, and the pivotal role citizens attach to his office. These include a marriage scene where he is invited to stand in the family picture (despite having just arrived the day before), the frequent salutations he receives on the street even when he is not dressed in his habit, and his being accorded a special table at the local pub. His location in everyday German life is made more believable through his interaction with the town's longhaired youth. In one scene, the priest asks a group of teenagers for change at the cigarette machine, and he seems knowledgeable about the rock music they enjoy. In his Sunday school classes, he makes light jokes and endears himself to the rebellious 1968 generation with his philosophical, open-ended answers to skeptical questions about the existence of God and the importance of bourgeois morality. Storz thus rejects the oft-assumed irrelevance of religious figures in modern everyday life in favor of a progressive, softer version of the Catholic priest. But these accommodation strategies are tested with the arrival of the semi-repentant mass murderer. The priest begins to see his choice as one between God and justice. A deus-ex-machina ending spares him from ultimately choosing (the mass murderer disappears before his identity is discovered), but the viewer is left to consider the difficulty of his position.

Whatever the priest's moral culpability, the village itself seems to bear an even greater portion of guilt in fostering an atmosphere in which the perpetrator can roam free. The town's teenagers have money to buy Credence Clearwater Revival records in the local shop, the café bursts with patrons, and several characters drive expensive BMWs. The director's decision to include panoramic shots of the picturesque village, with its neatly appointed row houses, gardens, and city square, reinforces the notion that the location is not just idyllic or oblivious (though the producers of course also intended to cultivate this idea); the relative wealth and prosperity have created an ideal sanctuary for a mass murderer. The juxtaposition between the priest and other villagers, who seem unaware of their hero's searing moral conscience, gives even greater weight to the notion that the villagers bear some of the responsibility. He may go to great lengths to ingratiate himself with his modern, affluent parishioners, but his austere lifestyle and Sunday school lessons about the limits of bourgeois sensibilities demonstrate he is cut from a different cloth. In sum, *Die Beichte* neatly weaves together multiples themes, combining a question about *Vergangenheitsbewältigung* with some of the foundational changes affecting postwar Germany at the end of the 1960s.

Religious tropes, which often concurrently dealt with questions of materialism, prosperity, and frugality, pervaded television programming throughout the late 1950s and 1960s. Some of these references emphasized the role of religious institutions in modern life. Others focused on

Christianity—in isolated instances on other religions—as a source of *values* in modern Germany. The latter instances ranged from overtly Christian to nearly universal touchstones. Finally, religious values and identities were sometimes, as in *Die Beichte*, contrasted with competing ideals such as materialism, overabundant affluence, or, in the case of West German programs, Marxism. In each of these cases, religion acts as more than a mere vehicle through which to express other, ostensibly deeper moral questions. Rather, program makers took religion seriously, both as a marker of identity and as an ethical framework in and of itself. Television producers and writers on both sides of the Wall incorporated religious holidays and events, as well as simple visual cues like preachers, monks, or crucifixes, in their programs. Even amid the turbulent end to the 1960s, West German television continued to highlight religious figures, for example, in two well-publicized ZDF plays: Paul Fechter and Günter Gräwert's *Der Zauberer Gottes* (God's magician, 1966) and the French existentialist philosopher Gabriel Marcel's play *Un Homme de Dieu* (*Ein Mann Gottes* [A man of God], 1967).[60]

Because historians have usually emplotted the history of the East German Protestant Church (by far the largest church throughout the existence of the GDR) within a paradigm of repression and subversion, explanations of religion in East German media have likewise been confined to models that account for the "aberration." One such model holds that religious representations occur only to disparage and discredit traditional Christianity. This position assumes the openly atheist Marxist government saw the Protestant (and sometimes, by extension, the Catholic) Church as a reactionary institution and hence a threat to the revolution. Because the state closely controlled media, including television, these scholars also assume most mediatic references to religion were intended as negative depictions.[61] To be sure, political documents reveal the existence of such officially intended persecution through television. For example, at one meeting of the Staatliches Komitee für Fernsehen (State Committee for Television), the delegates hoped to counter "rising participation at church services among the youth . . . through the medium of dramatic arts."[62] At another meeting of the same body, one committee member noted, "The leading role of the working class increasingly slides into the background . . . Churchgoers are being voted into pioneer councils."[63] Authorities within both the SED Politburo and at the DFF Executive Committee promoted programs such as F. K. Kaul und Walter Jupe's long-running propagandistic series *Fernsehpitaval* and Gerhard Jäckel's *Die Wahnmörderin* (The crazed murderess, 1962) to disparage religion through televisual means.[64]

Nevertheless, programs in the GDR frequently used religious language and imagery. On the one hand, this points to a far more nuanced, complex vision of the socialist project than has been assumed.[65] Consider the Austrian priest from DFF's *Gerichtet bei Nacht* (Tried by night, 1960). He starts the film as frail and despairing, brooding over imminent doom and dispensing acid comments toward the hero, a left-leaning war deserter.[66] Later, however, the priest transforms, no longer frail but energetic, optimistic, and likeable. His constant references to God reinforce his connection with religion. During his bouts with negativity and despair, he asks why God has not intervened in the disastrous war or saved the Jews who were deported to concentration camps. When he becomes helpful and positive, he talks about a moment of real conversion (when he picked up the shovel and worked while the others slept) as a return to God and as a faith-promoting experience. His admonitions to the soldier include assurances that God is on their side and that faith has an inestimable power. Thus, though not the major hero in the piece, the priest becomes a role model, and the promise inherent to his conversion and later optimism is grounded in a transformative faith. Now working together, the priest and the soldier form a united front against the antagonist in the group, a Nazi scientist who desperately wants to escape the bomb shelter they find themselves trapped in, not so much because he wants to resume his duties but because he has recently made a breakthrough in nuclear science and he wants to make sure he gets paid.

Viewers easily comprehended the priest's simple, yet complete, transformation; it provided them with a concrete pattern to follow. Moreover, the film wove Marxism, a moral language familiar to many viewers, into another familiar, specifically religious, language. The producers expanded the Marxist project (a common exercise throughout 1960s GDR television history), in this case with a language well suited to describing conversion and reconciliation. However, as was often the case in the East, the producers' and politicians' schemes also had the unintended consequence of redrawing the boundaries of acceptable religious morality, in essence giving such language a new set of terms from which to draw. A medium instrumentalized by the officially atheist SED thus participated in the reinvention of religious identity.

Conclusion

German elites on both sides of the border perceived a connection between the moral failings related to the rise of postwar prosperity and the spiritual vacuum left behind by the Third Reich. Television, appearing in Germany in the wake of the economic miracle, was well placed to address these ills. Three themes spoke to the perceived vacuum most prominently: the concern that excessive consumption and commercialization had led to decadence resembling that of the Weimar Republic, the worry that a combination of the scarcity-induced materialism of the immediate postwar years and the ongoing obsession with consumption would give rise to a lack of empathy, and the notion (mostly in the West) that Christianity was the best bulwark against both excess and apathy. In terms of quantity, negative representations of wealth, excess, and interpersonal apathy remained constant throughout the period under study. Producers from East and West found common ground on these points, as each side saw much to criticize in contemporary Germany.

While the diagnosis differed little between the two sides, the prescribed treatment in the FRG looked quite different from the GDR's calls for a socialist mentality. Many plays advocated Christianity as the proper medicine for excess and apathy. Church representatives at each of the West German stations, as well as the churches' continued relevance well into the 1960s, despite the 1963 *Stellvertreter* scandal and other public setbacks (declining church attendance, for example), facilitated this narrative. The complexity of the messages, highlighted by the ways that expressions of religiosity intersected with modernity, increased as television expanded, and became more important in the everyday lives of Germans. Representations of religious doubt and theological anguish, represented perhaps most vibrantly by the West German *Ein gewisser Judas* and, as a kind of inverse, in the East German *Die Wahnmörderin*, gradually gave way to agonizing questions about faith and religiosity framed within the context of other moral dilemmas. *Die Beichte* functions as a prime example of how questions of faith intersected with the more universal concerns of German society, in this case *Vergangenheitsbewältigung*. The televisual reinvention of Christianity took place at an uneven pace, and throughout the 1960s, producers seemed to approach religion with uncertainty. But the reinvention did take place, as representations of religion grew to include other vertices of German cultural and social life.

Paradoxically, the nearly universal concern about prosperity did not prevent myriad representations that *reflected* consumer culture and its values. This was not an accident but rather a result of conflicting political goals. In the FRG, the economic miracle functioned as a symbol of political-ideological superiority over the Communist Bloc and as a sign that the West Germans had wholeheartedly adopted the Western European alliance system (NATO and the European Coal and Steel Community), notably influenced by the United States. Moreover, the economic miracle proved useful in reconstructing West German collective identity. Unable to find many national institutions that had survived the Nazi regime without blemish, historians, social critics, and consumers instead turned to more recent events, together building the myth that German hard work and ingenuity could overcome the Nazi catastrophe and form an essential part of the international crusade against communism. At the same time, however, this desire to flaunt wealth and affluence as a sign of restructured German identity and obeisance to American capitalism was tempered by the equally strong political goal of reeducating German citizens along moral lines. In the 1950s and 1960s, a *religious* backdrop to this mission pervaded the discourse. Even removed of its overt trappings, the fear that the economic miracle had gone too far was everywhere evident, including in television studios. The implicitly celebratory television plays were thus allowed to air side by side with programs that criticized those same messages.

In the GDR, this paradox revolved around the SED's quest to establish popular legitimacy within the strictures of a Marxist ideology. On the one hand, party elites condemned the economic miracle as decadent and West German affluence as evanescent. Official channels of propaganda and information, including television, presented the Marxist economic system as more just and, in the long run, more viable. On the other hand, the state absorbed some aspects of West German consumer culture and a taste for a limited version of affluence and wealth. Some of these absorptions were determined politically, others independently. In both cases, the state permitted the subtle celebration of materialism and money because it wanted to compete with the West. This project became much more overt in the 1970s; nonetheless, its origins can be seen in dramatic television from the 1960s. In the GDR's later years, this paradox reached unsustainable levels as the state began to lose the battle for legitimacy. Each new unqualified representation of West German affluence signaled a defeat, but each instance of criticism against the West began to seem hollow, as the public witnessed, often via West German television, how the material quality of life in the FRG had improved much more rapidly than in the East.

East German attempts in the late 1960s and early 1970s to demonstrate affluence and material well-being among its own citizens occurred concurrently with increasingly prominent West German portrayals of decadence and an *over*abundance of material wealth in the West. Neither strand of East German appropriation of consumer culture nor West German concern over an unhealthy materialism appeared suddenly: both had long roots in the 1950s and in many of the moral lessons preached during the Weimar Republic. Moreover, the moral strategies used to disseminate these messages changed little over the course of the time frame in question. East German appeals to material wealth in the early part of this period, seen for instance in the 1960 comedy *Papas neue Freundin*, resolve simple, almost petty, moral dilemmas while simultaneously inserting wealth as an implicit value, as when Klaus, a middle-aged married man, successfully woos the younger Irene with a convertible and expensive dinner appointments. The same pattern takes place almost a decade later in the 1968 program *Gib acht auf Susi!* (Pay attention to Susi!): Susi must resolve a simple dilemma—choosing between an older TV repairman and a younger, more age-appropriate zookeeper—within the confines of various overt markers of material well-being. The television itself, for instance, acts as a sign of prosperity, as does the beach resort, frequent ice cream trips, and Susi's persistent attention to her suitors' expense in courting her.[67] Thus, East German comedies, unlike the more serious Marxist critiques of consumer culture, changed little in terms of substance over the course of the 1960s.

Notes

1. Karl Wittlinger, *Dr. Murkes gesammelte Nachrufe*, dir. Rolf Hädrich (HR, 5 October 1965).
2. Karl Wittlinger, *Seelenwanderung: Eine Parabel*, dir. Rainer Erler (WDR, 2 October 1962).
3. Adelbert von Chamisso and Harald Zusanek, *Peter Schlemihls wundersame Geschichte*, dir. Peter Beauvais (ZDF, 25 December 1967)
4. Historisches Archiv des Westdeutschen Rundfunks, "Jahresbericht des Intendanten," 1962, 68.
5. *epd—Kirche und Fernsehen* 40, 6 October 1962.
6. As Jonathan Zatlin notes, Germans on both sides associated pure capitalism with the failed Weimar Republic, the Jews, and even National Socialism itself. See Jonathan Zatlin, *The Currency of Socialism: Money and Political Culture in East Germany* (New York: Cambridge University Press, 2007), 7.
7. For examples of how the East Germans partook in the culture of the economic miracle, see Katherine Pence, "'A World in Miniature': The Leipzig Trade Fairs in the 1950s and East German Consumer Citizenship," in *Consuming Germany in the Cold War*, ed. David F. Crew, (New York: Berg, 2003), 21–49; Judd Stitziel, "On the Seam between Socialism and Capitalism: East German Fashion Shows," in Crew, *Consuming Germany*, 51–86.
8. Bundesarchiv (BArch), DR 8 17 Vorlage Nr. 5/60. The "and" is underlined in the original document. Advertising television existed in the West, but before the 1970s made up only a very small portion of the stations' revenue (direct broadcasting taxes constituted most of the income).
9. Zatlin, *Currency of Socialism*, 3.
10. Erica Carter, *How German is She? Postwar West German Reconstruction and the Consuming Woman* (Ann Arbor: University of Michigan Press, 1997), 8.
11. Arnold Sywottek, "Wege in die 50er Jahre," in *Modernisierung im Wiederaufbau: Die westdeutsche Gesellschaft der 50er Jahre*, ed. Axel Schildt and Arnold Sywottek (Bonn: Dietz, 1998), 36.
12. Michael Wildt, "Privater Konsum in Westdeutschland in den 50er Jahren," in Schildt and Sywottek, *Modernisierung im Wiederaufbau*, 280.
13. Shelley Baranowski, *Strength through Joy: Consumerism and Mass Tourism in the Third Reich* (New York: Cambridge University Press, 2004), 5; S. Jonathan Wiesen, *Creating the Nazi Marketplace: Commerce and Consumption in the Third Reich* (New York: Cambridge University Press, 2011), 41.
14. Friedrich Meinecke, *Die deutsche Katastrophe* (Zürich: Brockhaus, 1946), 35–36, 89.

15. Mark W. Clark, "A Prophet without Honour: Karl Jaspers in Germany, 1945–48," *Journal of Contemporary History* 37, no. 2 (2002): 204–208.
16. For a small sampling, see Editha Klipstein, "Das Armenhaus," *Frankfurter Hefte* 1 (April 1946): 91; Oswald von Nell-Breuning, "Kapitalismus und Sozialismus in katholischer Sicht," *Frankfurter Hefte* 2 (July 1947): 665–681; Walter Dirks, "Das tägliche Brot," *Frankfurter Hefte* 3 (September 1948): 826–835.
17. Best evident in *The Forgotten Factor*, shown in Germany during the spring of 1948.
18. Max Horkheimer and Theodor Adorno, *Dialectic of Enlightenment*, trans. John Cumming (New York: Herder, 1944), 135–144.
19. Manfred J. Enssle, "Five Theses on Everyday Life after World War II," *Central European History* 26, no. 1 (1993): 18.
20. Peter Bender, for instance, notes that the concept of a *geistige Leere* (spiritual vacuum) existed in both states. Peter Bender, *Deutschlands Wiederkehr: Eine ungeteilte Nachkriegsgeschichte, 1945–1990* (Stuttgart: Klett-Cotta, 2007), 17.
21. Konrad Jarausch, *After Hitler: Recivilizing Germans, 1945–1995* (New York: Oxford University Press, 2006), 140.
22. Friedrich Schiller and Walter Dörfler, *Die Räuber*, dir. Fritz Umgelter (BR, 26 February 1959); August Strindberg and Wilhelm Semmelroth, *Nach Damaskus*, dir. Semmelroth (WDR, 26 November 1966).
23. Karl-Georg Külb, *Die Spur führt in den siebenten Himmel*, dir. Rudi Kurz (DFF, 12, 14, 15, 17, 19 December 1963).
24. *Fernsehdienst* 50/63, 16.
25. Renate Holland-Moritz, *Funk und Fernsehen der DDR*, 12 January 1964.
26. E. Schmidt Novotay, *Berliner Zeitung*, 15 September 63.
27. Arnold Sywottek, "From Starvation to Excess? Trends in the Consumer Society from the 1940s to the 1970s," in *The Miracle Years: A Cultural History of West Germany, 1949–1968*, ed. Hanna Schissler (Princeton, NJ: Princeton University Press, 2000).
28. Susan Reid, "Cold War in the Kitchen: Gender and the De-Stalinization of Consumer Taste in the Soviet Union under Kruschev," *Slavic Review* 61, no. 2 (2002).
29. Gerhard Bengsch, *Irrlicht und Feuer*, dir. Horst E. Brandt and Heinz Thiel (DFF, 21, 23 August 1966). Based on the novel by Max von der Grün, *Irrlicht und Feuer* (Recklinghausen: Paulus Verlag, 1964).
30. "Aus eines Bergmanns Feder," *Television Fernsehspiegel*, undated.
31. Letter from Heinz Glade to *Volksstimme*, undated.
32. Letter from Lutz Strauß to *Neues Deutschland*, undated.
33. Letter from Siegfried Bey to *Lausitzer Rundschau*, undated.
34. Elvira Mollenschott, "Klassenbruder an der Ruhr," *Neues Deutschland*, 29 August 1966.
35. Thomas Beutelschmidt, "Von West nach Ost—von Ost nach West: Irrlicht und Feuer," in *Alltag: Zur Dramaturgie des Normalen im DDR-Fernsehen*, ed. Henning Wrage (Leipzig: Leipziger Universitätsverlag, 2006), 102.
36. Eckart Kronenberg, "Irrlicht und Feuer," *Die Zeit*, 5 September 1966.
37. Hans Schubert, *Stadtpark*, dir. Klaus Wagner (NDR, 6 October 1963).
38. *Infratest Wochenbericht*, October 1963, 64–66.
39. Jan L. Logemann figures that in 1955, car ownership per capita was ten times higher in the USA than in West Germany. By 1970, the gap had closed to 2 times higher ownership in the United States. In the mid- to early 1960s, then, automobiles were not ubiquitous among working class households in the FRG. Jan L. Logemann, *Trams or Tailfins? Public and Private Prosperity in Postwar West Germany and the United States* (Chicago: University of Chicago Press, 2012), 79.

40. *Infratest Wochenbericht*, March 1964. Viewers rated the program extremely low (–1, with 53 percent viewership), and the comments reveal many viewers failed to comprehend the piece.
41. *epd—Kirche und Fernsehen* 12, 21 March 1964. The same publication, perhaps infected by the pessimism of the program, also doubts whether viewers really paid attention.
42. JonDavid K. Wyneken, "Driving Out the Demons: German Churches, the Western Allies, and the Internationalization of the Nazi Past, 1945–1952" (PhD diss., Ohio University, 2007), 66–68.
43. Maria D. Mitchell, *The Origins of Christian Democracy: Politics and Confession in Modern Germany* (Ann Arbor: University of Michigan Press, 2012), 174–175.
44. Rüdiger Steinmetz, *Freies Fernsehen: Das erste privat-kommerzielle Fernsehprogramm in Deutschland* (Munich: UVK Medien, 1996), 82, 91, 188–189.
45. Mitchell, *Origins of Christian Democracy*, 35.
46. Karl Heinz Voigt, *Freikirchen in Deutschland (19. und 20. Jahrhundert)* (Leipzig: Evangelische Verlagsanstalt, 2004), 159.
47. Christian Kuchler, *Kirche und Kino: Katholische Filmarbeit in Bayern, 1945–1965* (Paderborn: Ferdinand Schöningh, 2006), 136.
48. Klaus von Bismarck, *Christliche Präsenz in einer säkularen Rundfunkanstalt* (Cologne: Westdeutscher Rundfunk, 1968).
49. Nicolai Hannig, *Die Religion der Öffentlichkeit: Kirche, Religion und Medien in der Bundesrepublik, 1945–1980* (Göttingen: Wallstein, 2010), 161–171.
50. Evangelisches Landeskirchliches Archiv Berlin 1/861, Letter from Robert Geisendörfer to the Evangelische Kirche in Berlin-Brandenburg, 22 July 1964; Leopold Ahlsen, *Der arme Mann Luther*, dir. Franz Peter Wirth (WDR, 21 January 1965).
51. Archiv des Erzbistums Köln, KRD 103, Letter from Becker to Schröder, 15 March 1962.
52. Herbert Reinecker, *Unterm Birnbaum*, dir. Gerhard Klingenberg (WDR, 3 October 1963).
53. *epd—Kirche und Fernsehen* 39, 5 October 1963.
54. Claude André Puget and Oskar Werner, *Ein gewisser Judas*, dir. Oskar Werner (SWF, 19 November 1958).
55. "Ein gewisser Judas," *Funk-Korrespondenz* 48, 26 November 1958; "Ein gewisser Judas," *epd—Kirche und Fernsehen* 24, 1 December 1958.
56. 2 Corinthians 5:7.
57. Oliver Storz, *Die Beichte*, dir. Eberhard Itzenplitz (ZDF, 11 November 1970).
58. Oliver Storz, *ZDF Programmdienst* 46/70, 11 November 1970.
59. Historisches Archiv des Zweiten Deutschen Rundfunks, Oliver Storz, "Die Beichte 6335/1001," letter, undated.
60. Paul Fechter and Günter Grävert, *Der Zauberer Gottes*, dir. Günter Grävert (ZDF, 26 December 1966); Gabriel Marcel and F. K. Wittich, *Ein Mann Gottes*, dir. Oswald Döpke (ZDF, 22 March 1967).
61. Rotraut Simons, *"Der Pfarrer bleibt vom Bild her problematisch": Ausgewählte Dokumente der Auseinandersetzung mit der Darstellung von Christen in Kinofilmen in der DDR 1956 bis 1989/1990* (Berlin: Staat-Kirche E.v., 2003), 3.
62. BArch, DR 8 30 Staatliches Komitee für Fernsehen, Protokoll Nr. 8/63.
63. BArch, DR 8 77 21.2.1968, Stichwortprotokol der Intendanz-Sitzung vom 9.2.1968.
64. Gerhard Jäckel, *Die Wahnmörderin*, dir. Martin Eckermann (DFF, 9 October 1962).
65. Most standard narratives of the intersection between religion and the SED have highlighted the SED's antagonistic relationship to the Protestant churches. See, e.g., Mary

Fulbrook, *A History of Germany, 1918–2014: A Divided Nation* (Malden, MA: Wiley Blackwell, 2015), 204–205.
66. Günter Kaltofen, Hans-Joachim Kasprzik, and Hermann Rodigast, *Gerichtet bei Nacht*, dir. Hans-Joachim Kasprzik (DFF, 11 September 1960).
67. Hermann Rodigast, *Gib acht auf Susi!* dir. Klaus Gendries (DFF, 25 December 1968).

Chapter 4

RESETTING GENDER ROLES

Women's Equality, Reinvented Masculinity, and the
Nuclear Family

Many of the television plays described in this book faded from public memory long ago. Stations did not record the earliest broadcasts because of the prohibitive cost of the required technology. Both sides began filming almost every production in 1960 (thus ensuring an archival record), but rebroadcasts remained uncommon until the 1970s (with a few notable exceptions for extremely popular shows). Even among the former writers and directors themselves, few could in later years recall the details of any production other than one of their own. Not so with the East German program *Steine im Weg* (Stones in the way, 1960). One of the show's producers, Hans Müncheberg, even declared in a 2008 interview that every DFF worker employed at the station in the early 1960s, including the janitors, would remember that particular broadcast in detail.[1] Embellishment aside, the gist of his statement is probably accurate. DFF did tout *Steine im Weg* as one of East German television's first real highlights. Several of the actors, including Jochen Thomas and Mathilde Danegger, were recognizable stars from the big screen. More importantly, though, *Steine im Weg* was one of the first dramatic pieces to capture the attention of high-ranking political authorities. Censorship on television before 1960, an era in which the vast majority of plays were performed live, consisted mainly of station-internal executives reading scripts and, rarely, of discussions between executives and politicians after the fact. Even after some plays were recorded on celluloid before being broadcast in the late 1950s and early 1960s, there was no real program of pre-broadcast political censorship for television, and most criticisms or alterations were couched in artistic considerations.² With *Steine im Weg*, authorities from the SED finally took notice (during the actual television broadcast) and demanded ex post facto alterations. Because of the nature of the request, however, this meant the cast and crew had to refilm the show months after completion, at enormous expense and, it must be assumed, to the great frustration of everyone involved.

Steine im Weg had been one of the first victims of a rapidly evolving East German rhetorical strategy during the late 1950s. In most respects, the broadcast was not at all unusual. Helmut Sakowski, a young (and promising) screenplay writer and novelist, wanted to show how typical Germans might come to terms with agricultural collectivization. The SED had from the mid-1950s made agriculture a point of special emphasis. After the 1953 uprising had been crushed with the help of Soviet tanks, the regime felt the greatest obstacle to building a socialist nation lay in the rural areas. These regions required indoctrination and, authorities hoped, a taste of the benefits of centralized planning. Some communities had already (willingly) embraced collectivization by the late 1940s, but the project met widespread low-level resistance in most locales.³ Starting in 1952, but accelerating by 1955, the regime began an agitprop blitz, depicting happy, collectivized farmers in pulp fiction, posters, brochures, and films. Television largely targeted an urban audience, but Sakowski successfully convinced DFF authorities that a show depicting farmers' issues (rather than workers') would resonate with the regime and at the same time sell more television sets in smaller towns and villages. *Steine im Weg*, first broadcast in November 1960, was the result.

The show follows the struggles of a young single mother, Lisa Martin, to find acceptance within her local Landwirtschaftliche Produktionsgenossenschaft (Agricultural Production Cooperative—LPG).⁴ Lisa stems from a poor family that had practiced subsistence farming for generations. She previously fell in love with one of the area's richest farmers, Alfred Bergemann, and gave birth to a child during the early postwar years. But the romance ended less than a year after the child's birth and, to make matters worse, Alfred's new wife encourages him to maintain an attitude of pride and aloofness in the face of the coming LPG. The LPG council recognizes that not every farmer will immediately take to the new system, so participation is at first optional. Lisa joins the LPG and quickly establishes herself as the most competent farmer and hardest worker in the village. The council assigns her control over the village's pigs, widely considered the LPG's most valuable property. When Alfred's independent farm bleeds money, he ignores his wife's pleas and approaches the council about joining the collective. Ecstatic to welcome an experienced farmer, and one of the area's last holdouts, the council quickly accepts his terms. Unfortunately, this means demoting Lisa to a different position. Furious, she quits the collective, only to be talked out of her decision by the LPG's new head, a handsome man named Paul. Paul convinces the council to make Lisa and Alfred cooperators. Alfred, however, refuses to work with his ex-girlfriend. He decides to abandon his farm and move to the West. Lisa and Paul, now lovers, become the de facto leaders of a now-thriving community.

In the world of Soviet-style propaganda films, Alfred's character type—the kulak, or rich peasant—has a long history. The rich peasant occupied a place of contempt second only to the Russian boyars (aristocrats) in Stalinist films and literature from the 1930s to the 1950s. In such works, the kulak rarely reforms; instead, he flees or finds himself in prison. Sakowski's *Steine im Weg* follows this well-established Marxist tradition, perhaps adding a bit more nuance to Alfred's character to make the program more believable to West German (and skeptical East German) viewers. But what worked in the Soviet Union, and what had been popular in the early GDR, no longer made sense in the late 1950s, when millions of East Germans left for the other Germany. The population drain would, less than a year later, lead to the creation of the Berlin Wall and a more strongly fortified border. In the meantime, the SED recognized the program as exceedingly problematic. Alfred was no monster, or a fascist. Proud, perhaps, and no explicit role model, but his decision to leave had been painful and complex. In the minds of Ulbricht, Albert Norden, and other SED authorities who watched the first version, some viewers might identify with Alfred and, by extension, wonder whether they really had a place in the GDR.[5] Ulbricht himself wrote to the station, requesting an updated version in which Alfred would decide to "stay and adapt to life in the GDR."[6] To make this conciliatory ending possible, however, Sakowski, Müncheberg, and Gröhl decided they would have to rewrite and reshoot the entire play, as Lisa, Alfred, and Paul's relationship had been much too fraught in the original.[7] The new version aired in May 1961 and, in addition to a completely new end scene in which Alfred resolves to stay in the village, portrays Alfred's wife as the main source of the family's unhappiness with collectivization.

For East German producers, *Steine im Weg* represented an extraordinary broadcast because of its connection to the contemporary political situation. For viewers, however, the broadcast must have seemed remarkable for an entirely different reason: a single mother in a traditional, largely patriarchal subset of German society had risen to a position of prominence. Simply put, *Steine im Weg* appeared as the most outstanding example of the GDR's push to represent women as equals in the workplace. By placing Lisa at the center of the story, and by assigning her a typically male position (as the collective's pig herder), the creators intertwined agricultural-political imperatives and the reformulation of "proper" gender roles, both within and outside the context of those imperatives. Lisa's manner of dress and appearance in the program, including overalls and tied-back hair, reinforced and emphasized these presented changes. Such visual evidence established a clear message: communist societies treat women as equals and allow them to earn traditionally male jobs based on merit.

Moreover, a careful look at the marginalia from the screenplay manuscript reveals conscious decisions at the production level to emphasize Lisa's masculine qualities. For example, when Lisa comes home to eat in one of the opening scenes, the script directions call for a richly laden table. An older man, a guest at the table, declares, "He who works like a man must eat like one," referring to Lisa, still decked out in her work clothes.[8] The man does not necessarily confuse Lisa for a man but considers the work she does, accentuated to the audience by her dirty overalls and hands, as a "man's" job and accepts Lisa as competent in her occupation. Without question, the dialogue itself contains the elements of a new, more open attitude toward gender roles in the communist farm or workplace, but these verbal points are significantly enhanced televisually, in this case by showing piles of sausages laid out for the slim but hardworking Lisa. The point was not lost on viewers; Heinz Schlerz at the *Volksstimme* in Magdeburg gushed over Lisa as the star of the show, in large part because she was *derb* (earthy or strong) and *reif* (ripe or seasoned), words that could connote strength and masculinity.[9] Katja Stern described Lisa as the perfect example of the new, improved farmer: strong, capable, and socialist.[10] Sakowski's main message may have been about building socialism, but the discourse surrounding the program pointed to a rethinking of the nature of women and of their role in the GDR.

One of the major legacies of the Third Reich's collapse was a wide-reaching, complicated national discussion about gender roles and anxieties. That such a discourse existed can hardly come as a surprise to historians. War commonly leads to social upheaval and chaos, and gendered concerns often work their way into the public eye. In modern wars, women have found themselves thrust into the role of breadwinner and provider, whether through their husbands' deployment or through unexpected death at the front. In some cases, they have also fought alongside male soldiers. In a sense, they become masculinized.[11] Male prisoners of war and (male) refugees, in contrast, become demasculinized to a degree, as personifications of the nation's defeat.[12] The unique nature of gender relations in Nazi Germany served to amplify these two issues. Authorities in the Third Reich actively avoided mobilizing women for the war effort, electing instead to outsource factory work to concentration camps in the East.[13] Some women did work during the war years, of course, but not to the same degree as in Great Britain, the Soviet Union, or the United States. By 1945, the imperative to shield women from the workforce had broken down, and the end of the conflict brought little change to the situation, with millions of German men dead, missing, or imprisoned. One legacy of the regime, therefore, was the creation of strongly defined gender roles and the subsequent destruction of those same ideals that came with defeat. To many Germans, this was nothing less than a national emergency.

At the same time, able-bodied women featured heavily in the nation's self-image during the Nazi regime. Girls and young women participated in youth camps and attended rallies alongside their male compatriots. A woman's primary function within this system was to conceive and rear healthy German children. For Hitler and his inner circle, this vision had a definite purpose: resettlement and repopulation in the East. National Socialism even embraced promiscuity and nonnuclear families as an ideal.[14] However, few Germans, even in the right-wing circles allied to National Socialism, embraced this extreme vision. For many commenters after 1945, Hitler had unleashed a perverse view of women's sexuality, one that constituted a major symptom of Germany's ongoing illness.[15] The postwar period seemed to bring an even greater amount of indiscriminate, extramarital sex than during the war years.[16] The real culprit, they argued, was fascism itself. To heal the nation, women must be restored to the domestic sphere, as the centerpiece of a revitalized nuclear family. This discourse appeared in both states but found greater resonance in the West. As the CDU politician and parliament member Bernhard Winkelheide bemoaned, "More than any other social institution, the family has fallen into the whirlpool created by the collapse."[17] Teleplays in the FRG reflected this prevailing sentiment that the traditional family needed repair and restoration after the Third Reich.

Restorative trends dominated discussions about sexuality and family life, but they certainly did not monopolize the broader discourse about women's rights and equality. In the FRG, a tension emerged between two distinct women-as-consumers ideal types. On the one hand, women were touted, in line with the bourgeois model sketched earlier, as caretakers and managers of the domestic sphere. According to this model, they purchased clothing, cooked food, and scrubbed the house using new, heavily advertised soaps and detergents. This ideal of a female homemaker, despite changing, more progressive attitudes about women in the workforce, permeated 1950s West German culture.[18] For example, the 1949 Family and Marriage Code (not revised until 1977) explicitly enshrined the ideal of the housewife into law and gave husbands some control over their wives' decision to work.[19] Aspects of this ideal type also appeared in the GDR. On the other hand, some voices touted female West German consumers as "new girls," independent of their husbands' whims (and incomes).[20] This modern woman remained largely feminine but disliked the conservative, even restorative culture fostered by the male-dominated postwar German elite.[21]

Historians of East Germany, on the other hand, have understood the GDR during the Ulbricht era as more deeply committed to reshaping women's roles, giving them greater rights and responsibilities (especially in the workforce).[22] To be sure, the male authorities still perceived women as the masters of household consumption, and the SED valued the nuclear family as much as their Christian and liberal counterparts in the West. Women's employment here, as in the FRG, had soared during the 1940s because of the demographic shortfall of men. While many women in time returned to the home, though, a great number kept working in the GDR.[23] Women's equality took on greater urgency in the GDR, which, by the early 1960s and the erection of the Berlin Wall, suffered from a crisis of legitimacy. Millions of East Germans had already left for the West. Hoping to drum up support, SED leaders consciously courted women as partners in building socialism, a trend that continued throughout the Ulbricht regime.[24] And positive representations of independent workingwomen extended beyond television, emerging as a central theme in DEFA films in the 1960s as well.[25]

The reformulation and reinvention of gender norms went beyond the issue of women's equality. The Third Reich's defeat had damaged German masculine ideals and stereotypes, based heavily on aggression and militarism. Hundreds of thousands of men found themselves in POW camps in the late 1940s and, to Germans accustomed to Hitler's hypermasculine rhetoric, feminized. Therefore, one of the major challenges of the postwar period was the "reconstruction of men."[26] Only with a revitalized, reformulated masculinity could Germany heal its wounds. The path to a new masculine ideal, moreover, followed a similar trajectory in East and West. Doctors on both sides, for instance, diagnosed deficient masculinity in returning soldiers, for example, by detecting female pubic hair.[27] Homophobia persisted, evidenced by the continued enforcement of Paragraph 175, the Nazi-era criminalization of homosexual acts.[28] Above all, as with the reconstruction of proper femininity, authorities touted family life as the primary solution to Germany's gender ills.

Broadly speaking, gendered spheres of power and control in postwar Germany existed in a series of acentric, overlapping circles. At the highest levels, legislators devised laws that clearly defined the roles of men and women. For example, the FRG's Gleichberechtigungsgesetz (Equal Rights Act) in 1957 ended the husband's "right of final decision" and allowed women to maintain sole possession of property obtained before the marriage. Political figures formed action committees that attempted to regulate and control men and women according to a top-down structure, as with the GDR's Demokratischer Frauenbund Deutschlands (Democratic Women's League of Germany).[29] Belonging to the same general discourse were activist organizations that lobbied for the recognition of women's rights (such as the West German umbrella organization Deutscher Frauenrat).

As an emergent mass medium and primary instrument of shaping domestic life in Germany, television played an important role in linking these overlapping circles of power and discourse. At the elite level, for instance, the women's editorial office Frauenredaktion (Mrs. Editors) at DFF grew in importance and size over the course of the 1960s.[30] No such statewide institution existed in the West, but individual stations did form similar editorial committees. On the other side of the spectrum, the viewers themselves mediated televised norms through viewing choices and letters to the stations, sometimes pushing back against representations and sometimes accepting them. Because so many participants affected the direction and tenor of televisual representations, and because the end product, the television play itself, presented such a highly complex visual representation of these mediated conversations, television is an ideal medium in which to explore the reformulation of the rapidly changing moral currents in post-fascist Germany.

Three gender-related themes dominated during this period. First, from the very start, many dramas represented and idealized the nuclear family. Not all programs cast women as obedient housewives; the GDR in particular sought to demonstrate ways women could work yet continue to act as managers in the domestic sphere. Still, the trope proved durable on both sides of the German-German divide throughout the 1960s. Second, TV fiction explored the aforementioned reinvention of masculinity. Men walked fine lines, for example, between destructive aggression and confident assertiveness or between abusive husband and family decision-maker. West German programs such as *So weit die Füße tragen* (1959; see chap. 2) may have set the tone of these sorts of discussions, but two East German shows, *Egon und das achte Weltwunder* (1964) and *Columbus 64* (1966) provide more poignant examples in that they visually contrast the two sides of masculine behavior. Third, television explored women's equality and liberation. As noted earlier, DFF assigned this imperative greater importance. As time went on, however, West German programs treated issues related to women's equality with greater regularity. By the late 1960s, the two sides' representations on this topic aligned much more than they diverged.

* * *

Despite their leaders' promiscuity and experiments in radical eugenics, many Germans living during the Third Reich strongly valued the family as one of the nation's bedrock values. Conservatives explicitly associated broken homes with communism and, more broadly, with Jewish degeneracy.[31] For them, Hitler's regime provided a bulwark against the leftist assault on family life. Germans of all stripes undertook research on their family history to prove their Aryan heritage and secure a valuable *Ahnenpass* (ancestor passport).

National Socialist propaganda furthermore stressed the home as the one of the most important locations for learning about Germany's destiny as conqueror and culture-bringer. Despite that era's abundant affinity for the family—whether in sanguineous or domestic terms—many postwar Germans perceived of the nuclear family as an institution in need of restoration and nurturing. Even in the GDR, where bourgeois values were not always held in the highest esteem, residents and authorities alike valued the unitary family as a healthy safeguard against the possible resurgence of fascism. Why the sudden emphasis on what remained an intact institution? There are several reasons. First, some Germans indeed remembered the exceptional programs, in which unwed mothers reared children from dedicated Nazi ideologues.[32] While not widespread, such circumstances shocked Germans' sensibilities, especially among the pious. Second, the huge numbers of missing fathers, sons, and brothers instilled in many a very real sense that the war had torn or even destroyed their families. Dead, missing, or captured at the front, these men left behind a physical and emotional void that in turn sparked a widespread cultural emphasis on the sanctity of the nuclear family.[33] Third, the re-Christianization project in the West enlisted the nuclear family as a natural ally and source of a religious upbringing. Even in the East, the increasingly beleaguered churches constantly preached about the centrality of family life. This lesson may have been so popular because it dovetailed with the Ulbricht regime's conservative social mores.[34]

Hermann Rodigast's comedy *Papas neue Freundin* (Papa's new girlfriend), broadcast on Christmas Day in 1960, provides an excellent example of East German Communism's ideas about family life.[35] Franz Bach, an architect, husband, and father of three sons, is attracted to one of his young female apprentices, Irene. He flirts with her and, after a few days, invites her to dinner. For her part, Irene appears a willing object. She beams at Franz's convertible and, when he asks her where she wants to eat, suggests the most expensive restaurant on the block (to the father's consternation). Her acquiescence emboldens Franz, who starts to contemplate adultery. At this point, however, the three children become aware of the relationship. They sabotage Franz and Irene's dates and attempt to rekindle the dormant romance between their parents. Franz's eldest son, Klaus, steps in to court Irene instead (at first to separate her from his father and later because he has fallen in love with her). Irene proves difficult to sway. For example, she shows obvious annoyance when Klaus takes her on a "mere" picnic instead of the expensive restaurant she frequented with Franz. In the end, though, Irene selects the more age-appropriate companion, and unsurprisingly, Franz patches his relationship with his wife, Margo.

Inasmuch as the lighthearted program has a theme or message, it is the restoration of the nuclear family. Rodigast paints Franz as a sympathetic character. He and Margo have a cool, somewhat distant relationship at the start of the piece, but he obviously loves his children, at one point dropping his briefcase before leaving for work and playing soccer with them, and at another juncture playing a board game with them. This picture of relative domestic tranquility is upset as soon as Franz starts seeing Irene. He gets into a shouting match with Margo, and when one of his boys asks for help with his homework, he slaps him and tells him his work is more important right now. The children notice the difference and decide to take turns shadowing their father. Much of the show's humor derives from these scenes, as the two younger kids wear sunglasses and hats to observe their dad undetected. They first try to sabotage his outings with Irene, for example, by puncturing his tires. They also try to make their mother more attractive by scheduling an appointment with the hairdresser and buying her a new dress for her birthday. When these measures prove ineffective, they convince Klaus to try to steal her away from their father. The children, including Klaus, are largely animated by the desire to preserve their loving family. While Klaus also develops feeling for Irene, this aspect of his intentions is revealed in the play's climatic scene, a fight between father and son after Franz discovers that Klaus has been seeing Irene. Franz is indignant and slaps his son, but Klaus retorts, "What are you thinking!? You're twice her age! Go back to Mom!" Franz does exactly that, and the program's end strongly implies that Klaus and Irene are in a serious relationship.

Given the program's main purpose, the restoration of a happy nuclear family, and given DFF's recent representation of a strong-willed, independent woman in *Steine im Weg* (which first aired a month before *Papas neue Freundin*), Irene's character seems a bit incongruent. She appears reasonably talented at her job, but the program avoids addressing the question of her expertise, instead marking her as a mere object of sex appeal. By agreeing to meet with the much older Franz outside his office, she comes across as "loose" and flirtatious. Her ultimate selection of Klaus softens this impression. Nevertheless, her role as a sex object far outweighs her merits as an employee. Clearly, the program's creator, Rodigast, never intended it as a commentary or referendum on women in professional capacities. And viewers did not seem to notice this side to her character. In response to a 1969 survey that asked, "Which DFF television play of the past ten years did you find the most exciting?" 7 percent of the viewers chose *Papas neue Freundin*, even though the piece was almost ten years old.[36] Traditional conceptions of gender, it seems, persisted despite pieces advocating women's equality.

Not all productions valorizing the nuclear family followed this pattern of light-hearted comedy. The title character ZDF's *Das Unbrauchbare an Anna Winters* (The incorruptible Anna Winters, 1963), for instance, doggedly adheres to a set of conventional gender norms, even when those beliefs no longer seem tenable. A Silesian refugee who works as a maid at a NATO facility in Germany, Anna has long been separated from her husband, who also now lives and works in the vicinity. She copes with her separation by means of mantras: "A husband belongs where the wife is, and a wife where the husband is . . . home is only where my husband is, and where Lisa (her daughter) is . . . there is only one table, and that's ours."[37] She repeats these words over and over throughout the course of the program, to her NATO employer, to her husband, who comes to her demanding a divorce, and to her neighbor friend, who tells her to move on. But she persists in setting the table for two every night, and tells all who will listen that he will come back one day. When the situation becomes more serious (GDR operatives start blackmailing her with threats against Lisa, still captive in the East), she persists in her simplistic formulations. She succumbs to the blackmail because her greatest value, the inseparability of her family, takes precedence over allegiance to her adopted state and employer. Even after she is caught spying, she holds tightly to her mantra and the value that lies behind it: the nuclear family above all else. In the end, despairing over the paradox in which she feels trapped, she commits suicide by throwing herself down the staircase at work.

Interestingly, *Das Unbrauchbare an Anna Winters* received heavy support from the church representatives at ZDF.[38] The reasons for this are now unclear, but perhaps its romantic depiction of the nuclear family, and how both World War II and the Cold War had torn at it, played a role. The promulgation of the nuclear family had been a particularly important project in both major churches since 1945. Fearing a drastic sociological shift in their constituency in the face of urbanization, postwar prosperity, and women entering the workplace, Christian churches pressured television stations to project "traditional" family values onto their programs. Nevertheless, Anna Winters's eventual suicide, caused by her inability to reunite her family, calls the effectiveness of the old, mantra-based form of moral understanding into serious question. As numerous critics noted, the disconnect between her ultimate simplicity (often termed "stupidity" in the press) and the complicated Cold War situation in which she finds herself must have given viewers pause and caused them to reevaluate their own basic values.[39] Still, Anna Winters generated significant sympathy among viewers. The show garnered a +6 approval rating, among the highest of the year.[40] Some of the attached comments are also telling: It was a "teaching piece" and had a "deep seriousness, a deep meaning." The viewers also liked Anna's character, showering praises on the main actress, Edith Schultze-Westrum, and on the fact that the viewer "had to set him (or her) self into this woman . . . and it was terrifying." Clearly, the public found her simplicity endearing, and her core value perfectly tenable. In this sense, the moral lesson presented here resonated positively in the general television discourse, especially among viewers.

Moreover, the above viewer's "terror," while undoubtedly referring to Lisa's imprisonment and Anna's anguish over the blackmail, seems inextricably bound up in Anna's gender. Only through the eyes of a woman, who cannot easily come to terms with the simultaneous collapse of family and loyalty to the state, can the difficulty of the situation truly be understood. Anna cannot adapt precisely because she is a woman. In this sense, Anna's liturgy of traditional gender norms in the face of an obviously hopeless situation shows the (supposed) weakness and non-adaptability of her sex. One TV critic implied as much when he commented that "the primitive hardness of the woman (or wife)" just wants to do the right thing.[41] "Primitive" could refer either to Anna in the specific or (and this seems to apply either way) to women in general, a sex unchanged for millennia.

At the same time, however, *Das Unbrauchbare an Anna Winters* also makes it clear that this premise is no longer tenable in modern society. Rapidly changing economic circumstances have forced both Anna and her estranged husband to work, a situation with which the lower classes in Germany had long been familiar but that had only recently penetrated the nation's psyche. At a very different level, Anna's catechistic obsession with traditional family values and gender roles is debunked by the show's location in the center of the Cold War struggle between East and West. Anna's desire to save her daughter from the Stasi's clutches trumps her devotion (if any even exists) to the FRG. But her choices are futile, shown to be naive against the stark reality of totalitarianism and the West's war against it. At no point does the program suggest the NATO officials who fire her and drive her to suicide or the West German state's insistence on the primacy of patriotism above family are responsible for the tragedy. Rather, the East German spies who use her, as well as Anna's own naive assumptions about the inviolability of the family, cause her tragic downfall and death.

Germans valued the nuclear family long before the Cold War, of course. The 1969 West German televisual dramatization of a 1917 Hermann Sudermann short story, *Reise nach Tilsit* (Journey to Tilsit), for example, starkly depicts the pitfalls of a husband abandoning his family for another woman.[42] The original story, part of Sudermann's volume *Litauische Geschichten*, or "Lithuanian Stories," describes an extramarital affair between a moderately wealthy fisherman (Ansas) and his household maid, Busze. Indre, Ansas's wife, learns of his transgressions and tells her wealthy bourgeois father, Jaksztat, who in turn rebukes Ansas and casts Busze from the estate. However, the affair continues, and Busze convinces Ansas to murder Indre on a ship voyage to Tilsit, a medium-sized city on the Baltic Sea. Along the way, he remembers his love for Indre and aborts the plan, only to unintentionally fall victim to the waves himself. Some literary critics have interpreted Sudermann's story as a complex, nuanced study in female contrasts between Indre and Busze.[43] Despite her transgressions, they argue, Sudermann writes Busze as vibrant and healthy, a kind of liberation for the weak, rudderless Ansas. Indeed, inasmuch as the short story probes the depths of Ansas's psychological despair and real sense of conflict, the tale transcends the simplistic moral caution implied by the binary between the two women.

The ZDF version hardly differs from the short story in its essential plot elements; however, the television program foregrounds the virgin/whore dichotomy between the good, honest housewife and the sexually promiscuous maid. On the one hand, Indre maintains a clean household, never joins her neighbors (and husband) at the local bar or *Gasthaus*, and pines for her husband, even when she knows that he has committed adultery. Busze's role as the temptress or seductress, on the other hand, is solidified visually and dramatically by the bright colors she wears and her frequent, loud laughter (some television plays on the ARD and ZDF were broadcast in color, starting in 1967; DFF followed suit in 1968). She calls Indre *scheinheilig* (hypocritical), thus deflecting Ansas's guilt back on her rival and cultivating the audience's emotional disdain for her character. The dramatically repeated opening and closing scene of Busze's former lovers washing up on the shore, each time discovered by a mentally handicapped villager, points to her supernatural ability to destroy suitors. In sum, the ZDF version paints Busze as an unrepentant, even demonic seductress. The masculine protagonist Ansas, in contrast, appears as a tragic figure, otherwise courageous and likable. The young seductress seems more blameworthy, and the moral message for men seems to be: choose your lover carefully (not: be faithful to your spouse). The message for women seems to be a choice: purity and chastity versus deceit, frivolity, and infidelity. A woman can be faithful or can whore herself, but she cannot walk a middle ground.

This paradox for women was not lost on critics. The *Frankfurter Neue Presse*, a centrist regional paper, declares that in this program, "men are still men, and women are either chaste, diligent, and good, or abysmally rotten and evil."[44] The anonymous author(s) likens this situation to those found in the *Heimatfilm* genre, where women were also forced into such paradoxes and dichotomies. By pointing out the inescapable paradox in which women find themselves, the *Frankfurter Neue Presse* implicitly brings the representation of gender categories to the reader's/viewer's attention. Fred Diehl at the *Rheinpfalzer Zeitung*, another regional daily, also compares *Reise nach Tilsit* to a *Heimatfilm*, but in this case, Diehl claims superior acting and a general sense of gravity redeem the production.[45] Despite these critics' proclamations, Sudermann's tragic story itself does not fit the pattern of West German films produced in the 1950s; the piece's almost melodramatic elements and bitter ending, which affects even the innocent Indre, give both story and film greater emotional depth than a *Heimatfilm*. But even if *Reise nach Tilsit* cannot be read as the belated product of repressive 1950s West German *Leitbilder* (a guiding model or example), the contrast between the two women could hardly be greater. With such moralizing figures as Indre's father displayed so positively in the teleplay (a critique also voiced in the *Frankfurter Neue Presse*'s review), the film assumes a position of moral dispenser, and one of the most prominent lessons involves the ideal woman, Indre. The only alternative the film presents to this ideal is Busze. Viewers (both male and female) are encouraged to choose Indre, an embodiment of the restoration of bourgeois values and a rejection of promiscuity.

While the *feminine* whore/virgin dichotomy is perhaps more strongly presented in *Reise nach Tilsit*, the program also contains an essentialized *masculine* duality. Over the course of the show, the audience learns that Ansas, while independent in some ways, owes much to Jaksztat (his father-in-law) for his wealth, estate, and social standing. Jaksztat is not a nobleman but a highly "Germanized" member of the Lithuanian bourgeoisie. The villagers fear him (though he actually lives some miles away in another town), and he represents the traditional moral and social order. In the television version, he appears as a large, well-fed man, quick to laugh with his grandchildren and give his horses sugar, but also quick to anger. In short, the strong-willed Jaksztat is the standard by which Ansas is measured. Ansas's failure to maintain a strict order in his household, even when his wife comes across as such a meek and submissive figure, is an affront to Jaksztat's ideal of masculinity. Despite his wrath, however, Jaksztat is happy to forgive Ansas: "Now you have to make whole again, that which you have broken." The possibility of repentance is visually reinforced by Ansas kneeling in Jaksztat's presence and asking God for forgiveness: "I am a sinner before the Lord!" For Busze, however, Jaksztat has only a beating and sharp words: "[You] dirty beast, we'll show you." Not only does he dehumanize the "seductress," but Jaksztat also invokes a larger social order in which he stands as a mere enforcer. For "the devil's child," there is no hope of repentance. This situation, particularly in its ZDF visualization, demonstrates the deep cleft between sexual mores for men and those for women.

The 1967 DFF adaptation of Hans Fallada's *Kleiner Mann—was nun?* (*Little Man, What Now?*) follows a similar trajectory, providing a setting for two contrasting types of female *Leitbilder*.[46] Klaus Jörn and Hans-Joachim Kasprzik's adaptation, the most widely watched East German dramatization of a Hans Fallada novel in the 1960s, highlights certain aspects of the novel and downplays others. Both novel and television play depict the struggles of a young clerk from Stralsund, Johannes Pinneberg, and his young wife, Emma (usually referred to as Lämmchen, "little lamb"). They face oppression from Johannes's miserly bourgeois employer, extortion at the hands of his creditors and even his alcoholic mother in Berlin, and the couple's race against time to save their child from starvation. The novel's final scenes establish Johannes's reliance on Lämmchen as the basis of their hope; only through her love can they overcome desperation. The DFF version, however, brings their decision to join the Communist Party to the forefront of the conclusion, in the form of Lämmchen's constant prodding and Johannes's Marxist "conversion." The voice-over narration at the end of the two-part program, while, taken directly from the novel, further emphasizes the present mission of the Marxist GDR state: "There is no peace between poor and rich . . . but millions are stronger than the legionary." "Millions" could be interpreted here as a reference to the numerical superiority of the poor in Weimar Germany, but, as Gisela Hermann's review article makes clear, it could be, and was, interpreted as a description of the millions of Germans in the GDR and as a continuing call to arms.[47] Furthermore, a recent interview with Jörn demonstrates the East German censors consciously omitted the final embrace between Johannes and Lämmchen and instead depicted Johannes running to the Communist Party, the true safeguard against the police brutality he had just experienced.[48]

The press reception of *Kleiner Mann—was nun?* pays the same attention to the present, even though neither novel nor television show makes anachronistic reference to the postwar period. The *Pressedienst*, a description of future programs circulated by DFF to help newspaper critics prepare their reviews, makes moral judgments about the past even in its more objective descriptions. A paragraph that begins in an ostensibly objective, almost journalistic shell—"Germany. July 1930. Berlin"—becomes the vehicle for the more interpretive sentence, "The lords of high finance plan a new treason against the nation."[49] The article thrusts the standard East German historical interpretation of the stock market crash and the impoverishment of the lower classes in the Great Depression on Fallada's work, despite the same publication's earlier assessment of the author: "He rarely pondered. He was always completely absorbed in the fullness of his embattled characters."[50] A review article in the *Sächsische Zeitung*, at the time an official SED daily, similarly inserts Marxist history as a moral assessment of the situation: "Johannes is lucky his 'Lämmchen' proves herself to be a dedicated, virtuous, brave proletarian child, whose grasp of class consciousness is just enough to hold the somewhat failed man and their child above water."[51] To be sure, Marxist ideology would have offered the same appraisal of the situation during the early 1930s, "class consciousness" and all. Again, however, the communist context, though it corresponds well with Fallada's work, is thrust to the center of the plot, despite the author's inclusion of multiple parties and factions in the Weimar Republic (although the Social Democrats and the

Communists do feature heavily). The "moral" of the original, if one is to be drawn at all, is that the "little men" must learn frugality in the face of adversity to survive. Marxism acts as an addition or literary interpretation of the text, one that neatly lines up with DFF's mission to educate its viewers about the universality of the Marxist message. Hermann wondered how the piece would remain true both to the original work and "to today's vantage point, without becoming . . . a mere copy or . . . an actualization, and thus not corresponding to the true Fallada."[52] One of her answers to this question proves illuminating: "We are grateful for the . . . cleverly formulated commentary [apparently the aforementioned voice-over], which opens a view to the present parallels in West Germany." She then proceeds to bemoan the fate of the poorer, but affluent, members of society, whose dreams of social mobility have been dashed by the rules of capitalism. Apparently, Hermann's idea of a balance includes enough condemnation of capitalism to make the "parallels" to West Germany clear to the viewer.

Johannes's mother, Mia, in a sense represents the FRG. She tries to extract exorbitant rent and special favors from her son and his wife. Not necessarily a villain, and certainly among the most intriguing characters in the piece, Mia nonetheless acts as an example of what *not* to do. In addition to the more universal moral infractions, Mia engages in prostitution, speaks loudly and obnoxiously, drinks heavily, and badgers her boyfriend, the generous but criminal Holger Jachmann. In short, she embodies multiple negative female stereotypes, including the whore and the henpecking, nagging wife. Exquisitely performed by the accomplished stage actor Inge Keller, Mia emerges as a wholly believable character, full of color and vitality, but all the more cautionary for prospective admirers. Her clothing, extravagant pearl necklaces, hats, and flapper dresses, as well as Keller's exuberant, loud performance, dramatically magnify Fallada's character for viewers and, in the process, teach female viewers how *not* to act.[53]

In contrast, Lämmchen functions as a positive *Leitbild*. Quiet and easygoing, Lämmchen seems a veritable Madonna compared to Mia. Her patience with Johannes persistently surfaces in the television version, and except for one scene where she panics because she fears for the life of her child, she never raises her voice. In contrast to Mia's prostitution, she remains faithful to her husband, despite continued economic hardship. Her diligence and frugality also shine through, as she knits socks from the couple's shabby apartment in Berlin to earn extra money. She thus conforms to a traditional division of labor but excels at what she does and holds the struggling family together in a time of crisis. This quiet, firm, highly moral nature is reinforced by the fact that she frequently disagrees with Mia. She disapproves of her mother-in-law's manners, her demeanor, and especially her extravagant spending. Even her pet name, Lämmchen, is indicative of her character. Jutta Hoffmann, the actor who played Emma, understood her character as "the moral strength," and as Johannes's "rudder."⁵⁴ Mimosa Künzel echoes this view at the East German CDU's official paper, *Neue Zeit*, declaring Lämmchen as "the ray of hope" in the production.⁵⁵

DFF also produced modern, "updated" representations of the traditional woman, of course. *Egon und das achte Weltwunder* (Egon and the Eighth World Wonder, 1964) is a typical—and popular—example along these lines.⁵⁶ The program itself, based on a popular 1962 novel of the same name by Joachim Wohlgemuth and brought to television by Christian Steinke, depicts a somewhat rebellious East German teenager (Egon) and his efforts to disassociate himself from his friends (whom he increasingly considers a bad influence). After a chance encounter with a beautiful young woman named Christine, he resolves to fit in with her friends, a more socially desirable group of FDJ youth. Though he gradually finds acceptance in his new cohort, Egon struggles to hide both his checkered past and the ulterior motive for his "conversion" (infatuation with Christine). After he earnestly but unsuccessfully attempts to understand and explain the intellectual underpinnings of Marxist-Leninism at an FDJ retreat, his socialist leaders and peers begin to express greater sympathy for the young man's plight. They encourage him to persevere in his new lifestyle. He does, eventually inviting his older, more rebellious friends to join.

Wohlgemuth's novel constantly describes Christine as attractive, elegant, and worthy of the title "Eighth World Wonder."⁵⁷ Newspaper reviews universally noted the show's tendencies in this direction. Georg Zivier at the West Berlin paper *Der Tagesspiegel*, for instance, says, "[Christine] is spun of finer material than Egon, cute and even blonde."⁵⁸ Here, as Zivier makes clear, the "finer material" refers to her attractiveness, and not to her role as an agent of change in Egon's life. Another critic's first choice of adjective for Christine is also "cute," ignoring any other qualities she might possess.⁵⁹ In fact, though every press report about *Egon und das achte Weltwunder* described Egon's self-transformation into a socialist worker with class consciousness (unsurprisingly, as the major publications in the GDR relied on the state for their very existence), not one publication mentions Christine's role in effecting his change of heart, except as a little extra encouragement. For example, Werner Schwemin at the *Berliner Zeitung* explains, "[Christine's] love helps Egon to discover his own personality" and, eventually, his purpose as a socialist worker.⁶⁰ Reviewers thus understood Christine purely as an object of sexual attraction, not as a partner for intellectual exchange.

The show itself gives numerous visual and verbal clues that corroborate this assessment of Christine's character. The title of the program, taken from a description of Christine within the novel, sets the tone for the young woman as an object to be revered and sought after, not as an agent in her own right. In televisual terms, the directors highlight her status as a trophy or possession in several ways, including a bar fight for the right to dance with her, a gratuitous nude swimming scene at the FDJ camp, and a sequence in which she asks for a male chess teacher, without really seeming interested in the game at all. This is not to suggest Christine never expresses or asserts herself, but in general, her role seems to be as an object of affection and adoration for Egon and the other male youths. The major result of this objectification is not the union of Egon and Christine; rather, the members of Egon's rebellious gang see the scales fall from their eyes and convert to socialism. Christine's sex appeal is thus a means to a nobler end.

Part of that noble end is the reclaiming and repurposing of Egon's strongly masculine character. At the beginning of the program, he fashions himself as a *Halbstarke*, or beatnik, by wearing leather jackets, drinking and smoking heavily, and performing provocative jazz music with his comrades (these visual and aural cues are absent from the novel). His independence and rejection of authority are a type of self-assertion, particularly in light of his relatively stable home and upbringing. As viewers quickly learn, Egon is an accomplished auto mechanic, marking him as an ideal candidate for the "proletarian" FDJ. Moreover, he seems to have already embarked on the path to reform. One newspaper critic maintains, "We sympathize from the start with him, because . . . Egon takes it upon himself to overcome his past and to . . . join the socialist society."[61] His self-identification with rebellion, therefore, seems to derive from a lack of satisfaction with his proletarian potential, and ultimately from his rejection of the FDJ's patterns of lifestyle because they are not masculine enough. An unnamed local FDJ youth, part of a rival group to Egon's *Halbstarke*, surprisingly (for an East German production) reinforces this very point by punching Egon at a local dance and failing to win Christine's affection. Indeed, the West German press noticed this fact, expressing surprise that an East German program, let alone one so lighthearted, could offer any kind of self-criticism.[62] As the show progresses, however, Egon slowly embraces socialism, standing up to his friends and observing the quiet, dignified figures of his leaders and his erstwhile opponent, Paul. The DFF's liaisons to the Zentralkomitee understood the program in these latter terms, declaring the station needed to plan more pieces like *Egon* in order to promote "historical consciousness" among the country's youth.[63] A competing ideal of masculinity thus emerges, supplanting the rebellious version with one more suited to the socialist workforce, to the chagrin of the same West German critics who praised *Egon*'s light criticism of the FDJ.[64] The new ideal also offers a corrective to the warlike, impatient version of masculinity commonly seen during the 1930s and early 1940s.

On the one hand, the essentialization of men and women fits into the Cold War struggle for the viewers' allegiance. Egon's "socialist" masculinity is presented as superior to the aimless, rebellious masculinity of his erstwhile friends. Likewise, Christine, the "Eighth World Wonder," acts as an attractive object, which is then harnessed to the more desirable FDJ youth; she functions as bait for the untamed *Halbstarke* youth. On the other hand, Egon's and Christine's characters simultaneously reflect the postwar (and post-Nazi) reformulation of gender norms. Producers place the sexualized Christine on a pedestal, and she is in no way the intellectual equal of her male counterparts. Egon's combative, delinquent behavior can be explained as indicative of a lack of a proper outlet for his masculine tendencies. The FDJ youth camp, it is assumed, will give him direction. Importantly, Egon experiences difficulty in coming to terms with this new assignment, briefly stepping down from the podium and trying to quit the camp. Parents and youth leaders are thus given instructions as well, encouraged to demonstrate patience with the process of reinventing German masculinity after the Nazis' hypermasculine worldview.

Perhaps the most interesting vision of masculinity in the GDR, however, features two contrasting models in a 1966 Ulrich Thein piece called *Columbus 64*.[65] The film follows the story of a young, frustrated writer and poet, Georg, played by the acclaimed actor Armin Müller-Stahl. His editor (he works for a newspaper) feels he possesses a clear aptitude as a writer but explains he hasn't learned enough about the world to write about any meaningful subjects. The editor recommends he spend time in a factory or mine to gain firsthand experience about workers. Georg rejects the idea, but when his debts begin to mount on account of his relatively carefree lifestyle, he reluctantly takes a job as a truck driver at a mine in Saxony. Here, he gradually learns the value of hard work and acquires what the show calls a "socialist mentality."

On the surface, the program is less a critique of gender roles than the story of a spoiled, bourgeois writer's conversion to socialism. One sub-narrative to this general plot, however, is a standoff between a communist "worker's hero" and a jobless, ex-Nazi villain. The ex-Nazi, Gundel, beats his wife and daughter daily. When Georg discovers this, he brings the daughter to his mentor and working-class inspiration, the "worker's hero" Sepp. Sepp confronts Gundel and accuses him of laziness, drunkenness, and a perverse love of violence. Gundel, in a panic, tells Sepp to leave or else he will call the police. Sepp laughs at this suggestion and says they are going to settle this personally. Gundel refuses to fight, and Sepp, having cowed his adversary, tells Gundel he will check up on him regularly. Throughout the sequence, Gundel is given several negative masculine traits. He physically abuses female family members, refuses his proper role as the breadwinner, and drinks heavily. Moreover, he lacks courage and seems, because of his past (explicated by Sepp in a previous scene), to be a man without proper convictions, having joined and then distanced himself from the Nazi party as the climate dictated. In contrast, Sepp personifies many positive masculine characteristics: protecting the female family members from abuse and mistreatment, working hard, taking justice into his own hands rather than hiding behind a support network (Gundel tried to invoke police protection, though they almost certainly would have sided with Sepp), and consistently allying himself to the Communist Party (demonstrating his unwavering convictions). The notion of a negative and positive masculinity is given further credence by the political affiliations of each man: as an instrument of the state, DFF naturally depicted the positive figure as a committed communist and the negative figure as a Nazi, a last vestige of a failed type of masculinity unleashed in 1930s and 1940s Germany. *Columbus 64*, in terms of both the Sepp/Gundel contrast and Georg's thorough transformation, thus carefully redefines the ideal masculine figure along socialist lines. Obviously, not all early television plays followed this pattern of political appropriation. But there can be little doubt that both the Cold War and the failed Nazi regime contributed to a necessary redefinition of proper masculinity. And this was not unique to the East. West German broadcasts such as *So Weit die Füße tragen* (discussed in chap. 2) and *Stadtpark* (chap. 3) display a similar concern with reclaiming masculinity in a post-fascist era.

The parallel redefinition or reassessment of women and their proper role in modern society followed a different trajectory. During the immediate postwar years, state mechanisms, whether controlled by the Allies or by the nascent German governments after 1949, attempted to curb and/or limit the number of women employed in traditionally masculine jobs. The authorities' most effective mechanism for enacting these withdrawals involved redirecting women's labor to the consumption, instead of the production, front.[66] Food shortages and painful reconstruction projects made this task easier, as women could now recast themselves as household budget managers and consumption experts. By the mid-1950s, however, this arrangement increasingly came under question. Women returned to work, often as "buffer" workers for certain sectors of the economy.[67] Television plays still depicted plenty of women in the home, but a far greater number were depicted as having entered the workforce in one capacity or another. In early West German television, women often appeared as secretaries or auxiliaries in the office. A real discussion about the possibility of women as career equals did not occur until the late 1960s.[68] By contrast, East German programs, in the mold of *Steine im Weg*, wrestled with this theme even in the medium's earliest days. And these discussions were not limited to the workplace, central though the topic was in the Marxist worldview. The discussion about workingwomen often quickly shaded into a more general discussion about women's rights and the push for equality.

Still, it is sometimes difficult to show direct connections between political messages and the actual production of teleplays. In March 1962, the drama division at DFF presented the executive committee with a list of programs that corresponded with the station's new mission to present "women's problems through artistic means," but none of the programs mentioned ever seem to have been produced.[69] Later in the letter, the department also expressed its support for a planned series called "Portraits from the German Past" and explained which female historical figures might best fit; however, the series never reached production stage and the names, with the prominent exception of Rosa Luxembourg, never found their way onto the small screen. Nonetheless, more progressive visions and messages of women's equality saturated fictional television in the East, some well before the SED, the intendant, or the Frauenredaktion addressed the issue directly. Internal discussions in the winter of 1962 about the newly accorded political importance attached to "women's equality" surely reached producers' and writers' ears before the official pronouncements circulated.[70] Moreover, well before 1962, East German programs such as *Steine im Weg* had presented women as capable and equal partners in their respective spheres and in the socialist building project. Another early program conceived before the SED and station executives pushed women's programming at DFF was Rudi Kurz's multipart series *Das grüne Ungeheuer* (The green monster, 1962, see chap. 2), which inserted equality of the sexes as an undertone. The program's lead female character, Isabel, is introduced as the beautiful, silent daughter of the left-leaning journalist Dr. Guerra. She wears a short, revealing dress and sports long, dark hair. When right-wing insurrectionists capture her and the show's protagonist (Morena), Isabel begins a transformation. She knocks out her captor with a soda bottle, takes the lead in helping the two captives escape, cuts her hair so that she will not be recognized, starts wearing pants, and finally, successfully impersonates a young male soldier. In other words, she adopts a masculine persona, one she wears even at the celebratory conclusion.

This projection of women as equals, without political intervention, began even earlier. Helmut Sakowski's play *Die Entscheidung der Lene Mattke* (Lene Mattke's decision, 1958), a predecessor to the more famous *Steine im Weg*, for example, revolves around a woman finding courage to resist her abusive husband and become a productive (and working) member of her village.[71] Lene Mattke, a hardworking mother of four in a GDR farming collective, has lived for years with an abusive, drunken husband. She avoids eye contact with other adults, regularly receives beatings at home, and struggles to cover her husband's lazy, extravagant lifestyle. When a new collective leader decides to focus his efforts on helping the family, however, Lene springs into action. She accepts a job at the collective's granary, works hard to impress the skeptical men at the combine, and transforms her whole demeanor from submissive and defeated to diligent and outgoing. When her husband, who has been in the hospital with a liver sickness, comes home and wants to move to another town, she confronts him and tells him she and the children will stay. She resists his attempts to hit her, and kicks him out of the house. Finally, the husband meekly returns and asks forgiveness, apparently repentant at the sight of his wife's newfound independence.

References to freedom in *Lene Mattke* operate at several levels. First, the SED's collectivization project is presented as enabling, rather than restricting, for independent farmers. Individual wealth and affluence, here represented by a new wardrobe for Lene and a place at the local school for her teenage daughter, come only once the family joins the collective, despite its traditional breadwinner's (the husband's) wishes. The LPG's role in creating freedom for the family (and, by extension, the conditions under which freedom can flourish) is enhanced when the villagers make fun of the new collective leader's attempts to raise the Mattke family out of poverty by comparing him to Jesus: "A second Jesus, we have here!" and "It is written, love your enemies!" Despite their jibes, he accepts the mantle and offers the family a chance of freedom through "redemption" by association. Second, and more importantly from a gender perspective, Lene transforms herself from a stereotypical downtrodden housewife to an assertive, contributing member of society. Lene proves herself able to take care of the cows, to work hard (not unlike Lisa in *Steine im Weg*), and to support her family without her husband's help. This lesson reverberated with newspaper critics, one of whom remarked, "She found her own strength."[72] Third, Wilhelm Gröhl, the director, dropped visual cues and markers to highlight her change. These include a new, shorter hairstyle, makeup that removes the bags under her eyes (applied after she starts her job at the stalls), and her newfound love of reading. *Lene Mattke* thus presents freedom for women on its own terms, separated from the more usual "freedom for women within their own sphere."

By 1964, the project of representing women's equality reached a kind of zenith on East German television with Sakowski's *Sommer in Heidkau*.[73] Hete, widely reputed to be sexually promiscuous in her fictional East German village, works as a maid at the local tavern. When Robert, an SED party functionary, comes to improve agricultural production in the agrarian community, he recognizes Hete's talent and promotes her to oversee a new method of harvesting potatoes. She works hard at her position, switching from her usual dress to pants, rolling up her sleeves as she works, and telling the men assigned to her how to do their jobs. Potato output increases under her supervision, and she is finally able to purchase a larger house for herself and her three children. Here, then, viewers witness a woman performing a man's work, a reformulation of the division of labor based on merit, not gender. Furthermore, Hete adopts a masculine position with all its trappings, including pants, sweat, and forcefulness. No longer must she conform to her own limited sphere of work; now she can also adopt masculine tasks to suit her abilities. *Sommer in Heidkau* discards the strict division of labor, favoring instead a new kind of value—in this case one more suitable to the Marxist-Leninist emphasis on the equality of the sexes. Indeed, political authorities lavished a fair amount of praise on *Sommer in Heidkau*. One anonymous document in the Federal Archives in Berlin reads: "One must mention Helmut Sakowski's *Sommer in Heidkau* as the most outstanding [television] experience of the week. You could even say the play is a high point in contemporary socialist television drama."[74] Sakowski won the station's annual prize for his efforts, the *Goldene Lorbeer des DFF*.

Indeed, perhaps unsurprisingly given the SED's support for *Lene Mattke* and *Sommer in Heidkau*, the GDR led the way in representing equality between the sexes as a value on television. In January 1962, DFF, under the direction of the SED Zentralkomitee, reorganized the long-standing Frauenredaktion. A short while prior, DFF had received the following communiqué from the Politburo: "The equal rights of the woman are an indispensible principle of Marxist-Leninism. Therefore, the realization of this mission cannot be left to women and girls alone, rather it must become an affair of the public as a whole."[75] Accordingly, station functionaries responded with "the necessary (re)establishment of a Frauenredaktion." Before this shift, the Frauenredaktion's organizers, as well as the station executives, clearly intended the body to promote something other than equality: the planning, organizing, and producing of women's programming. For example, one memo, mentioned earlier, suggested educational topics traditionally assigned to women.[76] To be sure, not all these plans centered on women in the home. The same memo also included a more progressive suggestion, "Masters of Chemistry," implying women might also learn about a traditionally male occupation in the sciences through women role models in the field.

Sommer in Heidkau may have been a bridge too far for the public, however. In contrast to Sakowski's widely acclaimed *Steine im Weg* and *Wege übers Land*, his 1964 piece drew significant criticism in viewer letters and responses. Along Hete's path to self-confidence and gender equality, she starts an affair with Robert. Given their devotion to socialism and agricultural innovation, this relationship seems relatively natural. As viewers learn toward the end of the broadcast, however, Robert is married. His relationship with his wife, Irene, is rocky, in no small part because she is proud and materialistic. He took the job at this remote village, it transpires, because he felt trapped by the marriage. When Irene arranges a surprise visit, however, she quickly learns about her husband's affair and confronts Hete. During the encounter, she exclaims, "You've broken our marriage, you slut!" Hete retorts, "What do you want from me? It's not my fault your husband hates you!" The show essentially ends on this note, with Irene going back to Berlin and Hete happy with Robert at her side. Many of the press reviews for *Sommer in Heidkau* are overwhelmingly positive. Katja Stern at *Neues Deutschland*, for example, praises Sakowski for writing another compelling play about rural life. She furthermore acclaims Robert's love for Hete, and Sakowski's willingness to paint Irene as a complex, nuanced figure, with vices and virtues.[77] Other reviews, submitted by amateur writers and viewers to the rural *Bauernecho*, were less thrilled. Paul Körner of Malchin, for instance, chastises Sakowski for presenting Robert as a role model: "A man such as Robert, who so easily leaves his family for another woman, cannot be a good example for us . . . He can motivate and inspire hundreds of people, but not his own wife?"[78] Direct viewer letters to the station were even less kind in their denunciation of the show's adultery.

By no means did the East Germans maintain a monopoly over women's equality as a value. Characters such as the cheeky teenage girl in NDR's *Die Kette an deinem Hals* (1965; see chap. 2), the sympathetic young German woman who falls in love with and marries an African American GI in *Gottes zweite Garnitur* (1967; see chap. 5), and the hardworking mother in *Ein Ausgangstag* (A day off, 1965) testify a movement toward equality had begun to take shape.[79] One of the most typical programs in this vein is ZDF's *Hanna Lessing* (1970).[80] Hanna, a contemporary West German woman, gives up her job because her husband earns so much. As with Renate in NDR's *Wilhelmsburger Freitag* (A Friday in Wilhelmsburg, 1965), however, Hanna begins to feel isolated from society. These feelings intensify when the couple learns, in a painful scene, they cannot have children, for medical reasons. She later tries to get her job back, but the position has been filled. The play ends with an argument between Hanna and her husband, in which she declares her life has been stolen from her.

But the limits of the building commitment to women's equality in the FRG are forcefully demonstrated in a scene from WDR's 1967 *Wie verbringe ich meinen Sonntag?* (How do I spend my Sunday?).[81] During the piece, a household's mother goes out with friends on a Saturday night, leaving her hardworking husband behind, the couple's child asks why they do not both go out. The mother replies the father needs to work so that they have money to buy things, which elicits the following response from the child: "But there is *Gleichberechtigung* [equal rights]!" implying the *father* deserves an equal opportunity to join in the family's recreation. By applying the term *Gleichberechtigung*, popularized by the aforementioned 1957 FRG law, to the father, the producers criticize the women's equality movement, implicitly promoting a different value, the clear division of labor and gender roles in the family unit, in its place. Although programs representing gender equality as a value often simultaneously demonstrated women's freedom, such freedom was a value unto itself. In the example from *Wie verbringe ich meinen Sonntag?*

the ironic use of *Gleichberechtigung* prefigures a supposedly equal relationship without laying any emphasis on the freedom of either partner. Indeed, the child's point is that the pair ought to work in tandem, a situation that, while not diametrically opposed to marital freedom, does not necessitate it. This concretely shows that gender equality, as represented in television discourse, is not contingent upon freedom. Conversely, freedom does not presuppose equality, even though they are often paired in practice.

Dieter Meischner's *Das Arrangement* (The arrangement, 1967), a ZDF production, likewise demonstrates the limits of the women's equality movement in the FRG. A married couple, Tom and Eva, have agreed to arrange their "sexual relations like rational people."[82] Both partners engage in multiple extramarital romances, and neither seems, on the face of it, to be jealous of the other. However, while *Das Arrangement* acknowledged the 1960s trend toward nontraditional gender relationships that featured liberation and sexual equality, it did not necessarily present them in a positive light. The program unfolds in the police commissar's office, where Tom is trying to come to terms with Eva's suicide. At first convinced she must have been happy *because* of their sexual freedom, he realizes, while describing the situation and assumptions that went into the marriage to the police, there were some warning signs before her suicide and that some of them may have been caused by the nature of their relationship. For example, one of her lovers, a prominent writer, admits to the commissar that Eva seemed intellectually secure, particularly happy to have achieved financial independence as a writer herself but that she seemed emotionally unstable at times. The chief editor at her newspaper, meanwhile, suggests negative reader letters as the possible cause of her unhappiness, a claim dismissed by one of Eva's fellow writers who instead insists she worried Tom was drifting away from her (the writer does not know about the "arrangement" between the couple). Finally, the viewer learns about the origins of the couple's agreement: Eva had expressed her physical attraction to a famous writer. Tom, who now wonders aloud to the commissar if he had not made a mistake here, encouraged Eva, telling her plainly he was not concerned about her sex life. He admits harboring similar desires toward other women, and the two come to a mutual understanding. Eva, judging by her reaction in the flashback, is relieved they can continue their marriage without pressure, and the two merely continue as they had before, now liberated from their worries.

These scenes, nonsequential flashbacks from different points in the marriage, thoroughly confused many viewers. One called it a "mess" (*Durcheinander*), and another wondered whether they had missed something, as the ending seemed out of place. This confusion, though, seems to have been precisely what Meischner had in mind. The open relationship practiced by Tom and Eva is not disparaged as an outright moral evil. One can certainly bring such a reading to bear on the story, but the disorganization of the piece, the lack of specific answers, and the way Eva is presented as such a multifaceted character muddy such a simplistic explanation. Nontraditional, open marriage is scrutinized but not necessarily condemned as a moral evil (Eva's suicide does potentially suggest such a relationship may not be advisable in terms of psychological health). Some viewers noticed this: "The film showed that tolerance is good, but that it has limits."[83] In addition to the ambiguous, perhaps even negative, ending to the film, *Das Arrangement* further limited the legitimacy of new marital and sexual "arrangements" by depicting what seemed, in fact, to be a very traditional set of gender relationships contained within the radical new formulation of sexuality and marriage. The couple's sexual freedom is called into question by the husband's lack of interest in his wife's escapades. The wife, in contrast, obsesses about his love life, carefully framing her interest, however, as something she is trying to overcome. The husband thus assumes a masculine position, aggressively seeking new conquests, while the wife's reciprocations seem to exist only as an imitative shadow of the husband's affairs. Moreover, the viewers witness a breakdown of the *woman's* confidence and self-esteem, not the man's. *She* despairs, suggesting the presence of an inalienable gender "arrangement" behind all of the posturing and talk of sexual freedom. The climax of this despair, which the audience witnesses toward the end of the piece, is punctuated by strong brass music and close, almost panicked camera angles in Eva's room before her suicide.

Taken as a whole, Meischner's piece does not necessarily dismiss the reformulation of marriage along the tragic lines illustrated here; there is nothing pathological or deeply disturbing about either the husband's or wife's behavior, and the whole scene in the criminal investigator's office paints an ambiguous official response from the policeman, arbiter of the public's mood. However, the ethics with which the arrangement is put into force are called into serious question, as if some rules are never meant to be broken. As with Anna Winters, the tragic emplotment suggests the presence of gendered preconditions, which, while shaken, still assert themselves at inopportune moments. Both pieces seem to call for a nuanced, flexible ethical system that accounts for the naturally existing gender differences, as well as the new values and norms that had come to the forefront in the 1960s, such as women's equality and sexual liberation. In any case, *Das Arrangement* seems to support Elizabeth Heineman's widely cited thesis that marital status itself acted as the single biggest divide between women in the East, who felt less pressure to wed, and in the West, where single women were seen as a problem to be overcome in the postwar period.[84]

At least in terms of the depiction of women, the essentialization of gender roles also took place in television executive and political planning sessions.

For example, despite the many "progressive" programs locating women as equals within the Marxist workforce, top DFF station decision-makers compiled lists of possible programs for its Frauenredaktion, or women's editorial section. For the fall and winter of 1959, the *Kollegium* (council) suggested programs like "Looking into the Pot," "Cleanliness Is the Trump," and "Health for Mother and Child."[85] The suggestions emphasize the traditional role of women in the home, responsible for cooking, cleaning, and rearing children. Thus, despite GDR state-mandated efforts to depict women as fully incorporated into the workforce, executives planned at least some programs as reinforcements of traditional gender-based divisions of labor, under the guise of educational programming aimed at women (as evidenced by the fact that the document specifically directs suggestions at the Frauenredaktion).

Conclusion

This chapter has demonstrated the televisual reinvention of gender norms and values on late 1950s and 1960s German television. The scope of these changes, however, was neither uniform nor unidirectional. Some new values and understandings transcended state boundaries between East and West, for example, the emphasis on the nuclear family. In other instances, East and West German understandings and representations diverged, as on the point of women in the workplace (the East Germans laid far greater emphasis on women's professional equality). In any event, the Cold War itself does not seem to have been the principal factor in the nature of any particular station's representation of gender norms or ideals. The tension between traditional and progressive representations persisted throughout the 1960s, at times spurred in one direction by new organizations like the DFF Frauenredaktion, at other times redirected by the patriarchal station executives and politicians. This reflects a broader phenomenon: women's rights, gender norms, and the relationships between men and women in Germany came under increasing scrutiny in the 1960s but did not become the loci of fiery political and societal debates until the 1970s and 1980s.[86]

In the GDR, progressive representations of well-integrated women in the workplace aired alongside programs that drew clear divisions between the sexes. Television, perceived as a more accurate mirror of public and official opinions than film or other mass media (because of its presumed strengths and limitations as an intimate, visual, conversational medium), reflected the ambiguity that accompanied both East and West German representations.[87] As Marilyn Boxer and Jean Quataert have argued, the emergence of women's movements and second wave feminism during the 1960s was probably *caused* by the increased participation of women in labor, not the reverse.[88]

In other words, neither decision-makers and television stations nor the mass of viewers who participated in television discourse realized the full import of these developing movements and institutions, though they certainly sensed the growing concern, as evidenced by programs such as *Steine im Weg* and *Das Arrangement*. In a political and institutional sense, the 1970s, with the increased importance and visibility of feminist organizations, would prove a far more radical era for the development of programming reflecting women's rights and gender reformulations.[89]

Nonetheless, certain aspects of gender roles as represented by television fiction changed drastically between the late 1950s and the late 1960s. The question of women's work, for instance, became a question of "how," not "if." Equality and freedom for women became a commonly represented theme in both East and West German television systems. However, in many ways, the ontological preconditions that moored men and women to their distinct spheres overshadowed such moral reformulations. In the GDR, progressive programs like *Steine im Weg* and *Die Entscheidung der Lene Mattke* gave way to the forerunners of Honecker's consumer-oriented mandate for television. To cite just one example, the 1968 DFF production *Gib acht auf Susi!* essentialized the female title character, presenting her as one of the most intelligent girls of her class but also blinded by riches, cars, and other material possessions. In the West, *Das Unbrauchbare an Anna Winters* deconstructed traditional family ties in the face of modern realities but did not leave any alternatives in its place. The paradoxical nature of women as both wives and workers actually seems to be strengthened as Anna throws herself down the stairs to escape this undesired reality. Television plays in the late 1950s and 1960s hinted at functional equality and women's rights, but only social movements such as second-wave feminism and the establishment of more radical women's rights organizations in the 1970s paved the way for more consistent representations of women as equals in German society.

Notes

1. Hans Müncheberg, interview with Stewart Anderson, Berlin, 15 November 2008.
2. Heather Gumbert, *Envisioning Socialism: Television and the Cold War in the German Democratic Republic* (Ann Arbor: University of Michigan Press, 2014), 116–117.
3. Arnd Bauerkämper, "Collectivization and Memory: Views of the Past and the Transformation of Rural Society in the GDR from 1952 to the early 1960s," *German Studies Review* 25, no. 2 (2002): 221–222.
4. Helmut Sakowski, *Steine im Weg*, dir. Wilhelm Gröhl (DFF, 16 November 1960).

5. Their fears were confirmed when Katja Stern, a TV critic at *Neues Deutschland*, criticized Sakowski's play on precisely that point in a 23 November 1960 article and again when the same newspaper printed several letters sympathetic to Stern's critique on 24 February 1961.
6. Bundesarchiv (BArch), DR 8 18 Vorlage 44/60.
7. As noted by Bernt Eckhoff, *National-Zeitung*, 7 June 1961.
8. Archiv Müncheberg 1.65.1, "Steine im Weg, Gelungene Neufassung," 1961, 17.
9. Schlerz, "Steine im Weg," *Volksstimme*, 2 June 1961.
10. Heinz Stern, "Steine im Weg," *Neues Deutschland*, 23 November 1961.
11. For an example of how war creates gender fluidity, see Katrin Schreiter, "Revisiting Morale under the Bombs: The Gender of Affect in Darmstadt, 1942–1945," *Central European History* 50, no. 3 (2017).
12. Maria Höhn, "Frau im Haus und Girl im Spiegel: Discourse on Women in the Interregnum Period of 1945–1949 and the Question of German Identity," *Central European History* 26, no. 1 (1993): 63.
13. Jill Stephenson, *Women in Nazi Society* (London: Croom Helm, 1975).
14. Dagmar Herzog, *Sex after Fascism: Memory and Morality in Twentieth-Century Germany* (Princeton, NJ: Princeton University Press, 2005), 27–42.
15. Ibid., 101–107.
16. Ibid., 66.
17. Quoted in Elizabeth Heineman, "Complete Families, Half Families, No Families at All: Female-Headed Households and the Reconstruction of the Family in the Early Federal Republic" *Central European History* 29, no. 1 (1996): 19.
18. Christine von Oertzen, *The Pleasure of a Surplus Income: Part-Time Work, Gender Politics, and Social Change in West Germany, 1955–1969*, trans. Pamela Selwyn (New York: Berghahn Books, 2007), 1, 30.
19. Patricia Davis and Simon Reich, "Norms, Ideology, and Institutions: (En)gendered Retrenchment of *Modell Deutschland?*" in *The Postwar Transformation of Germany*, ed. John S. Brady, Beverly Crawford, and Sarah Elise Williarty (Ann Arbor: University of Michigan Press, 1999), 237.
20. Michael Schwartz, "Frauenpolitik im doppelten Deutschland: Die Bundesrepublik und die DDR in den 1970er Jahren," in *Lieschen Müller wird politisch: Geschlecht, Staat und Partizipation im 20. Jahrhundert*, ed. Christine Hikel, Nicole Kramer, and Elisabeth Zellmer (Munich: R. Oldenbourg Verlag, 2009).
21. Höhn, "Frau im Haus und Girl im Spiegel," 59
22. Donna Harsch, *Revenge of the Domestic: Women, the Family, and Communism in the German Democratic Republic* (Princeton, NJ: Princeton University Press, 2007). At the same time, Harsch also points out that the state pursued its commitment to women's equality in the workplace in an inconsistent manner, often because of the tension between granting women new rights and establishing an always precarious legitimacy.
23. Eva Kolinsky and Hildegard Maria Nickel, "Introduction: Reinventing Gender after the GDR," in *Reinventing Gender: Women in Eastern Germany since Unification*, ed. Eva Kolinsky and Hildegard Maria Nickel (New York: Routledge, 2002), 5–6.
24. Gunilla-Friederike Budde, *Frauen arbeiten: weibliche Erwerbstätigkeit in Ost- und Westdeutschland nach 1945* (Göttingen: Vandenhoeck & Ruprecht, 1997), 9–10. To be fair, women in the GDR often found themselves working not because they subscribed to messages of equality or freedom (though this may have been true as well) but because the difficult economic circumstances found in the East dictated that women would need to contribute. See Elizabeth Heineman, *What Difference Does a Husband Make? Women and*

Marital Status in Nazi and Postwar Germany (Berkeley: University of California Press, 1999), 211.
25. Andrea Rinke, *Images of Women in East German Cinema, 1972–1982: Socialist Models, Private Dreamers and Rebels* (Lewiston: Edwin Mellen Press, 2006), 7.
26. Frank Biess, "Men of Reconstruction—The Reconstruction of Men: Returning POWs in East and West Germany, 1945–1955," in *Home Front: The Military, War and Gender in Twentieth-Century Germany*, ed. Karen Hagemann and Stefanie Schüler-Springorum (New York: Berg, 2002), 335–336.
27. Ibid., 340.
28. Herzog, *Sex after Fascism*, 88–95.
29. Marianne Ehlenbeck, *Geschichte des DFDs* (Leipzig: Verlag für die Frau, 1989).
30. BArch, DR 8 25, Vorlagen Nr. 1/62 bis 16/62, "Die Frau—der Frieden und der Sozialismus," 17 January 1962.
31. Claudia Koonz, *The Nazi Conscience* (Cambridge, MA: Belknap Press, 2003), 232.
32. Herzog, *Sex after Fascism*, 58–61.
33. Heineman, "Complete Families, Half Families, No Families at All," 19–23.
34. Ute Schneider, *Hausväteridylle oder sozialistische Utopie? Die Familie im Recht der DDR* (Cologne: Böhlau, 2004).
35. Hermann Rodigast, *Papas neue Freundin*, dir. Georg Leopold (DFF, 25 December 1960).
36. BArch, DR 8 38, Vorlag 20/65, "Perspektivplan des Deutschen Fernsehfunks bis 1970," 6 February 1970. It is unclear how authorities reacted to this information, though one surmises that such surveys informed the Honecker regime's directive to "overcome boredom" in television programming and films by the early 1970s.
37. Herbert Reinecker, *Das Unbrauchbare an Anna Winters*, dir. Eberhard Schröder (ZDF, 22 May 1963).
38. Historisches Archiv des Zweiten Deutschen Rundfunks, Das Unbrauchbare an Anna Winters, 3/2/031.
39. E.g., *Hessische Allgemeine*, 24 May 1963; *Deutsche Zeitung*, 4 June 1963.
40. *Infratest Wochenbericht*, May 1963.
41. *Münchner Merkur*, 24 May 1963.
42. Günter Grävert, *Reise nach Tilsit*, dir. Günter Grävert (ZDF, 16 November 1969); Hermann Sudermann, "Die Reise nach Tilsit," in *Litauische Geschichten* (Stuttgart: J. G. Cotta, 1917).
43. Helmut Motekat, "Hermann Sudermanns 'Die Reise nach Tilsit,'" in *Hermann Sudermann: Werk und Wirkung*, ed. Walter T. Rix (Würzburg: Königshausen & Neumann, 1980), 192.
44. *Frankfurter Neue Presse*, 18 November 1969.
45. Fred Diehl, "Erstklassiger Darsteller," *Rheinpfalzer Zeitung*, 18 November 1969.
46. Klaus Jörn and Hans-Joachim Kasprzik, *Kleiner Mann—was nun?* dir. Kasprzik (DFF, 16, 17 December 1967).
47. Gisela Hermann, "Die Frage blieb nicht offen," *Berliner Zeitung*, 20 December 1967.
48. Norman Ächtler and Werner Liersch, "'Autoren genossen doch eine gewisse Achtung': Ein Gespräch mit Klaus Jörn über die Fallada-Verfilmungen des DDR-Fernsehens," in *Hans Fallada und die literarische Moderne*, ed. Carsten Gausel and Werner Liersch (Göttingen: V&R Unipress, 2009).
49. DFF, *Pressedienst* 50/67, "Kleiner Mann—was nun?"
50. DFF, *Pressedienst* 42/65, "Wolf unter Wölfen."
51. Gerhard Dittmann, *Sächsische Zeitung*, 26 January 1968.
52. Gisela Hermann, "Die Frage blieb nicht offen," *Berliner Zeitung*, 20 December 1967.

53. An anonymous author at the *Märkische Volksstimme* was particularly glowing in his review of Mia's character, declaring it a particularly "human" performance. "Die Kunst in der Sprache des Fernsehens," *Märkische Volksstimme*, 19 December 1967.
54. Ibid.
55. Mimosa Künzel, "Ein Strahl der Hoffnung," *Die Neue Zeit*, 21 December 1967.
56. Christian Steinke, *Egon und das achte Weltwunder*, dir. Christian Steinke (DFF, 27 December 1964).
57. Joachim Wohlgemuth, *Egon und das achte Weltwunder* (Berlin: Verlag Neues Leben, 1963), 32–33.
58. Georg Zivier, *Der Tagesspiegel*, 30 December 1964.
59. Günter Ebert, "Eine lustige Liebesgeschichte," *Freie Erde*, 9 January 1965.
60. Werner Schwemin, *Berliner Zeitung*, "Auf dem Bildschirm: Egon und Kristine," 1 January 1965.
61. Ebert, "Eine lustige Liebesgeschichte."
62. René Drommert, "Diskussionen wenige Schritte hinter der Mauer," *Die Zeit*, 5 February 1965.
63. BArch, DR 8 38, Vorlage 22/65, 25 January 1965.
64. See Michael Lentz, *Bonner Rundschau*, 12 February 1965.
65. Ulrich Thein, *Columbus 64*, dir. Ulrich Thein (DFF, 1, 2, 4, 5 October 1966).
66. Katherine Pence, "Labours of Consumption: Gendered Consumers in Post-war East and West German Reconstruction," in *Gender Relations in German History: Power, Agency and Experience from the Sixteenth to the Twentieth Century*, ed. Lynn Abrams and Elizabeth Harvey (Durham, NC: Duke University Press, 1997), 211.
67. David Kucera, *Gender, Growth, and Trade: The Miracles Economies of the Postwar Years* (New York: Routledge, 2001), 33–38.
68. Negative portrayals of the career woman as an assault on the natural order also surfaced, albeit less frequently. See, e.g., the SDR program *Zeitvertreib*, 24 September 1964; ZDF's *Das Rendezvous* (7 November 1965).
69. BArch, DR 8 489, "Kollegiums-Vorlage 19/62, March 1962, Frauenredaktion."
70. BArch, DR 8 25, Vorlage 1/62, "Berlin, 17 January 1962."
71. Helmut Sakowski, *Die Entscheidung der Lene Mattke*, dir. Wilhelm Gröhl (DFF, 6 July 1958).
72. "Die Entscheidung der Lene Mattke," *BZ am Abend*, 8 October 1958.
73. Helmut Sakowski, *Sommer in Heidkau*, dir. Martin Eckermann (DFF, 4 October 1964).
74. BArch, DR 8 34, Vorlage 88/64, 5. October 1964.
75. BArch, DR 8 25, Vorlage 1/62, "Berlin, 17 January 1962."
76. BArch, DR 8 15, Vorlage 33/59, "Vorschläge für die Frauenredaktion Winter/Herbst 1959."
77. Katja Stern, "Freude am echten Wagnis: Sommer in Heidkau," *Neues Deutschland*, 10 October 1964.
78. Paul Körner, "Die Liebe in unserer Literatur," *Bauernecho*, 21 November 1964.
79. Leck Fischer and Erland Erlandsen, *Ein Ausgangstag*, dir. Werner Schlechte (ZDF, 12 November 1965).
80. Herbert Knopp, *Hanna Lessing*, dir. Eberhard Itzenplitz (ZDF, 9 December 1970).
81. Helmut Pigge, *Wie verbringe ich meinen Sonntag?* dir. Rainer Wolffhardt (WDR, 16 March 1967).
82. Dieter Meischner, *Das Arrangement*, dir. Günter Gräwert (ZDF, April 5 1967).
83. *Infratest Wochenbericht*, April 1967, 21–22.
84. Heineman, *What Difference Does a Husband Make?* 211.

85. BArch, DR 8 15 33/59.
86. Marilyn J. Boxer and Jean H. Quataert, *Connecting Spheres: European Women in a Globalizing World, 1500 to the Present* (New York: Oxford University Press, 2000), 7.
87. Günter Kaltofen, *Das Bild das deine Sprache spricht: Fernsehspiele* (Berlin: Henschelverlag, 1962), 4.
88. Ibid., 252.
89. Schwartz, "Frauenpolitik im doppelten Deutschland," 27, 34.

Chapter 5

EMBRACING DIVERSITY

Racial Tolerance and Integration

In contemporary Germany, no aspect of the Third Reich's legacy commands more attention than the murder of six million Jews. In particular, National Socialism's race-based program of discrimination and annihilation horrifies all but the most extreme neo-fascist adherents. A student today might therefore suppose that if German television in the 1950s and 1960s was created with an eye to overcoming the Nazi past, then it would likely have emphasized the dangers of racism and xenophobia. As chapter 1 demonstrates, television plays indeed grappled with the Third Reich and its evils, but relatively few programs, particularly in the medium's early years, directly promoted a message of anti-racism. In both East and West, German victims of Hitler's regime featured more heavily than Jews or non-Germans. As generational tensions simmered toward the end of the 1960s, however, some plays began to address the issue much more directly, and with a greater eye to the Holocaust and Germany's murderous past. It is in this context of relative silence that Ulf von Mechow and Julius Tinzmann's ZDF play, *Frei bis zum nächsten Mal* (Free until next time, 1969), must be understood.[1]

The plot in *Frei bis zum nächsten Mal* revolves around a gypsy, Josef Gayschek, and his attempt to buy a house in a small, somewhat isolated Bavarian village called Emsbach (in the present day). Most of the villagers, police included, assume Josef must have stolen the money, especially as he is looking to pay in cash. This skepticism turns to overt racism and xenophobia when a maverick villager decides to offer one of his properties as an option. Josef is arrested and detained on a theft charge, though the police cannot find any evidence of wrongdoing. The revelation that the buyer received his money as a reparation payment from the West German government, his whole extended family having perished in Nazi death camps, does nothing to sway public opinion in the town. Even the fact that his birth certificate was printed in their district in Bavaria means little to the unsympathetic inhabitants. Josef's children are ostracized by students in the local elementary school, and the mayor promises to find a "solution" to the new "problem." Only the local Catholic priest supports the newcomer, and he receives significant flak for his troubles. The prospective seller sticks to his plan to sell, but only because he desperately needs the money. The village council therefore decides, over objections from the priest, to seize the initiative and buy the property before Josef has the opportunity to close the deal. With little alternative, Josef and his family pack their van and travel to another location.

Frei bis zum nächsten Mal drips with criticism of German society and attitudes about unwanted ethnicities. For example, it constantly refers to, and attempts to repudiate, common cultural stereotypes about gypsies. One of the village police officers calls Josef a "huckster" or peddler, without any evidence to support this claim. When the gas station attendant tells the police about the "crisp" hundred mark bills the family uses as payment, they agree the money must surely be stolen. Finally, one local truck driver calls the gypsies *Landstreicher*, or vagabonds, and warns they will steal from the village "like ravens." These instances reflect common European stereotypes about gypsies: they cheat, swindle, steal, and leech off hardworking natives. Such misperceptions and prejudices provided a justification for the genocide perpetrated against Roma and Sinti peoples, an atrocity initiated by the Nazis but embraced by groups of Poles, Romanians, and other peoples in Eastern Europe.[2]

Several mothers in the town raise another stereotypical concern: they complain to the priest that Josef's children will corrupt the local school with "magic" and other evil practices. Christian communities had for centuries harbored fears that Romani possessed supernatural powers granted by the devil. This brief scene hints at those fears by the use of visual and aural reinforcement. Close camera angles of the mothers' faces and rabid, almost incomprehensible shouting accompany their complaints. The camera also pans over a set of German children, innocently playing with dolls and toys in the yard behind the gathered crowd. Korbinian Köberle, the show's director, thus harnesses the medium's strengths—facial close-ups and recorded sound—to help the audience understand the mothers' angst. Right after this scene, however, the priest jarringly responds: "Gypsies are, as a rule, religious Catholics." The gypsy family's Catholicism underscores the religious commonality between gypsies and Bavarians. The writers' appeal to identification based on religion also surfaces later, as the priest, in defense of

Josef's desire to buy a house before the town council, quotes from a Catholic encyclical on pastoral guidance for gypsies. The council's response to this tactic, apparent boredom, is interspersed with camera shots of the gallery, which features deranged hecklers and visual disbelief (indicated by shaking heads). Thus, the program bases at least part of its argument for tolerance on religious grounds, both because of the strong, caring priest figure and because the unruly crowd is presented as more of a mob than a town council. Given the church's position, then, the mothers' fears of gypsies practicing sorcery or dark magic appear all the more absurd. A child's question, "Why do the people have something against gypsies?" further accentuates this dynamic, as he is not old enough (or indoctrinated enough) to harbor suspicions or stereotypes. His mother's response, "Because the gypsies are different from us," reinforces the priest's claim. As she cannot put her finger on any real difference, the play infers the village's response to the situation, a purge of the "problem," is absurd.

The townspeople's actions are made to seem even more ludicrous when they learn about Josef's reparation money. Instead of feeling ashamed, the mayor continues to prosecute the case, looking for a legal technicality or loophole to prevent the sale of the house. When the frustrated (and incarcerated) Josef says, "That's all exactly like before. He who wears the uniform is right," the mayor retorts, "That is defamation of a civil servant. It will be recorded." The overt reference to German Nazi aggression does not deter or upset the mayor in the slightest. His response not only suggests indifference to past injustices and almost unbelievable stubbornness but also appears to confirm Josef's criticism of the bureaucratic system that so meticulously and efficiently classified, relocated, and murdered undesirables under the pretense of legality and strict obedience.

The social criticism of German attitudes in *Frei bis zum nächsten Mal* implies a plea for tolerance. However, the program goes further, making a strong case for integration. For example, at one point, the mayor asks Josef, "Why specifically in our village? There are houses to buy everywhere."[3] The question is more than a mere dismissal of Josef's plight; the mayor feels the need, though it may not be conscious, to justify his refusal *morally*. In the background, a universalized sense of fairness guides his actions. When faced with a concrete dilemma, he feels he must pay homage to this ethical framework. In this case, he tries to reassign the undesirable moral responsibility (but a responsibility nonetheless) to another town. But while the notion of commuting responsibility might have carried weight with the audience in another setting, Josef's response, producing a birth certificate notarized in Emsbach, makes commutation impossible. This deepens the dilemma for the mayor, and thus for any possibly sympathetic viewers. Mere tolerance, it seems, may not be an option. In light of the birth certificate and the persecution of Josef's people, revealed several minutes later in the program, the villagers and the mayor seem to have an unavoidable moral responsibility to go one step further and *integrate* Josef and his family into the village. The authorities, however, do not give up their attempts to halt Josef's plan to settle down and integrate, forfeiting whatever credit they might have still had with many viewers. In the process, the program argues in favor of integration as a moral imperative.

This emphasis on integration (and not mere tolerance) represented a stark about-face from earlier dramas. *Frei bis zum nächsten Mal* does not leave moral lessons about integration at a foreign, non-German, and abstract level (as, for example, occurs in *In einem Garten im Aviamo*, a 1964 West German play about a romance between an African American GI and a (white) Italian girl); rather, it focuses directly on a German case, forcing viewers to reevaluate what they hold to be the boundaries of moral responsibility. As one viewer puts it, "It held the mirror up to the people's face[s]." Others noted, "I was furious at such stubborn villagers," and "it showed how deeply rooted prejudices are."[4] The probing, stark moral imperative raised by the program is reinforced by producers' insistence, both in the official press release and in a short description at the start of the broadcast, that they based the screenplay on a real experience. Proper names and locations have been altered, but police officers and even village residents helped corroborate the story in the hopes that "the story will not repeat itself."[5] Perhaps as an indication of the piece's much more conscious condemnation of German intolerance, Rainer Werner Fassbinder, one of the founders of New German Cinema and a revolutionary voice of the turbulent late 1960s, advised Von Mechow and Tinzmann and even had a cameo as one of the police officers. In echoing some of the themes from New German Cinema (marginalized groups, generational tensions, and reconciling the German past) and confronting West Germany's ongoing inability to overcome racism, *Frei bis zum nächsten Mal*, along with other plays from the late 1960s, such as *Die Beichte*, presaged a new, more explicit phase in the ongoing process of *Vergangenheitsbewältigung*.

This chapter examines the representation of race in German television fiction during the 1960s. As with the other four themes discussed in this book, many decision-makers understood racist attitudes as a major symptom of the nation's ongoing sickness. Indeed, some historians have claimed postwar Germans even used the same biological and racial nomenclature employed by the National Socialists in describing non-Germans to explain how the German nation itself had fallen ill at the hands of fascism.[6] In other words, they repurposed Hitler's epidemiological rhetoric in diagnosing the nation's own shortcomings. While East and West Germans disagreed on the cure, in broad terms they concurred that Hitler's extreme brand of nationalism and racial thinking had thrown down very deep roots and that these attitudes would not be easily remedied.[7] Some authorities in the GDR, for instance, promoted a policy of assimilation toward non-German *Vertragsarbeiter* (contract workers). But these same officials also realized their program, at least regarding non-Germans, would not gain traction easily, given persistent attitudes about the inferiority of other races and ethnicities.[8] Similarly, when local officials in Stuttgart concluded that the guest worker program would not prove temporary, they pursued policies of integration. These attempts proved uneven, however, both because federal and state-level policies continued to treat foreign workers as temporary guests and because Stuttgart's residents proved less than enthusiastic about the newcomers.[9]

Teleplays throughout the period under examination aimed to alter what many authors perceived as persistent Nazi racial thinking, but earlier broadcasts approached the topic far more indirectly than *Frei bis zum nächsten Mal*. East German productions from the early 1960s highlighted the fact that Germans, Jews, and other peoples had worked together to overcome National Socialism, under the banner of communism. But they almost never mention the widespread nature of racism in Germany, instead attributing such attitudes to a small, hardened core of Nazi adherents. Some early West German programs advocated tolerance and understanding, but often marginalized the issue by locating the message in another culture (Italy and the United States, for example). Moreover, perhaps cognizant of the term's extremely negative connotation during the Third Reich, contemporary writers and producers rarely spoke of "race" or "racism" as they crafted their programs. The word itself had become taboo, complicating producers' desire to engage viewers in an open discussion about what they perceived as a clear, real problem.[10] Television broadcasts about racism thus followed a marked trajectory, from indirect messages about tolerance in the late 1950s and early 1960s, to more explicit integrationist messages in the late 1960s and early 1970s. This process, moreover, followed a more radical curve toward integration in the West than in the East.

The slowness of this process should come as no surprise to careful observers of postwar German history. Allied denazification efforts, including in the Soviet zone, did emphasize the evils of anti-Semitism, but in most respects, the German worldview remained unabashedly racialized. Both East and West German governments, for instance, continued to determine citizenship almost wholly based on blood.[11] Instances of violence toward non-Germans occur throughout the history of postwar Germany. Xenophobia clearly persisted, particularly against Afro-Germans, who sometimes replaced Jews as the object of exclusionist diatribes.[12] The "Steinstraßen-Affäre" in Kaiserslautern, where clerics and other concerned German citizens campaigned against allowing African American GIs into the city center (in which they allegedly met with German prostitutes and contributed to a decadent urban culture), provides a stark reminder that the same set of authorities who bemoaned the nation's moral vacuum often harbored racist attitudes themselves.[13] Despite these continued attitudes, it would be misleading to draw a simple line between Nazi Germany and the two Cold War successor states. At the political level, European integration in both West and East changed attitudes about diversity in fundamental ways. The CDU, itself a compromise between the two major churches' political interests, promoted integration and reconciliation along the lines of a Christian *Abendland* (occident). In doing so, they tacitly acknowledged the importance of non-Germans (French, Dutch, and Belgians) in the FRG's society and commerce. These attitudes among party officials eventually led to the arrival of Spanish and Italian guest workers.[14] The GDR, moreover, enacted an about-face from the Nazi years, embracing both Eastern European peoples and, as Quinn Slobodian has noted, nations in the Global South in the name of socialist friendship.[15] These integrationist impulses accelerated toward the end of the 1960s.

Whether these messages were accepted at the individual or group level is less clear. The aforementioned violent incidents involving foreigners must be tempered with evidence that new attitudes were beginning to take hold. For example, Heide Fehrenbach describes the discourse surrounding the more than three thousand mixed-race German children as a reformulation of the race question entirely: "Simply stated, German response to the children was far from monolithic. Rather, for the decade following 1950, biracial occupation children became a nexus around which social, cultural, and scientific debates about the meaning of race—and its implications for postwar German society—whirled."[16] A wide range of strategies and methods were proposed to address the issue, including, in the late 1950s, seeking out the fathers for possible adoption and issuing "anthropological" calls for integration (some scholars claimed the children of Americanized black fathers and German mothers would maintain a better work ethic than previous generations of Afro-Germans). By the late 1960s, the strategies seemed much more positive and inclusive. Progressive films such as Rainer Werner Fassbinder's *Katzelmacher*, for example, showed Germans it was possible to properly integrate these children through schooling and education.

It is precisely at this intersection—where individuals, families, and smaller groups received, interpreted, and acted on political and official messages of tolerance—that television fiction can provide important insights. The visual record does not necessarily mirror popular attitudes and practices (it more often indicates political imperatives from producers and executives), but it certainly speaks to how decision-makers and gatekeepers understood behaviors regarding diversity playing out in practice. It also indirectly reflects social practice by visualizing negative examples, making racist and integrationist attitudes believable and comprehensible through drama. In this chapter, I argue the televisualization of race, ethnicity, and otherness acted as a kind of drawing board for the reformulation of proper behavior toward non-Germans, particularly those living in Germany. The specific racial hierarchies developed during the Third Reich fell into disuse (though racist attitudes did not), but new conceptions had not yet coalesced to take their place. Dramatizations redrew the bounds for acceptable prejudices, and, in many cases, simultaneously preached tolerance.

* * *

Many early programs advocated tolerance toward non-Germans. The most common mechanism for presenting this lesson involved emphasizing the relative unimportance of race, religious heritage, or ethnicity as defining categories for an individual's value or potential. A typical example in this vein was Heinz Kamnitzer and Alexander Stenbock-Fermor's East German *Mord an Rathenau* (The murder of Rathenau, 1961).[17] True to its title, *Mord an Rathenau* depicts the final weeks of Walther Rathenau, the Weimar Republic's foreign minister in 1922. Heroic speeches and bravery attributed to Rathenau before his assassination paint the title character as a kind of martyr. At one point, for instance, the television Rathenau (played by Harry Hindemith) wins over a group of heckling students with a fiery, patriotic speech in which he declares his allegiance to Germany, even if it means his death. While his ultimate devotion reinforces his martyr status, his statement of allegiance to Germany identifies the crux of the students' heckling and suspicions, which is his Jewish heritage, and quashes their fears in one swoop. Another scene has him entertaining an industry executive in his office while a portrait of Abraham Lincoln hangs in the background, foreshadowing his impending death. Whatever their intentions in celebrating Rathenau's martyrdom, however, the program's creators circumscribed the fallen minister within the Marxist canon of heroes, in essence appropriating his legacy. The film itself contains much evidence for this interpretation, for example, during a carnival scene where one of the future assassins shoots out three candles, verbally calling the three "Liebknecht, Luxembourg, Rathenau." Karl Liebknecht and Rosa Luxembourg had long been established as Communist heroes (and martyrs). Rathenau, though not a socialist, is included by association, the third target on the hit man's list of enemies. In addition to the visual evidence, production documents attest to the station's intentions to use the piece as Communist propaganda. Under the "responsibilities [*Aufgaben*]" of DFF, the drama department mentions the usefulness of *Mord an Rathenau*: "A television film in which the bearing of two people, who travel between two ideological worlds, is presented ad absurdum [*sic*] and the necessity of these people's orientation toward the working class, which can only be hindered by militarism and war, is clear."[18] The plan to depict a "working-class" consciousness, to be hindered only by "militarism and war" (common East German synonyms for fascism), locates the film firmly within the construction of modern socialism. Kamnitzer and Stenbock-Fermor use Rathenau, in addition to the two reluctant heroes, to further that project. An earlier description of the work in progress corroborates this assessment: "This film is a convincing picture of the German past and its connections to the present."[19]

But the moral education for viewers goes deeper. Two fictional characters, artificially inserted into the plot, bridge the gap between the well-known, formal history of the assassination and an emotional attachment to the events, achieved through pathos and association with more everyday characters. These two interlopers, Horst Bergmann and Lilly Deutsch, know the plotting assassins from school, and they arrange to personally meet with and warn Rathenau of the danger. Out of fear, however, Bergmann does not reveal the specifics of the plot, only stating a vague feeling that someone is plotting against the minister. Rathenau dismisses the information, as he has already received numerous death threats. After the murder, Bergmann feels terrible that he did not reveal his friends more quickly and, in atonement for his inaction, becomes more involved with the local communist youth group. *Mord an Rathenau* thus caters to viewers' emotional investment in the protagonists as a way of driving home the anti-fascist message. Bergmann, played by Jürgen Frohriep, is simply accessible and believable.

Deeper even than this political-moral level, however, lies another: Rathenau, a secularized Jew, appears as normal and "class-conscious" as any other progressive member of German society. He is far too famous and distanced to generate much of a personal message, a fact acknowledged by the director's reluctance to depict him in many close-ups (a standard technique of early television dramas).[20] But the dialogue repeatedly reinforces his status as a Jew. In one scene, Rathenau argues with his mother about the appropriate place of his Jewish heritage. His mother laments, "You should not have taken the foreign minister post. You forget you belong with the Jewish people." Rathenau replies, "My people are the Germans. The Jews are only a tribe, like the Saxons." Rathenau's remarks here, in the context of a political, almost documentary, character sketch, point to the film's lessons about race. Kamnitzer and Stenbock-Fermor affirm Rathenau's background but simultaneously set it aside in favor of other aspects of his nature. It indicates his natural propensity for moving oratory not only through the short speech given in the program, which takes place in a contemporary setting, but also through various hints he had long been a gifted public speaker. Rathenau's Jewish heritage is explicitly mentioned but dismissed as trivial, or at least as unimportant in the increasingly national sentiments of the twentieth century. In this sense, *Mord an Rathenau* acts as an easily digestible lesson in tolerance.

Pointed explanations about the unimportance of race and religious identification were by no means limited to East German television fiction. Paul H. Rameau's 1963 *Menschen helfen Menschen: Zwei Tage von Vielen* (People Help People: Two Days out of Many) forwarded much the same lesson, though, in this case, the attempt backfired.[21] In simple terms, *Menschen helfen Menschen* highlights Roman Catholic attempts to rescue Jews from the Holocaust. However, it also aired in the immediate wake of the *Stellvertreter* controversy. Scrutiny over the Catholic Church's role in facilitating or allowing the Holocaust had reached a high water mark, and leaders from both Churches had begun to publish stories and memoirs about their role as rescuers to combat the negative publicity. The ZDF television board, like those of the ARD member stations, included several high-ranking clerics. The decision-making process behind this particular program has not been preserved at the current ZDF Historical Archive, but the presence of concerned church leaders at the highest levels of the station seems to have pushed the piece into a more prominent role. The text ZDF provided to press outlets ahead of the broadcast further demonstrates the program acted as an "answer" to Hochhuth's play: "More men and women were found ready to donate protection and help to the victims of the terror regime than has been made known to the wider public."[22] The producers thus intended the program to make known the extent of the churches' (particularly the Catholic Church's) assistance, in an effort to alleviate the controversy.

At its core, the play's message is that ethnicity and creed do not matter in the context of Christian charity and aid. The leader of the Berliner Bischöflichen Ordinat's Hilfswerk, or help organization, goes out of her way to assist the Jews being rounded up in 1941 Berlin. She and the other members "give tireless help to the persecuted Jews," as the *Programmdienst* puts it, even putting their own freedom in peril to stop the Gestapo from finding their charges. The program thus parades the universal Christian imperative of providing charity to others, espousing a simplified Christian ethos along the way (though it occurs in unusual and extreme circumstances), and encouraging viewers to do the same. In this Christian framework, Nazi categories of racial superiority are disparaged as morally evil.

This ethos, however, takes on a different character when placed in its televisual wrappings. The program casts the protagonists as stereotypical church disciplinarians. As the Catholic-run publication *Funk-Korrespondenz* acknowledges, the program presents the Hilfswerk leader (Frau Dr. Sommer) as an "ideologically driven camp commandeuse" and the bishop (Graf Preysing) as an "old-fashioned, condescending bishop."[23] While the *Funk-Korrespondenz* criticized these depictions because they did not help the church's image in the aftermath of the *Stellvertreter* incident, the kind of "tough love" portrayed here gives the impression that the German rescuers possess an aloofness and superiority compared to the Jewish victims, one of whom the *Funk-Korrespondenz* described as "an adoring, crying Jewish girl" who looked up to the stern Catholic organizers as saviors. *Menschen helfen Menschen* thus questions the Holocaust's morality (hardly a provocative position) but places its actors into a new, implicitly racialized relationship of power. The German Catholic overseers treat the Jewish victims not as vermin, as the Nazis did, but certainly worthy of contempt and condescension. This relationship might almost be termed colonial in nature. The Jews in the program say very little, and often appear submissive, much as in a European imperialist vision of African or Asian colonial peoples. The captives lack agency and are completely dependent on Germans for their escape. Apparently, however, no viewers complained about the reformulated relationship between Catholic liberators and Jewish victims in their comments to Infratest. Some praised the program for its depiction of the protagonists' heroes or for showing Germany's troubled past, while others disparaged it for bringing up that same past.[24] Two viewer remarks demonstrate this contrast: "One cannot show the moving fate of the Jews often enough," and "This old stuff about the Jews should be left alone." As a history lesson, the program seems to have thus touched a nerve, something the producers clearly intended in treating the subject of Jewish persecution. If it was intended as a lesson in proper attitudes about diversity in postwar Germany, however, the program seems to have failed. As noted in the viewer comments, some Germans applauded the representation of the Jewish persecution, but others, perhaps influenced by the depiction of dependent, needy Jewish characters under orderly German supervision, disregarded it.

Ulrich Thein's DFF production *Der Andere neben dir* (The other [person] beside you, 1963) likewise tries to come to terms with German prejudice during the Nazi era.[25] In this case, however, the protagonists are confronted with their shameful past directly and given the chance to apologize and atone for their errors. *Der Andere neben dir* takes place in contemporary (early 1960s) Berlin and Prague. An East German master surgeon (Dr. Marschner) and his wife travel to Prague to attend a conference on new medical technologies. A Czech surgeon (Dr. Melichar) takes Marschner's place as part of a scheduled "exchange" between East Germany and Czechoslovakia. Meanwhile, Melichar's wife, Frau Melicharová (a translator at the medical conference in Prague) recognizes the Marschners as her former employers (she had worked as a servant in their household). A flashback sequence depicts the Marschners' son's attempts to rape Frau Melicharová in 1944. When Marschner returns to Berlin, angry about Melichar's decision to perform a complex operation without his approval, Melichar reveals the identity of his wife. Marschner also learns his son had framed the young Czech servant for petty theft and that the Marschners had heartlessly handed her over to the Gestapo. She had been, in Melichar's words, mistreated, starved, and now betrayed. Marschner realizes his terrible mistake, calls his wife (still in Prague), and the two couples begin the process of reconciliation.

Der Andere neben dir functions in many ways as a simple fable or morality tale. Dr. Marschner is feared and hated by the nurses and other doctors as strict and too quick to judge. He fires a resident for tardiness, chews out the nursing staff for drinking coffee, and generally avoids contact with the support staff. After his experience with Dr. Melichar, however, he has a Scrooge-like change of heart, reinstating the resident, greeting the staff, including even the security guard, and inviting Frau Melicharová to Berlin. The program thus espouses kindness and charity by contrasting the hospital's atmosphere before the experience and after. The flashback involving Frau Melicharová creates a parallel between the surgery and the events in 1944 and pushes the characters' nationality to the forefront. Marschner's mistrust of Melichar, particularly his decision to perform surgery, is linked to his mistrust of the family servant almost twenty years prior. The object of his wrath in both cases was a Czech, a fact that an angry Melichar does not overlook. Melichar accuses him of a "lack of interest" but also of failing to understand his position of power as a German (in the first case) and as the hospital director (in the second).

Though couched within the rhetoric of socialist brotherhood among the Warsaw Pact states, newspaper reviews of the program corroborate this assessment. The *Film-Spiegel* says, "In summary: *Der Andere neben Dir* is a film worthy of the friendship between our two countries."[26] A *Sächsischer Zeitung* article, aptly titled "You and the Others" to reflect the statements made about those of other nationalities in this program, goes even further: "This was not a comfortable film for any of us, and especially those of us who work with colleagues from socialist 'brotherlands' will feel worked upon."[27] This observation that no one felt comfortable after watching the film, particularly those who have had frequent dealings with non-Germans, speaks to what producers (including Thein) and critics saw as wartime German complicity and guilt, as well as continued hatred, even concerning nationalities from states now considered close political allies. Surely the political imperative of establishing good relations with trading partners and fellow satellite states in the East played a hand in Thein's securing some of the most recognizable actors available to DFF for the lead roles (Erwin Gerschonneck and Inge Keller played Dr. and Frau Marschner, respectively).

Like these programs, Claus Hubalek's *In einem Garten in Aviamo* (In a garden in Aviamo, 1964) preaches racial and ethnic tolerance.[28] But it also represents the beginning of a much more overt discussion about race on West German television. The NDR play features an African American air force officer (George), stationed at a NATO base along the coast in southern Italy, and a blind but very attractive Italian girl (Anna-Maria). The two meet at her father's roadside restaurant, falling in love after an initial period of indecision on the part of the soldier. A jealous (white) American medical officer from the Deep South, however, approaches the girl and her father, offering to perform a procedure that might restore her sight. George offers to help pay for the costs. But when the jealous medical officer tells George he wants to perform the procedure only to separate the pair, George begins to fear she will not accept him (she does not know he is black). He applies for a transfer to another base, and the heartbroken Anna-Maria, who only learns George is black after he has gone, is left behind.

In einem Garten in Aviamo drips with progressive conceptions of race and tolerance. After the couple's first encounter, for example, George tells his black friend, "She talked to me, as if I were the same as her." A short while later, when he finally hears from her father she is blind, he rejoices, proclaiming, "Before God we are all the same." John Olden, the director, reinforces the notion of "same-ness before God" throughout the film and demonstrates its moral intention: race carries no ontological preconditions that would preclude romance, and thus can be discounted as an important category. During one outing at sea, Anna-Maria expresses her mental image of the scene, and the boat is pure white. George, uneasy at the double meaning of this phrase, asks what she thinks he looks like. She doesn't mention race at all, instead focusing on his voice. She thus avoids the more obvious external features that would tend to associate or label George as black. Finally, as the couple shop together on the main road in town, Anna-Maria tells George not to worry about the villagers, because no one will stare at her blindness. George, however, notices that everyone stares at them, and begins to feel uncomfortable. Here, the Italian townspeople notice the mixed-race couple immediately, but their staring is depicted in a negative light, made to seem inappropriate against Anna-Maria's blissful smile. Thus, because she is blind, Anna-Maria actually sees more clearly than her fellow Italians. In terms of subject matter, dialogue, and visualization, *In eimen Garten in Aviamo* addresses the question of race much more directly than any program before (West or East).

Hubalek, who also wrote the original radio play, clearly intended the piece as a type of moral instruction in tolerance for postwar Germans.[29] However, because it freely addresses the obstacles preventing an interracial romance from blooming while creating a "safe" distance between German viewers and the topic of interracial marriage (the entire film takes place in Italy and does not involve a single German), *In einem Garten in Aviamo* effectively distills and isolates the message from social practice in Germany. By explaining the topic in simple, phenotypical terms and removing it from a German context, the producers avoid dealing with German society's continuing racism(s) directly, instead projecting it onto another European society and crafting moral lessons at a more comfortable level. Unfortunately, no viewer letters survive to give clues about its reception. But the potential rhetorical power of such television representations of racial injustice, particularly when those depictions were highly visual, is suggested by the extremely high qualitative rating (+6) given by a large number of viewers (47 percent of those who could receive the ARD signal).[30] In at least some sense, then, *In einem Garten in Aviamo* fulfilled its purpose, discursively celebrating a romantic love that transcended outmoded notions about race. But *epd—Kirche und Fernsehen*'s one-line summation of the program neatly captures the piece's mood: "Pleasantly performed play."[31] Despite the seemingly controversial subject matter and the tragic ending, at least one critic saw fit to describe it as soothing or pleasant, an inkling perhaps indirectly caused by the exotic setting and the distance of the teleplay from everyday German life.

Such "pleasant" messages of tolerance occurred frequently during television's early years (before the mid-1960s). As the medium matured, however, more complicated lessons about integration and assimilation came to the fore. One of the earliest pieces in this vein, the remarkable Hans Oliva play *Das Mädchen Rahel* (The girl Rahel), appeared in 1961 on DFF.[32] It depicts two teenaged Jews, Rahel and her friend Rolf, as they hide from the Gestapo in 1942 Berlin. They live in a small, cramped apartment below street level, shielded by a Communist resistance cell. Oliva designs most of the dialogue in the style of a chamber play; Rahel and Rolf's interaction dominates the production, and very few scenes take place outside the apartment. In their solitude, they muse about their former German classmates (in particular, they wonder how many of them were really Nazis) and the far-fetched prospect that the Americans might free Berlin within the year. In one particularly poignant scene, they study the feet that pass by their door to the street. Rahel opines that some feet are dangerous, some friendly, and some honest or even depressed. Unlike faces, she explains, they do not lie. By the end of the program, which takes place over several weeks, Rahel and Rolf fall in love. They also each decide to help the communist resistance movement. They agree to set fire to an anti-communist demonstration. Unfortunately, Rahel's role in the partisan movement leads to her discovery, arrest, and execution. The prison guards ask if she wants to write any last words, to which she replies, "To whom? You've killed my whole family." She writes a farewell letter to Rolf (it is unclear whether he, too, has been captured), which she knows will never be sent, and the final shot shows her walking out of her prison cell, to meet her fate.

On the surface, Oliva's piece emphasizes the protagonists' German-ness. Both Rahel and Rolf (whose real name is revealed to be Ruben later in the program) speak openly about how they feel more German than Jewish, and they admit they've never been to synagogue before. This impression is reinforced when Rahel pretends to hold a guitar (in reality, she cradles a piece of wood for the fire) and the two sing "Kluge Sterne," a well-known German lullaby written by Heinrich Heine. When they fall in love, they fantasize about a Christian (not a Jewish) marriage. Rahel explains how the pretend marriage is supposed to work, with a priest (a *Pfarrer*) conducting the ceremony. Ruben points out that Jews don't have Christian priests presiding, to which Rachel replies, "Oh, in that book I read, there weren't any Jews. That's too bad." They also decide to pray during a bomb raid but realize they do not know how, a point that further emphasizes their distance from Judaism in practice. German viewers likely would have had little trouble identifying with what were, essentially, secular-minded German teenagers who happened to be Jewish. Ursula Genhorn, the woman who plays Rahel, even has blond hair.

A closer look, however, suggests Oliva intended more than a simple love story and tragedy. For one, the play is strangely forthright about the Holocaust for a program that aired in the early 1960s. A narrator at the start of the broadcast, for instance, explains the "final solution was in full swing, not four years after the pogroms of 1938." He furthermore references specific death camps such as Sobibór and Auschwitz, and the play includes brief footage of the cremation pits at such facilities. The references to the Nazis' Final Solution do not end with the opening narration scene; the play does not show Rahel's daring attempt to set fire to the street display, but it does depict Ruben and Rahel exiting the apartment and entering a raging fire, which has been superimposed on the shot. The scene implies the two Jewish protagonists' fate resembles that of their parents and other Jewish victims. Oliva's purpose in including these Holocaust references seems to have been to draw an equivalence between Jewish and Communist victims.

Even more remarkable is the way the piece suggests Germany could and should have been more welcoming to its Jews. During one scene, for example, Rahel says she believes "one day people will see there is another Germany, where Jews and Germans get along." Ruben, however, shakes his head and remarks, "This Germany!? It killed our parents! They treat us like animals! Should we die, just so that others will see this other Germany?" Ruben thus accuses not only Hitler and the National Socialists of crimes against his people, but also the nation itself. Though subtle, this was an unusual statement for an early television drama. It suggests to the viewer that mere tolerance toward Jews was not enough; only integration and real acceptance would have saved them. The teenagers disagree whether such a Germany could exist in practice, but Rahel seems convinced she can bring it to pass by helping the Communist cell.

While unusually blunt in referencing the Holocaust and accusing the German nation of a failure to integrate Jews, *Das Mädchen Rahel* adhered to DFF's socialist mission and perhaps may not have seemed that unusual to East German viewers accustomed to the regime's skin-deep attempts to appease Jews by proclaiming them "official victims" and funding the miniscule congregations that remained in the GDR.[33] An early West German play with an integrationist message, a 1963 NDR broadcast entitled *Die erste Lehre* (The first apprenticeship), proved far more controversial.[34] Written by Günter Rudorf and directed by Allan A. Buckhantz, the program describes the struggles of a mixed-race teenager, born out of wedlock in the fictional northern town of Moorstede to a German mother and African American father during the Allied occupation, to gain acceptance in West German society. Curiously, the ARD's *Deutsches Fernsehen Programmdienst*, which provided information about upcoming television offerings to press outlets, described the youth's childhood and school years as anything but underprivileged or difficult. The synopsis depicted German black children's situations as favorable: "As long as they were small, one found them [the children] 'sweet' and after all, 'they couldn't help it.'"[35] The children were well cared for by their German mothers, and the local schoolteachers did not discriminate against them. However, as Willy, the protagonist, prepares to train for a career as an electrician, latent racism suddenly surfaces everywhere in his life. His apprenticeship is canceled, most master electricians refuse to take him in, and villagers he has known for years suddenly look at him as an unwanted outsider, and competition for their own children. Willy is forcefully made aware he is "black." Willy eventually finds acceptance when he moves to Hamburg. "There," the *epd—Kirche und Fernsehen* reports, "no one asks about his skin color. There he will find his future."[36] This scenario locates racism as backwards, provincial, and as the sort of problem best rectified by increased exposure to the non-ethnic Germans in question. *Die Erste Lehre* marks the city as a nurturer of such values and thus as the proper venue for education in integration.

While Willy's projected future as a German citizen in Hamburg gives a blueprint for how other non-Germans (individuals) can best integrate, it also features in television's mission to simultaneously reformulate and relocate German national identity at the macro level. On the one hand, older variations of German nationalism, linked in previous decades to blood and race, had been discredited and needed to be torn down. A representative of this older form can be seen in the person of Willy's German grandmother, who never accepts her grandson because of his skin color. Nationalism in the postwar world now needed to be remade into a form compatible with the FRG's new role in NATO and in the nascent EU (then the European Economic Community). Acceptance of non-Germans had become a political imperative in the new order, and the most prevalent extant venues for this process, the major cities, featured prominently in televisual constructions of German national identity.

On the other hand, if the city was to become the focal point for moral lessons about racial and ethnic integration, television programs needed to show the shortcomings of other venues. Examples of provincial backwardness abound in West German television, from Maria Matray and Answald Krüger's *Standgericht* (1966) to Leopold Ahlsen's *Sansibar* (1962). *Die Erste Lehre* is merely the most poignant example among many that *relocates* the construction of German-ness to the metropolis, the antithesis of the province or periphery. This may well have been meant literally, but the figurative implications were also clear: being German had more to do with language, personal choice, and brotherhood in an abstract, anonymous community than with blood, ancestry, and familial attachment to plots of land. How viewers perceived and understood this lesson is less clear, however. The *epd— Kirche und Fernsehen*, having recognized the importance of the city in Willy's quest to find a place in German society, doubts the existence of a place as full of prejudice as Moorstede. "It doesn't have to be an entire city," the author reasons. "An individual can also make life hell for a person."[37] No viewer documents survive for *Die Erste Lehre*, but this sort of argument may well have resonated with many Germans. Other critics were even less careful than the editors at the *epd*. The *Funk-Korrespondenz* noted, "So arose a piece which [merely] forwarded the author's intentions."[38] For this reviewer, the racial moral lesson overshadowed both the dramatic unity of the piece and other aspects of the situation, such as the mother's dark past and the psychological state of the villagers. In this case, the reviewer not only marginalized the television play, he rejected its entire premise, clamoring instead for a toned-down version of German racism and an explanation of *why* these episodes *really* occur. Televisually presented norms about race could thus be called into question in multiple ways.

The "flight to the metropolis" solution may have provided an outlet for downcast *Mischlinge* (mulattoes) like Willy, but surely seemed less than ideal in other situations. The 1967 ZDF adaptation of Willi Heinrich's *Gottes zweite Garnitur* (*The Lonely Conqueror*, literally God's second string), for instance, depicts a romance between a German girl, Claire, and an African American soldier, John, in which the couple's intentions to escape family and community persecution by moving to Paris fall apart because of family pressure.[39] In the story, Fred (Claire's fiancé) and his family agree to host an American soldier for Christmas dinner. When the soldier (John) turns out to be black, however, the family members decide to withhold their intended present, an LP record, and get him back out the door as quickly as possible. Claire, ashamed by her future in-laws' behavior, storms out of the house. John offers to walk her home and, over the course of the evening, they fall in love. After an initial struggle with herself, Claire breaks off her engagement to Fred, and they spend John's leave together in France. Their plans to stay in France are thwarted, however, when Claire's father refuses to give her any money until she finishes school (the viewers also learn, however, his ulterior motive is to separate the couple). At this point, Fred, who has confronted Claire repeatedly, tells John's military superiors about the affair. The new and deeply racist company captain arranges for John to be transferred to Vietnam, a critique of American racism and foreign policy that would have surely resonated in Germany, a European center for anti-war demonstrations even before 1968. John quits the army to stay with Claire, but the military police break into his apartment after 11 p.m., allowing them to charge him with hiring a "prostitute."

The television version of *Gottes zweite Garnitur* visually and narratively links German anti-black racism to Germany's troubled colonial past and even to National Socialism.[40] Much as Heinrich intended in his original novel, the program presents these moral lessons as a form of blatant German hypocrisy. In the opening sequence, for instance, Fred's father claims not to harbor any prejudices against blacks, a point he makes without any prelude or cue from the conversation. This blunt statement seems to arise from his own feelings of uneasiness, however, and appears totally out of place against the backdrop of his shocked expression upon seeing John (and upon his wife's refusal to leave the kitchen with a *Schwarzer* (black person) in the house). A discussion about the differences between blacks and whites comes more naturally to Claire. When John starts to talk about racial prejudice in the United States, for instance, she declares she does not often think about race when considering a person. These two scenes offer starkly different, indeed opposite, reactions to John's black heritage. Fred categorically pushes it to the forefront of the discussion, whereas Claire (the producers' example of "correct" tolerance) considers it a category of far lesser import. A more combustible intersection occurs when Claire refuses to kiss John, even when they are far away from her family in France. She cries, "Not here! You aren't a European!" In this instance, Claire reveals her own mental limitations and racial-categorical thinking. John's shocked expression is designed to generate sympathy from the viewer, and the entire scene is portrayed as a socially natural, but nonetheless wrong, reaction to the situation. Claire's slip suggests, for Heinrich and Paul Verhoeven (the author of the teleplay, who began his career during the Third Reich), racial thinking remained an embedded aspect of German culture.[41]

Because of archival limitations, it is often difficult to ascertain how viewers reacted to a particular film. In the case of *Gottes zweite Garnitur*, the situation looks somewhat better. This can be attributed to the program's extremely high qualitative rating (+7; more than 90 percent of the viewers rated it "very good" or "excellent"). Infratest's summary of its collected responses corroborates what the film suggests: John comes across as an extremely sympathetic character, resulting in a positive review.[42] Viewers described the piece as dealing with a "racial problem" but never considered it a topic that should be avoided; rather, the Infratest responses tended to suggest the Germans in the program were at fault for John's treatment. Many viewers sent letters directly to the station, asking about Jimmy Powell's (who plays John) address, the future films and/or television programs in which he would be appearing, and, as Claire had done in the film, the origin of his excellent German (he studied for many years in Vienna).[43] Viewers also expressed the hope that their comrades had learned something from the film, and almost every letter in the archive folio expressed some form of support for the moral lesson imparted. Critical responses to the program were not filled with the same kind of showery praise but nonetheless tended to tout the piece for its "seriousness" and for John's sympathetic nature.[44]

By the end of the 1960s, television producers and executives at West German outlets seem to have understood television as an ideal medium for initiating discussions about foreigners living in Germany. The topic became all the more relevant in the wake of a massive labor recruitment program in the FRG, starting in 1955 and lasting through the 1970s. By the end of the 1960s, millions of "guest workers" (*Gastarbeiter*) had to come to Germany, mainly from Spain, Portugal, and Italy. Politicians and employers expected these foreigners to return home after a few years of service.[45] Many of the workers decided to stay in Germany permanently, however, rekindling long-repressed discussions about race and tolerance. The word race, now associated with National Socialism, had dropped out of common use, except in relation to the children of African American GIs and German women, the so-called *Mischlinge*. But, as Rita Chin has argued, racialized mentalities and modes of thinking continued to color discussions about foreigners living in Germany.[46] Starting in the early 1960s, isolated critics of the guest worker recruitment program, on both the right and the left, drew on racialized ways of thinking in framing their dissent. The very term guest worker denotes something alien and foreign to the German body public.[47] It was in this context that a series of pro-integration pieces on "guest workers" appeared during the late 1960s. These plays criticized xenophobic attitudes and sympathetically depicted foreign workers struggling to find acceptance in a strange new land. At least one historian has claimed the introduction of non-German workers in the 1950s did not spark a widespread debate because the workers were considered temporary by definition.[48] Television plays provide a strong counterexample, as a visible, highly public platform for discussing the presence of non-Germans in the FRG before the more well-known debates about Turkish immigration in the 1970s and 1980s. Such representations were by no means limited to television, as demonstrated by Rainer Werner Fassbinder's famous 1969 film *Katzelmacher*, about a Greek worker living in Germany. But television, with its public service model and willingness to address thorny topics in the name of education, played a prominent role in initiating this discussion in the public sphere.

Volker Koch and Philippe Pilliod's ZDF piece *Die Anpassung* (The adaptation, 1970), for example, depicts a small cohort of Italian laborers trying to adapt to life in the FRG.[49] One of the major plot points is the Italian protagonists' romantic connections to German women. The play presents these relationships as ephemeral. Two of the three girlfriends seem interested in the Italians only as long as they do not have to enter into a more serious relationship. The third, Eva, seems more genuinely interested, but her beau, Pasquale, has a wife and children waiting for him in Naples. This situation characterizes the relationships between Germans and foreigners as it is presented in the film: disrupted by the temporary status of the men in Germany and constantly shadowed by a culture gap. The publicity leading up to the broadcast corroborates and contributes to the impression of disruption. The ZDF *Programmdienst*, received by every major news outlet reporting on and announcing the television schedule, highlighted the guest worker problem with the first line, "The film follows the path of a southern Italian work [force] . . . which came into the Federal Republic seeking work."[50] ZDF thus located the guest worker "problem" at the forefront of its advertising for this program. The *Programmdienst* also asks a series of critical questions such as "Is it [the guest worker system] desired? On the part of the host country? On the part of the guest workers themselves?" These questions, which almost seem to contradict the authors' intentions to spur greater efforts to aid integration and "adaptation," contributed to the impression that the film, whatever its actual plot, genre, or content, first and foremost addresses the guest worker "problem." Multiple references to the workers as Southern Italians served to distance the protagonists even further, to "ethnicize" them in contrast to the far more affluent (and thus European) Northern Italians (the bulk of the Italian guest workers did, in fact, come from the south). With such information in hand, it should come as no surprise that newspapers followed suit in their descriptions and announcements of the program. The editors at *Die Welt* disdain the inclusion of an "amateur" film sequence shot in Sicily.[51] Not only do the production documents fail to mention non-studio material, but also this comment makes the scenes shot in Italy seem less professional, and thus less well suited for the supposedly more sophisticated German television audience. Wolfgang Paul at *Der Tagesspiegel* goes so far as to say the film describes social misfortunes in Italy more than any problems in Germany (even though almost the entire film takes place in Germany, in the German language).[52]

Die Anpassung's location within the evening's programming schedule also highlights the piece's social implications. The ARD had already aired, doubtless in honor of 1 May (International Workers' Day), a short documentary about guest workers entitled "Ein Land, 25 Jahre später: Die Gastarbeiter" (A Land, 25 Years Later: The Guest Workers).[53] By the time *Die Anpassung* aired an hour later, most viewers had already switched to the ARD's "Wenn der weisse Flieder wieder blüht," an annual (and popular) spring variety show (accordingly, Infratest reported a 9 percent viewership, extremely low for such a well-publicized and politically relevant piece).[54] Thus, *Die Anpassung* found itself following another television program about guest workers and competing against a completely apolitical and noncontroversial song-and-dance show. Viewers, perhaps, could not help but understand the program according to its comments about ethnicity. In this sense, the producers apparently achieved their objective: increased awareness of the guest workers' plight.

Precisely what the producers meant to do with this awareness, however, is not at all clear. To be fair, *Die Anpassung* generated an unusual amount of internal debate and communication at ZDF. The station director, Karl Holzamer, apparently sought the opinion of several colleagues and experts while the show was still in its production stage, indicating an uncertainty about whether to broadcast it at all. This correspondence, including both recommendations and warnings, reveals the tension involved in filming socially controversial material for what was perceived as a "conversational" or relaxing medium. This tension did not take the form of a debate about the morality of recruiting, employing, and integrating guest workers in Germany; rather, the correspondents expressed themselves as dramaturgical experts, bickering over the strengths and shortcomings of the (developing) piece in question. For example, in February 1969, Holzamer himself, apparently responding to complaints and suggestions no longer found in the archive, demanded to know, "Where in this material is the (for a television play) indispensable drama?"[55] In response, Hans-Jürgen Bobermin, an executive over drama, wrote:

> In the context of the increasingly clear tendency of modern television plays to draw suspense less from a collection of external experiences than out of social circumstances . . . we are therefore convinced the individuals, and the nonspectacular situations in which they find themselves, inspire more real, inner drama than the establishment of a conventional "body of effects."[56]

More was at stake here, however, than the dramatic integrity of one film. Both West German television channels regularly broadcast documentaries, many of them simultaneously contemporary and self-critical. These programs reflected the industry's moral-political mandate (from the beginning a *moralische Anstalt*—moral institution) and educational mission. But while documentaries, to say nothing of news magazines, found a wide audience, television fiction remained the dominant genre throughout the 1960s. To put it simply, viewer ratings demonstrate viewers wanted to watch *good* drama more than any other type of show. Producers universally understood the attraction of harnessing this popularity, which could allow them to fulfill their moral/educational mandate while simultaneously reaching and appealing to large numbers of viewers. Precisely how, and in what form, drama was to accomplish this was another question altogether. Holzamer knew full well the power of dramatic-based social commentaries, having authorized programs simultaneously divisive and popular, such as *Das Unbrauchbare an Anna Winters, Sonderurlaub,* and the entire *Kleines Fernsehspiel* series.

But *Die Anpassung* attempted to couple the teleplay more closely with pure social commentary. It pushed the limits of dramatic appeal to the extreme, as Bobermin makes clear with his idea of pulling drama out of "social circumstances." Social criticism, since ancient Greece a component part of drama, no longer needed to conform to dramatic convention. Producers tried to make drama out of the everyday, out of the social situation itself. Bobermin, speaking to the intendant, chose his words carefully. Two dramatists assigned to review the piece internally, Hans Gottschalk and Herr Dr. Knapp, felt less constrained to justify the new approach. They proclaimed, after one preview, "This production is . . . the best example of a '*Dokumentarspiel*' as it should be . . . we are agreed this teleplay formally indicates a path which one should tread in the future."[57] Gottschalk and Knapp praise the piece's documentary qualities as a possible model for future productions. These types of qualities, as Bobermin subtly explains, had the power to transform television fiction into a more potent ideological, political, and moral weapon. Because of the themes in *Die Anpassung*, the debate over the proper relationship between drama and documentary implicitly threw the guest worker debate into sharper relief. Dr. Gerhard Hannig, in a letter to Holzamer, demonstrates this connection:

> Journalists, who have already been shown this program, have apparently voiced the opinion that it is one-sided and may be capable of awaking false notions about the lives of foreign workers in Germany. On this topic, with which I am not familiar, I cannot and do not want to say anything. Despite this, I feel prompted to write the following: "If the [ZDF] should ever have the intention to broadcast a play that concerns Turkish workers, I would like to herewith offer my support, as an adviser."[58]

The question of dramatic presentation, in other words, the *packaging* surrounding the messages of tolerance and integration, becomes charged with the political-moral debate itself, as seen here, where Hannig inserts the much more volatile (and, until the mid-1970s, rarely addressed on television) question of Turkish guest workers into what was otherwise a lively debate about the nature of drama. In the end, the two poles in this discussion, one favoring an internally contained, traditional drama, and the other looking to push the program toward documentary-style social commentary, seem to have reached a compromise.

True to its reputation in the internal correspondence, the program is not easy to follow. It jumps from one aspect of the protagonists' lives to the next, and its multiple romantic relationships, seemingly important to the plot when introduced, never reach any kind of conclusion. The program's emphasis on modernism and disorientation (rather than on the narrative itself) may help account for the program's mediocre qualitative rating, +1.[59] The film became a sort of intellectual exposé on the problems of integration. On the other side of the compromise, the final version of the press release omitted the following statement (included in a May 1969 draft): "The thematic complexity corresponds with an unconventional element, constantly changes, breaks up the action, and expands critical perspectives."[60] The final version thus does not parade the intellectual, "unconventional" approach as clearly as had been intended. Despite these attempts to soften the show, however, unflattering stereotypes and depictions angered Italian viewers and critics alike, a fact noted by Hannig in his letter. Perhaps the stark depiction of real life inherent to a film about the everyday, combined with the necessary visual cues and markers signifying the characters as Italians—guest workers in a foreign land—combined to produce the opposite of what the producers intended; instead of a message about integration made more powerful by dramatic and intellectual innovation, the film delivered a set of Italians having difficulties in Germany without any comprehensible or clear moral message. Given this failure, xenophobic viewers (like the one from the Infratest survey) may have simply had their worst fears confirmed.

A second drama about guest workers in Germany, Dieter Waldmann's *Der Unfall* (The accident, 1968), avoided this pitfall by including an unequivocal moral message: innocent, newly arrived guest workers encounter unjustified prejudices and stereotypes.[61] *Der Unfall* depicts the arrival of a young Spanish laborer, Paco, who comes to take the job left vacant by his severely injured brother. He immediately encounters indifference and hostility, finding help at the train station, for instance, only from a group of Greek tourists. His troubles continue as he makes his way to the factory, to the unsanitary housing complex where he is forced to live, and as he tries to make friends with the natives. By the end of the film, Paco learns his brother's apparent accident on the job was really a hushed-up hate crime. He confronts the allegedly responsible German factory workers, and the movie ends ambiguously, with Paco being restrained by one of his few German friends.

The moral lessons intended for viewers, similar in scope and aim to those found in *Die Anpassung*, center on the failure of German society to admit and integrate foreigners. In this case, a rather simple telos—peaceful coexistence and integration for Paco and other innocent temporary workers—is advanced by way of a much more multifaceted set of normative examples and arguments. In effect, viewers witness a catalog of possible responses to the guest workers, almost all of which involve ethnic hatred of one kind or another. Right at the start, for example, Paco asks a rail official, in Spanish, where the exit is. The official, though sitting behind a desk with signs in German, French, English, and Spanish, replies (in German), "Don't be stupid! It's right here." This entrance sets the mood for the entire piece; even those seemingly charged with welcoming outsiders to Germany disdain the guest workers. This scene thus challenges the tolerance paradigm, at least in its non-integrationist incarnation. When Paco finally finds the factory, the manager tells him he has never heard of his brother, and to get lost. When one of his employees reminds him someone by that name had indeed recently been involved in a near-fatal accident, the manager agrees, but refuses to take a new employee on that basis or to let Paco stay in the foreign workers' home. He tells Paco, "In Spain, do you think the streets are paved with gold here?" This time, the token German's response to Paco's presence is one of extreme indifference to his familial or personal situation, mixed with a general disdain for his pool of guest workers. He perpetuates a commonly held assumption, that Northern Europe is wealthier than Southern and that Southerners want to steal Northerners' hard-earned prosperity.

Not all of Paco's encounters with Germans seem intolerant. For example, the Consortium for the Cultural Integration of Foreign Workers recruits Paco at one point, and the members seem genuinely interested in promoting its activities. But later, during one of their parties, the organizers give long, political speeches about integration, very much detached from these workers' everyday lives, and conclude by singing German folk songs and staging spaghetti-eating contests. On the one hand, the Consortium focuses its cooperative efforts on the German side of the coin; on the other, the organizers fail to recognize their particular chapter consists more of Spanish workers than Italian, and the spaghetti-eating contest evidences the lack of serious attention being paid toward integration. Thus, even the more tolerant or "multicultural" Germans (to borrow a term that gained wide usage only in the following decade) do not really espouse collaboration or discussion. Instead, they seem to promote integration for their own narrow political goals or to assuage their feeling that the guest workers are not given the best conditions under which to work. Finally, at one point during Paco's adventures, the camera lingers on a travel poster for "España," which features two swimsuit-clad women walking on the beach. Paco looks quizzically at the poster before returning to his own shabby apartment, which he shares with a dozen other Spaniards. The disconnect between Spain as a mental image for Germans and Spaniards coming to work in Germany could not have been stronger, as evidenced by the *epd*'s astonishment that a police officer in the film could say, "That's what they're like down there!" after a fight breaks out at the guest workers' house but in the next moment wonder how these foreigners could never have seen the Costa del Sol.

Indeed, some of the press responses to *Der Unfall* belie the same sort of disconnect or at least puzzlement on the part of the critics themselves. For example, the *epd—Kirche und Fernsehen* praises the piece for its condemnation of "new racism" in Germany, but the editors also worry the viewers will dislike the presence of so many foreigners at the center of the plot.[62] This fear probably arose from the fact that for much of the show, the main character, Paco, only speaks in untranslated Spanish. In any event, it appears to have been unfounded. Infratest reported only a 28 percent viewership (low for a television play) but also noted the viewers' reactions "were overwhelmingly very positive."[63] In fact, Waldmann specifically designed the film around the themes of alienation and uncertainty, feelings he wanted the viewer to experience firsthand through Paco's eyes. That almost none of the German characters express any warmth or real sympathy worked to bolster this mood. Klaus Hamburger at the *Funk-Korrespondenz* likewise gives the film a positive review.[64] Waldmann, Hamburger explains, is well placed to criticize (West) Germany's intolerance because he has lived in the United States for so long. But Hamburger also laments the lack of any solutions to the problems Waldmann raises, instead seeing only an indictment of German "intolerance," which, he says, led to far greater "accidents" than the one represented here. The moral lessons taught in *Der Unfall* are indeed implicit, imparted mainly through negative examples; at the normative level, however, these lessons do seem fairly obvious. As the *Kölnische Rundschau* puts it, "[*Der Unfall*] makes the viewer defiant against the indifference of others."[65]

Although the GDR experienced a similar period of self-criticism involving presuppositions about race and morality, the political landscape allowed fewer opportunities to put new schemas into practice. Without any period of sustained economic success, East Germany did not have a corresponding guest worker program at this time (they did contract workers from Vietnam and Mozambique starting in the 1970s). Moreover, official memory in the East refused to acknowledge the persistence of Nazi prejudices in the GDR. Nonetheless, some television programs did speak to the topic of integration and tolerance. These almost always involved other Warsaw Pact nations. The multipart program *Wege übers Land* (Ways across the country, 1968), for instance, prominently featured German-Polish relations.[66] Spanning thirty years of German history, viewers first encounter Poles as a family is forced out of its farm in 1941, to be replaced by German woman from a village in Brandenburg, Gertrud, and her collaborationist husband, Kalluweit. In one tearful passage, the evicted Polish father says to the incoming family, which he holds blameless in the forced removal, "never forget this night." The war scenes involving Poles promote tolerance, not integration (despite the long history of German land ownership in Poland, the film clearly denotes this particular farm as Polish). When Gertrud, the film's real protagonist, flees Poland in the face of the Soviet advance, however, the line between tolerance and integration becomes blurred. She has already rescued two children (one Jew, one orphaned Pole) from a death transport and now takes in a third, a Polish infant. She raises the children in the GDR. Her choices come to a head in the fifth and final part of the film, taking place in the early 1960s: the Polish mother discovers her son's identity and comes to take him back. Gertrud initially refuses, provoking a heated diatribe against German aggression from the Polish woman. Eventually, however, Gertrud agrees to let him go, and the two sides are reconciled.

The theme of ethnic integration in German society is explored here in two ways: one, through the seamless raising of the two Jewish children in an isolated German village, and two, through the reconciliation between Gertrud and her unnamed Polish counterpart. The first avenue remains implicit throughout. The second, however, involves a painful moral dilemma. Politicians readily latched onto Helmut Sakowski's screenplay because they realized it promoted German-Polish friendship, a politically desirable goal in the context of the Warsaw Pact.[67] Transcripts from the Kollegium des deutschen Fernsehfunks (German Television Council), the committee assigned to assist the DFF's station director in making decisions, demonstrate a constant imperative to produce or expand on programs about German-Soviet and German-Polish "friendship."[68] These imperatives carried latent—and potent—undertones of reconciliation with Poles, Russians, and Czechs. For example, one justification for the filmic representation of Bruno Apitz's well-known novel *Nackt unter Wölfen* stresses the potential benefit for viewers: "The people participating from East and West [in other words, viewers] thereby achieve insight into the mistakes of the past and thus understand today's political imperative: the unified action of all peaceful Germans toward a truly democratic Fatherland."[69] Given the program's theme, it seems clear the "mistakes of the past" are the extermination of Jews and the enslavement of Poles in concentration camps. The East German executives thus commissioned a piece aimed at the kind of *Vergangenheitsbewältigung* that the West so rarely approached in the pre-Eichmann trial years. The appeal to all "peaceful Germans" implies the necessity of new attitudes toward people of other nations while building a new, more tolerant Fatherland.

But what was politically expedient was also morally complicated. At one level, this was a universal moral question: should an ersatz mother be forced to give up her charges after more than fifteen years of care? Its corollary is perhaps even more difficult: what say should a teenage child have in the matter? At another level, however, the situation turned on the question of ethnic reconciliation. Germans and Poles had long lived side by side; now that they had been separated, how would they resolve these lingering cords of connection, inevitable even after so many years? *Wege übers Land* gives some insight via dramatic representation. Gertrud's rescuing actions of courage and charity give the (German) audience a sense of self-righteousness, an acceptable role model or outlet with which viewers can naturally identify. When the choices before her become more equivocal, but no less moral, Gertrud's character suggests to viewers several coping strategies: at one point, in her anger, she accuses the Polish mother of greed (this strategy is quickly rejected, as Gertrud herself apologizes). A few minutes later, she shares stories about the war, building up her credentials as an anti-Nazi. In this case, an official who had accompanied the Polish mother, apparently some sort of chief in the Polish village, corroborates her claims as he was forced to hide in her cellar for weeks. Finally, Gertrud reminds the woman she was a rescuer, that things could have been much worse, and that she really had no choice but to take the child. In the end, the real mother gives in and forgives Gertrud. These strategies for dealing with a specific situation not only resonated with viewers; they provided believable actions corresponding to morality at a national or community level. German anger over the new Oder-Neisse boundary between Germany and Poland, widely derided in the West for many years and unpopular even in the East outside of the political elites' circles, is here represented by Gertrud's initial, and understandable, anger. Gertrud's claims to anti-fascism relate directly to the nation-building process in the East, where the representations and machinations behind the state's attempts to direct collective memory constantly emphasized the *lack* of Nazis in the East, and used the communist resistance as a source of legitimacy. In other words, Gertrud's intentions can be seen as legitimate because she also fought against the very regime that brought her to Poland. Finally, Gertrud declares she had no alternative. This strategy might have had several parallels in contemporary East Germany, for example, the manifest evilness of Nazi Germany and the similarly self-evident righteousness of the SED.

Conclusion

While German television broadcasts regularly addressed questions of tolerance, integration, race, and ethnicity, they could not mask the obvious disconnect between television representations and popular attitudes. German xenophobia ran deep, even years after the war, as demonstrated by West German conceptions of race and citizenship, and East German hostility toward students from Mozambique.[70] This fact calls the notion of how and whether television *reflected* viewers' values and desires into serious question. In light of the evidence presented here that television fiction reflected (not merely reformulated) prevailing norms, how can this disconnect be explained? This question merits further, and more focused, exploration, but several possibilities come to mind. First, perhaps the expression of anti-Semitism or other kinds of racism was simply too dangerous in the postwar climate. Viewers who disliked the "good" Jews presented in *Das Mädchen Rahel*, for example, were unlikely to write or phone the station and voice their opinions. Second, as the constantly changing patterns have shown, notions about race and ethnicity did not necessarily remain constant over time, or even internally consistent. Attitudes about diversity, as *Die erste Lehre* demonstrates, were complex and often self-contradictory. Third, veiled intolerance was, in fact, present in many of these dramas, but the overt moral lessons covered some of these attitudes. For example, *Die Anpassung* catalogs German racist attitudes toward guest workers but at the same time essentializes, and thus marginalizes, those workers.

Fourth, as the atmosphere surrounding social criticism and television changed over the course of the 1960s, so did the programs, which increasingly criticized Germans as intolerant and pressed for greater integration (especially in the FRG). This suggests a possible generational shift, as younger viewers began to actively participate in television discourse, and themes about race and integration became more commonly represented. So, for example, guest worker dramas such as *Die Anpassung* or *Der Unfall*, as well as programs like *Gottes zweite Garnitur* and, to a lesser degree, DFF's *Wege übers Land*, signaled a new, more vocal era in television fiction, very different from the silence of the late 1950s and early 1960s. But while the very decision to produce these programs not only suggests new attitudes about acceptable programming, it also attests to the persistence of the problem. The television authorities wanted to combat intolerance, but viewer responses, carefully read, suggest continued antagonism. With few exceptions (*Das Mädchen Rahel*, for example), television plays began to highlight the problems but did not attempt to reformulate or challenge the notion that other people—be they black, Jewish, or Southern European—were different. By the latter half of the 1960s, producers had found apt and, based on the high rating given to programs like *Gottes zweite Garnitur*, popular ways to criticize racism as a practice and encourage new types of behavior but still shied away from striking at the root of the problem: essentialization and racial hierarchies, persistent attitudes that had been present for centuries and were heavily shaped by the Third Reich's racial imaginary.

Notes

1. Ulf von Mechow, *Frei bis zum nächsten Mal*, dir. Korbinian Köberle (ZDF, 23 July 1969). The play was produced by the Neue Deutsche Filmgesellschaft.
2. Gilad Margalit, *Germany and its Gypsies: A Post-Auschwitz Ordeal* (Madison: University of Wisconsin Press, 2002), 32–33.
3. Historisches Archiv des Zweiten Deutschen Rundfunks (ZDF-HA), *Frei bis zum nächsten Mal Drehbuch—9252*.
4. *Infratest Wochenbericht*, July 1969, 17.
5. *ZDF Programmdienst* 25/69.
6. Jennifer Kapczynski, *The German Patient Crisis and Recovery in Postwar Culture* (Ann Arbor: University of Michigan Press, 2008), 60; Uli Linke, *German Bodies: Race and Representation after Hitler* (New York: Routledge, 1999), 153.
7. Konrad Jarausch, *After Hitler: Recivilizing Germans, 1945–1995* (New York: Oxford University Press, 2006), 55–63.
8. Ibid., 247. See also Tanja R. Müller, *Legacies of Socialist Solidarity: East Germany in Mozambique* (Lanham, MD: Lexington, 2014), 86–89. Müller explains that racism did not exist in the "official parlance" of the GDR but that authorities acknowledged it implicitly in connection with contracted workers from Mozambique in the 1980s.
9. Mark E. Spicka, "City Policy and Guest Workers in Stuttgart, 1955–1973," *German History* 31, no. 3 (2013): 353–356.
10. Heide Fehrenbach, *Race after Hitler: Black Occupation Children in Postwar Germany and America* (Princeton, NJ: Princeton University Press, 2005), 6.
11. See Jost Halfmann, "Two Discourses of Citizenship in Germany: The Differences between Public Debate and Administrative Practice," in *The Postwar Transformation of Germany: Democracy, Prosperity, and Nationhood*, ed. John S. Brady, Beverly Crawford, and Sarah Elise Wiliarty (Ann Arbor: University of Michigan Press, 1999), 378–398.
12. Heide Fehrenbach, "Black Occupation Children and the Devolution of the Nazi Racial State," in *After the Nazi Racial State: Difference and Democracy in Germany and Europe*, ed. Rita Chin, Heide Fehrenbach, Geoff Eley, and Atina Grossmann (Ann Arbor: University of Michigan Press, 2009).
13. Maria Höhn, *GIs and Fräuleins: The German-American Encounter in 1950s West Germany* (Chapel Hill: University of North Carolina Press, 2002), 199.
14. Christopher A. Molnar, "Imagining Yugoslavs: Migration and the Cold War in Postwar West Germany," *Central European History* 43, no. 1 (Mar 2014). Molnar furthermore argues that West Germans did not view Spanish, Italian, and Yugoslavian guest workers in racial terms.
15. Quinn Slobodian, *Comrades of Color: East Germany in the Cold War World* (New York: Berghahn Books, 2015), 3–4.
16. Fehrenbach, *Race after Hitler*, 75.
17. Heinz Kamnitzer and Alexander Stenbock-Fermor, *Mord an Rathenau*, dir. Max Jaap (DFF, 23 November 1961).

18. Bundesarchiv (BArch), DR 8 22, Kollegiumsvorlage 51/61, 6 September 1961.
19. BArch, DR 8 280, Heinz Adameck, "Einige Gedanken über die Produktion von Fernsehfilm im Deutschen Rundfunk," undated.
20. BArch, DR 8 22, Kollegiumsvorlage 51/61, 6 September 1961.
21. Paul H. Rameau, *Menschen helfen Menschen: Zwei Tage von Vielen*, dir. Ralph Lothar (ZDF, 11 March 1963).
22. "Menschen helfen Menschen, Zwei Tage von Vielen: Ein Fernsehfilm," *ZDF Programmdienst*, 11 March 1964.
23. Trude Pfeiffer, *Funk-Korrespondenz* 13, 26 March 1964.
24. *Infratest Wochenbericht*, March 1964, 39–40.
25. Ulrich Thein, *Der Andere neben Dir*, dir. Ulrich Thein (DFF, 27 September 1963).
26. "Der Andere neben Dir," *Film Spiegel*, 18 October 1963.
27. Gerhard Dittmann, "Du und die Anderen," *Sächsicher Zeitung*, 5 October 1963.
28. Claus Hubalek, *In einem Garten in Aviamo*, dir. John Olden (NDR, 19 November 1964).
29. Hubalek's other pieces, including the NWRV's *Die Festung* in 1957, also treat difficult moral topics. *Die Festung* describes German soldiers who question increasingly insane orders along the Russian front.
30. *Infratest Wochenbericht*, November 1964.
31. *epd—Kirche und Fernsehen* 47, 21 November 1964, 11.
32. Hans Oliva, *Das Mädchen Rahel*, dir. Robert Trösch (DFF, 9 November 1961).
33. Thomas C. Fox, *Stated Memory: East Germany and the Holocaust* (Rochester, NY: Camden House, 1999), 79.
34. Günter Rudorf, *Die erste Lehre*, dir. Allan A. Buckhantz (NDR, 12 March 1963).
35. *Deutsches Fernsehen Programmdienst*, 11/1963, 10–11.
36. *epd—Kirche und Fernsehen* 11, 16 March 1963.
37. *epd—Kirche und Fernsehen* 11, 16 March 1963, 8.
38. *Funk-Korrespondenz* 12, 20 March 1963, 15.
39. Paul Verhoeven and Nicolaus Richter, *Gottes zweite Garnitur*, dir. Paul Verhoeven (ZDF, 13 December 1967).
40. Michelle René Eley, "Anti-Black Racism in West German Living Rooms: The ZDF Television Film Adaptation of Willi Heinrich's *Gottes zweite Garnitur*," *German Studies Review* 39, no. 2 (2016): 316.
41. See Eley's article for a much more exhaustive catalog of the film's anti-black racism.
42. *Infratest Wochenbericht*, December 1967. The summary also mentions "In einem Garten in Aviamo" as belonging in the same vein.
43. Letters collected in ZDF-HA, 3/1/062, "Gottes zweite Garnitur."
44. "Gottes zweite Garnitur," *Allgemeine Zeitung Mainz*, 15 December 1967.
45. Rita Chin, *The Guest Worker Question in Postwar Germany* (New York: Cambridge University Press, 2007), 6.
46. Ibid., 16.
47. Ibid., 48.
48. Christhard Hoffmann, "Immigration and Nationhood in the Federal Republic of Germany," in Brady et al., *Postwar Transformation of Germany*, 365.
49. Volker Koch and Philippe Pilliod, *Die Anpassung*, dir. Christian Rischert (ZDF, 1 May 1970).
50. "Die Anpassung," *ZDF Programmdienst*, May 1970.
51. "Lustlos in Deutschland: Gastarbeiter und Anpassung," *Die Welt*, 4 May 1970.
52. Wolfgang Paul, *Der Tagesspiegel*, 3 May 1970.

53. "Ein Land, 25 Jahre später: Die Gastarbeiter," (ARD: 1 May 1970, 19:15).
54. *Infratest Wochenbericht*, May 1970, 20–21.
55. ZDF-HA, 6335/0856, "Die Anpassung," letter from Karl Holzamer to Hans-Jürgen Bobermin, 25 February 1969.
56. ZDF-HA, 6335/0856, "Die Anpassung," letter from Hans-Jürgen Bobermin to Karl Holzamer, 6 March 1969.
57. ZDF-HA, 6335/0856, "Die Anpassung," Vorführung, 26 September 1969.
58. ZDF-HA, 6335/0856, "Die Anpassung," letter from Dr. Gerhard Hannig to Herr Professor Holzamer, 8 December 1969. Several dramas on the question of guest workers appeared in the 1970s, but, to my knowledge, Holzamer never took up Hannig on his offer.
59. *Infratest Wochenbericht*, May 1970, 20–21.
60. ZDF-HA, 6335/0856, "Die Anpassung," Bavaria Atelier Gesellschaft mbH, *Das Neueste in Kürze* 16/69, 23 May 1969.
61. Dieter Waldmann, *Der Unfall*, dir. Peter Beauvais (WDR, 7 November 1968).
62. *epd—Kirche und Fernsehen* 46, 16 November 1968, 12.
63. *Infratest Wochenbericht*, November 1968, 17.
64. Klaus Hamburger, "Gesellschaftskritischer Krimi," *Funk-Korrespondenz* 46, 14 November 1968, 17.
65. *Kölnische Rundschau*, 8 November 1968.
66. Helmut Sakowski, *Wege übers Land*, dir. Martin Eckermann (DFF, 22, 24, 26, 28, 29 September 1968).
67. BArch, DR 8 49, Vorlage 3 66, 15 March 1966.
68. BArch, DR 8 24, 2 Protokoll Vorlage 25/62, 2 July 1962, doc. 5.
69. BArch, DR 8 487, Dramatische Kunst, Programmvorschläge der Hauptabteilung Dramatische Kunst für Spielzeit 1959/60, 12 May 59.
70. Fehrenbach, *Race after Hitler*, 174; Müller, *Legacies of Socialist Solidarity*, 86–95.

Conclusion

The heyday of television fiction as a medium of moral instruction did not end suddenly or abruptly, but it did end decisively. When Erich Honecker became the head of the SED in 1971, he oversaw far-reaching changes in the GDR's attitude toward consumerism and entertainment. The new regime increased production quotas and slashed prices for popular, hitherto neglected consumables, from kitchen appliances to automobiles and even television sets. In exchange, he demanded unwavering political loyalty from his citizens, enforced by Erich Mielke's infamous Ministry for State Security, or Stasi. Because television now played such an important role in negotiating and mediating East German culture and values, Honecker saw the medium as a front line in the battle over the nation's soul. Accordingly, in the early 1970s, the regime instrumentalized the medium even more aggressively. Party officials issued a series of explicit directives on entertainment, deriving in part from Honecker's famous pronouncement that television had to "overcome a certain boredom" among its viewers.[1] Television plays remained a key fixture on the East German airwaves, but they increasingly served to entertain the public rather than to educate or instruct. Building on the foundation set by overly propagandistic news series such as *Der schwarze Kanal* (The Black Channel), nonfiction genres became television's primary means for disseminating political education.

Likewise, television fiction in the West underwent a fundamental transformation in the 1970s. The ARD's constituent stations, as well as ZDF, decreased funding for plays and instead diverted money to news magazine programs and game shows. Viewed as a percentage of television broadcasting hours as a whole, dramatic television declined only slightly in the early 1970s; in 1966, ARD devoted 18.8 percent of its air time to plays, ZDF 24.6 percent, compared to 17.2 percent and 23 percent, respectively, in 1976.[2] But the station workers who compiled these percentages included in this statistical category licensed, non-television films, which gained in prominence and popularity during the 1970s. Documentaries and docudramas, too, rose to greater prominence after 1970, replacing television plays as the most popular programs.[3] Television fiction, such a vibrant genre during the 1960s, had begun to lose some of its luster by the early 1970s.

During the 1960s, television had supplanted newspapers, radio, and even cinema as the premiere form of mass media. It enthralled huge national audiences, and arbitrated some of the most heavily discussed moral topics of the day, many of which were perceived to be a result of the Third Reich and its evils. Television plays sought to generate moral consensus by visually representing solutions to those dilemmas, making it an important tool in the hands of elites in the two German states. The medium seemed to speak with authority, projecting calm, convincing solutions directly to the living room and assuming the role of unifier, culture-bringer, and teacher between the late 1950s and the late 1960s. It corresponded precisely to the self-perceived mediatic and moral needs of the postwar population, projecting stability and offering the promise of reinvention through visualization and dramatization. In short, it became a crucible in which to grind the most important questions of the day.

At the same time, however, the rapidly changing moral environment of the 1960s meant the moral messages themselves, while often presented as coherent and perhaps even obvious within the context of each program, did not remain constant or homogenous throughout the period in question. Because the messages were so dynamic, it is possible to step back and identify broad diachronic trajectories. Programs that reflected on the nation's moral past became gradually but definitively more self-critical. For example, the "good Germans" featured in early productions such as *Nackt unter Wölfen* and *Waldhausstraße 20* gave way to more complex, nuanced depictions typified by *Dr. Schlüter* and *Mord in Frankfurt*. The former programs valorized German protagonists as selfless rescuers or resisters. The antagonists, Nazi prison guards or Gestapo agents, appeared in small numbers and as obvious aberrations next to the seemingly more typical German heroes. The latter programs depicted tainted protagonists, who might or might not find redemption. They did not come close to the candid representation of gas chambers and firing squads common in television programming during the 1980s and 1990s, but they did represent a significant departure from the sanitized, simplistic version of the past typified by the *Heimatfilm* genre popular in the 1950s.

Plays that dispensed lessons about politics likewise changed over time, often in response to developing Cold War events and circumstances. Portrayals of the righteous fugitive, prominent in programs such as *Die Flucht aus der Hölle*, became less common after the erection of the Berlin Wall in 1961. As the border hardened over the course of the 1960s, television plays increasingly focused on a somewhat different type of hero: the man (or woman) of conscience. This type of character stood firmly against the ills of fascism, be they manifest during the Third Reich or in the "other," false German state. This narrative device proved popular in both East and West, for example, in *Ohne Kampf kein Sieg* (East German) and *Die Kette an deinem Hals* (West). Of no less concern to television producers on both sides was the wave of postwar prosperity, accompanied by an unhealthy fixation on consumption and commercialization. Germans of almost all stripes agreed National Socialism had left behind a gaping spiritual and moral vacuum; the economic miracle in West Germany, which reached its zenith as television became a mass medium in both states, seemed dangerously poised to fill that void. In response, television revealed and cataloged the less savory aspects of consumer culture and hardened materialism. East German critiques of the miracle changed little over the 1960s. West German productions, in contrast, became more pointed in their criticisms over time. Lighthearted comedies such as *Seelenwanderung* thus gave way to more serious pieces such as *Wilhelmsburger Freitag*.

The way German programs represented gender norms and relationships changed much less drastically in the 1950s and 1960s. To be sure, some pieces such as *Die Entscheidung der Lene Mattke* and *Steine im Weg* visualized a new form of liberation and equality for workingwomen. But such depictions occurred more frequently in the GDR, and they did not necessarily become more common in the late 1960s. Another concern to contemporaries was the question of gender roles in the wake of what some saw as the rise of promiscuity in the Third Reich.[4] Television plays on both sides stressed, for example, the nuclear family. Many West German programs furthermore focused on the strict segregation of masculine and feminine tasks. Such representations became all the more urgent in light of the perceived crisis of masculinity after 1945. Huge numbers of POWs returned home bereft of their manhood (as conceived by National Socialist ideals). A new form of masculinity emerged, assertive but more refined.

While German television plays readily depicted non-Germans in the late 1950s and early 1960s, they almost never grappled with questions about tolerance or integration. Early representations of race and ethnicity commonly assumed the characters in question were, in most essential respects, German. In *Mord an Rathenau*, *Das Mädchen Rachel*, and *Die erste Lehre*, for instance, the protagonists appear as secular, well-adjusted Germans who happen to also be Jewish or black. By the second half of the 1960s, teleplays began to seriously engage with the question of otherness and difference. *Gottes zweite Garnitur*, *Wege übers Land*, and *Der Unfall*, for example, explore the complex relationship between race, ethnicity, and identity. The most progressive representations, like *Frei bis zum nächsten Mal*, still attempted to show the absurdity of classifying German citizens, whatever their background, as something other than German. In moral terms, however, later depictions of race and ethnicity sought to teach viewers about concepts such as tolerance and integration.

In a broader sense, moral representational strategies of all types changed from 1956 to 1970. In German television's formative years, program makers assumed a commonly held set of values and givens as they presented lessons to viewers (though this was by no means universal, even in the 1950s). Television plays resolved moral issues by recourse to these assumptions. As television matured, producers came to understand the medium as ideally suited for addressing more contentious societal and moral questions. They moreover assumed some of their programs would not receive universal acclaim but that they were nonetheless necessary. As Germans' values became more diverse and nuanced, so did their television programs.

Whatever the moral arguments' diachronic trajectory, however, the evidence presented here seems to clearly indicate a strong sense of moral renewal and reinvention. Producers, politicians, critics, and viewers sought to craft a new, improved German nation through television plays and moral lessons. Moreover, these lessons assumed many of the same characteristics on both sides of the German border, speaking to common themes such as gender, history, and materialism. The prevalence of this Germany-wide discourse can be overstated, of course. West Germans, in particular, could not universally receive the East German broadcasts because of technical and geographic limitations. But newspaper reviews, interstate authorship of certain plays, and viewer letters demonstrate that television signals readily transgressed the border. The Cold War spurred competition between the two German states, but this did not necessarily mean ideological polarity; on the contrary, Marxists in the East and liberals, conservatives, and socialists in the West in many ways envisioned the same moral universe.

Notes

1. Quoted in Knut Hickethier and Peter Hoff, *Geschichte des deutschen Fernsehens* (Stuttgart: Metzler, 1998), 384.

2. Ibid., 221, 333.
3. Ibid., 250–253.
4. Dagmar Herzog, *Sex after Fascism: Memory and Morality in Twentieth-Century Germany* (Princeton, NJ: Princeton University Press, 2005), 103–105. It is important to note, however, that National Socialists simultaneously promoted traditional gender roles as an aspect of regenerating the German nation.

Epilogue

Many of the programs highlighted in this book were never rebroadcast and therefore almost completely disappeared from the public's consciousness. But not all. The continued popularity of criminal thrillers, for instance, meant the stand-alone Durbridge productions saw multiple reruns and, within the last few years, DVD releases. Some of the early adventure plays, such as *So weit die Füße tragen* and *Nackt unter Wölfen*, have remained an occasional fixture on Saturday afternoons and have even been refilmed in recent years. The East German comedy *Papas neue Freundin* was rebroadcast fourteen times between 1961 and 1989 and is likewise now available for purchase. Indeed, many of the popular East German broadcasts have appeared in a digital format (which was not the case when I started research for this project in 2008). The situation with West German programs is less fortuitous because of tighter licensing restrictions.

The literal afterlife of individual programs (or the lack thereof) does not comprise the totality of the era's legacy, however. For example, one of the most celebrated turning points in the German culture of remembrance vis-à-vis the Holocaust—the translation and broadcasting of the 1978 NBC miniseries *Holocaust*—can be properly understood only in the context of the genre's prominence in the 1960s, and its long-standing willingness to grapple with real social and moral issues. Germans proved receptive to Holocaust memory culture in the late 1970s and 1980s for several reasons. One of these was a familiarity with the format. Even in the 1980s and 1990s, television documentaries about the Holocaust wove together narrative education with illustrative dramatic scenes. The legacy of television fiction can also be seen in the increasing number of plays filmed in a realistic mode. One of the pioneers of moral programming in the 1960s, Günther Rohrbach, made realistic, critical productions a priority when he became head of the WDR television play department in 1968. Films about workers' lives, gritty and uncompromising, proliferated as a result. The notion of the television broadcast as an "event" also maintained its currency for more than a decade after the Golden Age had ended. In 1983, for instance, competing East and West German television plays about Martin Luther, in honor of his five hundredth birthday, generated huge viewership and in some ways represented the pinnacle of that year's celebrations. These films, moreover, had a distinctively moral flavor, a legacy of German television's early years. The dramatic products of the Federal Republic's public service broadcasting system, and those of its now-absorbed competitor from the East, have left lasting shadows on German culture and society.

Appendix 1

TELEVISION PROGRAMS REFERENCED

DFF (East Germany), Chronological

Die Entscheidung der Lene Mattke (Lene Mattke's decision) (6 July 1958)
Nackt unter Wölfen (Naked among wolves) (10 April 1960)
Gerichtet bei Nacht (Tried by night) (11 September 1960)
Die Flucht aus der Hölle (Flight out of hell) (11, 18, 25 October 1960; 1 November 1960)
Steine im Weg (Stones in the way) (16 November 1960)
Papas neue Freundin (Papas new girlfriend) (25 December 1960)
Gewissen in Aufruhr (Conscience up in arms) (5, 7, 10, 12, 14 September 1961)
Das Mädchen Rahel (The girl Rahel) (9 November 1961)
Mord an Rathenau (The murder of Rathenau) (23 November 1961)
Der Schwur des Soldaten Pooley (*The Survivor*, lit. The oath of solider Pooley) (17 December 1961)
Tempel des Satans (Satan's temple) (1 March 1962)
Die Wahnmörderin (The crazed murderess) (9 September 1962)
Die Nacht an der Autobahn (Night on the Autobahn) (16 September 1962)
Geboren unter schwarzen Himmeln (Born under black skies) (21, 23, 25, 28, 30 October 1962)
Das grüne Ungeheuer (The green monster) (16, 18, 20, 22, 23 December 1962)
Fetzers Flucht (Fetzer's flight) (13 December 1962)

Carl von Ossietzky (1 September 1963)
Der Andere neben dir (The other [person] beside you) (27 September 1963)
Die Spur führt in den siebenten Himmel (The tracks lead to the Seventh Heaven) (12, 14, 15, 17, 19 December 1963)
Sommer in Heidkau (Summer in Heidkau) (4 October 1964)
Egon und das achte Weltwunder (Egon and the Eighth World Wonder) (27 December 1964)
Wolf unter Wölfen (*Wolf among Wolves*) (14, 16, 18, 21 March 1965)
Die Mutter und das Schweigen (The mother and the silence) (21 November 1965)
Dr. Schlüter (4, 5, 7, 8 December 1965; 27 March 1966)
Irrlicht und Feuer (Ghost light and fire) (21, 23 August 1966)
Ohne Kampf kein Sieg (Without struggle, no victory) (28, 30 August 1966; 2, 4, 6 September 1966).
Columbus 64 (1, 2, 4, 5 October 1966)
Kleiner Mann—was nun? (*Little Man, What Now?*) (16, 17 December 1967)
Wege übers Land (Ways across the country) (22, 24, 26, 28, 29 September 1968)
Gib acht auf Susi! (Pay attention to Susi!) (25 December 1968)
Krupp und Krause (Krupp and Krause) (5, 7, 9, 12, 14 January 1969)

ARD (West Germany), Chronological

Ein gewisser Judas (A certain Judas) (19 November 1958, SWF)[1]
So weit die Füße tragen (As far as your feet can carry you) (10, 24 February 1959; 10, 24 March 10 1959; 7, 21 April 1959, NWRV)
Die Räuber (The robbers) (26 February 1959, BR)
Waldhausstraße 20 (20 Waldhaus Street) (23 October 1960, NWRV)
Die Einladung (*The Invitation*) (16 January 1961, SWF)
Sansibar (*Flight to Afar*, lit. Zanzibar) (28 December 1961, SDR)
Das Halstuch (The scarf) (3, 5, 7, 10, 13, 17 January 1962, WDR)
Schlachtvieh (*Lambs to the Slaughter*, lit. Slaughter Cattle) (14 February 1963, NDR)
Seelenwanderung: Eine Parabel (Soul migration: A parable) (2 October 1962, WDR)
In der Strafkolonie (*In the Penal Colony*) (27 January 1963, SFB)
Die erste Lehre (The first apprenticeship) (12 March 1963, NDR)
Unterm Birnbaum (*Under the Pear Tree*) (3 October 1963, WDR)
Stadtpark (City Park) (6 October 1963, NDR)
Der Prozess Carl von Ossietzky (The trial of Carl von Ossietzky) (11 February 1964, NDR)

Wilhelmsburger Freitag (A Friday in Wilhelmsburg) (19 March 1964, NDR)
In einem Garten in Aviamo (In a garden in Aviamo) (19 November 1964, NDR)
Der arme Mann Luther (The poor man Luther) (21 January 1965, WDR)
Dr. Murkes gesammelte Nachrufe (Dr. Murkes's collected obituaries) (5 October 1965, HR)
Die Kette an deinem Hals (The chain around your neck) (17 October 1965, NDR)
Melissa (10, 12, 14 January 1966, WDR)
Standgericht (Court martial) (10 October 1966, NDR)
Nach Damaskus (*To Damascus*) (26 November 1966, WDR)
Wie verbringe ich meinen Sonntag? (How do I spend my Sunday?) (16 March 1967, WDR)
Mord in Frankfurt (Murder in Frankfurt) (30 January 1968, WDR)
Der Unfall (The accident) (7 November 1968, WDR)
Alma Mater (27 November 1969, NDR)

ZDF (West Germany), Chronological

Menschen helfen Menschen: Zwei Tage von Vielen (People help people: Two days among many) (11 March 1963)
Das Unbrauchbare an Anna Winters (The incorruptible Anna Winters) (22 May 1963)
Sonderurlaub (Special leave) (17 June 1963)
Nachtzug D 106 (Night train D 106) (17 June 1964)
Ein Ausgangstag (A day off) (12 November 1965)
Der Zauberer Gottes (God's magician) (26 December 1966)
Ein Mann Gottes (A man of God) (22 March 1967)
Das Arrangement (The arrangement) (5 April 1967)
Gottes zweite Garnitur (*The Lonely Conqueror*, lit. God's second string) (13 December 1967)
Peter Schlemihls wundersame Geschichte (*Peter Schlemihl's Miraculous Story*) (25 December 1967)
Frei bis zum nächsten Mal (Free until next time) (23 July 1969)
Reise nach Tilsit (Journey to Tilsit) (16 November 1969)
11 Uhr 20 (11:20) (8, 9, 11 January 1970)
Die Anpassung (The adaptation) (1 May 1970)
Die Beichte (The confessional) (11 November 1970)
Hanna Lessing (9 December 1970)

Note

1. This section includes the regional contributing stations BR, HR, NDR, RB, SDR, SFB, SR, SWF, and WDR, as well as the predecessor station NWRV.

Appendix 2

WEST GERMAN TELEVISION STATIONS

Public Service Stations Broadcasting on the Arbeitsgemeinschaft der Öffentlich-Rechtlichen Rundfunkanstalten der Bundesrepublik Deutschland (Channel 1)

Bayerischer Rundfunk (BR)
Hessischer Rundfunk (HR)
Norddeutscher Rundfunk (NDR)[1]
Radio Bremen (RB)
Süddeutscher Rundfunk (SDR)
Sender Freies Berlin (SFB)[2]
Saarländischer Rundfunk (SR)
Südwestfunk (SWF)
Westdeutscher Rundfunk (WDR)

Notes

1. A previous station encompassing all of Nordrhein-Westfalen split into the NDR and WDR in 1956. Until 1961, they continued a loose cooperation for the most expensive television productions, called the NWRV.
2. The SFB was first added to the ARD in 1958.

Appendix 3

TELEVISION LICENSES/SUBSCRIPTIONS, 1958–1970

German Democratic Republic

1958: 317,604[1]
1959: 593,479
1960: 1,035,030
1961: 1,459,300
1962: 1,892,500
1963: 2,378,900
1964: 2,800,800
1965: 3,216,400
1966: 3,600,400
1967: 3.932,900
1968: 4,173,400
1969: 4,337,000
1970: 4,499,200

Federal Republic of Germany

1958: 2,132,519[2]
1959: 3,375,003
1960: 4,634,762
1961: 5,887,530

1962: 7,213,486
1963: 8,538,570
1964: 10,023,988
1965: 11,379,049
1966: 12,719,599
1967: 13,805,653
1968: 14,958,148
1969: 15,902,578
1970: 16,674,742

Notes

Both German states required a yearly license or subscription to watch programming, even after purchasing a new set.

1. *Statistisches Jahrbuch der Deutschen Demokratischen Republik*, 1959–1971.
2. Knut Hickethier, *Das Fernsehspiel der Bundesrepublik Themen, Form, Struktur, Theorie und Geschichte, 1951–1977* (Stuttgart: J. B. Metzlersche Verlagsbuchhandlung, 1980), 17.

BIBLIOGRAPHY

Archival Sources—Printed

Archiv Müncheberg
  "Steine im Weg, Gelungene Neufassung," 1961
Bundesarchiv (BArch)—Lichterfelde
  Abteilung DDR, Bestand DR 8, Staatliches Komitee für Fernsehen, 1956–1970
Bundesarchiv—Stiftung Archiv der Parteien und Massenorganisationen der DDR (BArch-SAPMO)
  Bestand DY 30/IV, Büro Prof. Albert Norden
Deutsches Rundfunkarchiv (German Broadcasting Archive)—Babelsberg (DRA-B)
  DDR-F 456, Vorbereitende Plan-Materialen, Dramatische Kunst und Kulturpolitik, 1967–1968
  Personalia Archiv
  Pressearchiv
  Schriftgut 161/19/28/4/5
  Schriftgut 161/1/19/28/4/5: "Schatten über Notre Dame," 1966
  Schriftgut "Der Schwur des Soldaten Pooley," 1961
  Schriftgut "Tempel des Satans," 1962
  Schriftgut "Wolf unter Wölfen," 1965
  Schriftgut "Irrlicht und Feuer," 1966
  Schriftgut "Wege übers Land," 1968
Sender Freies Berlin (SFB)—Unterlagen, 1952–1960
Deutsches Rundfunkarchiv—Frankfurt (DRA-F)
  Programmbeirat für das Deutsche Fernsehen (ARD), 1956–1974
  Ständige Fernsehprogrammkonferenz, Fernsehspielprogrammbeirat, Akten A06
Hessischer Rundfunk
  Geschäftsbericht
Historisches Archiv des Südwestfunks (SWF)
  SWF R 09037, Ein Gewisser Judas
Historisches Archiv des Westdeutschen Rundfunks (WDR)
  13005 Klaus von Bismarck, Korrespondenz
  13050 Klaus von Bismarck, Korrespondenz
  13197 Infratest/Infratam
  13380 Hans Joachim Lange, Interne Korrespondenz
  13350 Hans Joachim Lange, Jahresbericht der Fernsehdirektion
  Bibliothek

Jahresbericht des Intendanten
Staatsarchiv Hamburg
    NDR 621–1/144 (Norddeutscher Rundfunk)
Zweites Deutsche Fernsehen Unternehmensarchiv (ZDF)
    Bibliothek
    Pressearchiv
    Schriftgut "Ein Mann Gottes," 1967
    Schriftgut "Das Rendezvous," 1965
    Schriftgut "Gottes Zweite Garnitur," 1967
    Schriftgut "Die Beichte 6335/1001"

Archival Sources—Televisual

Deutsches Rundfunkarchiv—Babelsberg
Institut für Theaterwissenschaft, Freie Universität Berlin
Norddeutscher Rundfunk—Hamburg
Radio Bremen
Südwestfunk (SDR)—Stuttgart (SDR)
Südwestfunk (SWF)—Baden-Baden (SWF)
Zweites Deutsche Fernsehen Unternehmensarchiv (ZDF)

Contemporary Periodicals

Allgemeine Deutsche Nachrichtendienst
Allgemeine Zeitung Mainz
Die Andere Zeitung
Badische Zeitung
Bauernecho
Berliner Zeitung
Bild-Zeitung
Bonner Rundschau
BZ am Abend
Christ und Welt
Deutsche Zeitung
Deutsches Fernsehen Programmdienst
epd—Kirche und Fernsehen
Fernsehdienst
Der Fernsehzuschauer
FF Dabei
Film Spiegel
Frankfurter Hefte
Frankfurter Neue Presse
Freie Erde
Freies Wort
Funk und Fernsehen der DDR
Funk-Korrespondenz
Hannoversche Allgemeine Zeitung

Hannoversche Presse
Hessische Allgemeine
Infratest Wochenbericht
Kieler Nachrichten
Kölnischer Rundschau
Lausitzer Rundschau
Leipziger Volkszeitung
Märkische Volksstimme
Münchner Merkur
National-Zeitung (Berlin)
Die Neue Zeit
Neues Abendland
Neues Deutschland
Ostsee Zeitung
Pressedienst
Rheinpfalzer Zeitung
Sächsische Zeitung
Schweriner Volkszeitung
Statistisches Jahrbuch der Deutschen Demokratischen Republik
Der Spiegel
Süddeutsche Zeitung
Der Tagesspiegel
Television Fernsehspiegel
Theorie und Praxis
Volksstimme
Westdeutsche Allgemeine Zeitung
ZDF Programmdienst
Die Zeit

Published Primary Sources

Ächtler, Norman, and Werner Liersch. "'"Autoren genossen doch eine gewisse Achtung': Ein Gespräch mit Klaus Jörn über die Fallada-Verfilmungen des DDR-Fernsehens." In *Hans Fallada und die literarische Moderne*, edited by Carsten Gausel and Werner Liersch, 207–213. Göttingen: V&R Unipress, 2009.

Apitz, Bruno. *Nackt unter Wölfen*. Berlin: Mitteldeutscher Verlag, 1958.

Baumer, Franz. *Carl von Ossietzky*. Berlin: Colloquium Verlag, 1984.

Bismarck, Klaus von. *Christliche Präsenz in einer Säkularen Rundfunkanstalt*. Cologne: Westdeutscher Rundfunk, 1968.

———. *Der Gesellschaftkritische Auftrag des Fernsehens für das Programm*. Cologne: Westdeutscher Rundfunk, 1969.

———. *Die nationalen Aufgaben von Rundfunk und Fernsehen*. Cologne: Westdeutscher Rundfunk, 1967.

———. *Der Rundfunk und sein Publikum*. Cologne: Westdeutscher Rundfunk, 1967.

Brauchitsch, Manfred von. *Ohne Kampf kein Sieg*. Berlin: Verlag der Nationen, 1964.

Burrichter, Clemens. *Fernsehen und Demokratie*. Bielefeld: Bertelsmann Universitätsverlag, 1970.

Emrich, Ernst. *Wir Schalten um*. Ravensburg: Ravensburger Taschenbücher, 1965.

Erb, Ute. *Die Kette an deinem Hals: Aufzeichnungen eines zornigen jungen Mädchens aus Mitteldeutschland.* Frankfurt: Europäische Verlagsanstalt, 1960.
Greuner, Ruth, and Reinhart Greuner. *Ich stehe links: Carl von Ossietzky über Geist und Ungeist der Weimarer Republik.* Berlin: Buchverlag der Morgen, 1963.
Grossmann, Kurt R. *Ossietzky: Ein deutscher Patriot.* Munich: Kindler Verlag, 1963.
Grün, Max von der. *Irrlicht und Feuer.* Recklinghausen: Paulus Verlag, 1964.
Haseloff, Otto Walter. "Über Wirkungen des Fernsehens." In *Wirkungen des Fernsehens,* edited by Otto Arzt, Bruno Krammer, and Bernhard von Watzdorf, 5–25. Mainz: Zweites Deutsches Fernsehen, 1972.
Hildmann, Gerhard. *Fernsehen—ein Trojanisches Pferd?* Stuttgart: Neske, 1963.
Hirsch, Kurt. *Kommen die Nazis Wieder?* Munich: Verlag Kurt Desch, 1967.
Hochhuth, Rolf. *Der Stellvertreter.* Reinbek: Rowohlt, 1963.
Horkheimer, Max, and Theodor Adorno. *Dialectic of Enlightenment.* Translated by John Cumming. New York: Herder, 1944.
Jolly, Cyril. *The Vengeance of Private Pooley.* London: Heinemann, 1956.
Kaltofen, Günter. *Das Bild das deine Sprache spricht: Fernsehspiele.* Berlin: Henschelverlag, 1962.
Kogon, Eugon. "Gericht und Gewissen." *Frankfurter Hefte* 1, no. 1 (1946): 25–37.
Kniffler, Carter, and Hanna Schlette. *Politische Bildung in der Bundesrepublik.* Neuwied: Hermann Luchterhand Verlag, 1967.
Longolius, Christian, ed. *Fernsehen in Deutschland: Gesellschaftspolitische Aufgaben und Wirkungen eines Mediums.* Mainz: Hase & Koehler Verlag, 1967.
Meinecke, Friedrich. *Die deutsche Katastrophe.* Zürich: Brockhaus, 1946.
Pfemfert, Franz. "Kino als Erzieher." *Das Blaubuch* 23 (1909): 548–550.
Rhotert, Bernt. "Das Fernsehspiel: Der Gang einer Fernsehspielproduktion (1959)." In *Theorie des Fernsehspiels,* edited by Claus Beling, 48–51. Heidelberg: Quelle & Meyer, 1979.
Rohrbach, Günter. "Bildungstheater oder Zeittheater: Probleme der Fernsehspieldramaturgie." In *In guter Gesellschaft: Günter Rohrbach, Texte über Film ud Fernsehen,* edited by Hans Helmut Prinzler. 86–91. Berlin: Bertz & Fischer Verlag, 2008.
SDR Geschäftsbericht 1961. Stuttgart: Süddeutscher Rundfunk, 1961.
Sudermann, Hermann. "Die Reise nach Tilsit." In *Litauische Geschichten.* Stuttgart: J. G. Cotta, 1917.
Wilhelm, Kurt. *Fernsehen: Abenteuer im Neuland.* Cologne: Grotesche Verlagsbuchhandlung, 1965.
Wohlgemuth, Joachim. *Egon und das achte Weltwunder.* Berlin: Verlag Neues Leben, 1963.

Secondary Sources

Anderson, Stewart. "Modern Viewers, Feudal Television Archives: How to Study German *Fernsehspiele* of the 1960s from a National Perspective." *Critical Studies in Television* 5, no. 2 (2010): 91–104.
Augustine, Delores, Heinrich Best, Axel Salheiser, Rüdiger Stutz, and Georg-Wagner Kyora. "Nazi Continuities in Easy Germany." Special section, *German Studies Review* 29, no. 3 (2006): 579–.619.
Bacherer, Karin. *Geschichte, Organisation und Funktion von Infratest.* Munich: Infratest, 1987.
Baranowski, Shelley. *Strength through Joy: Consumerism and Mass Tourism in the Third Reich.* New York: Cambridge University Press, 2004.

Bauerkämper, Arnd. "Collectivization and Memory: Views of the Past and the Transformation of Rural Society in the GDR from 1952 to the early 1960s." *German Studies Review* 25, no. 2 (2002): 213–225.
Bender, Peter. *Deutschlands Wiederkehr: Eine ungeteilte Nachkriegsgeschichte, 1945–1990*. Stuttgart: Klett-Cotta, 2007.
Bergerson, Andrew Stuart. "Listening to the Radio in Hildesheim, 1923–53." *German Studies Review* 24, no. 1 (2001): 83–113.
Betts, Paul. "Manners, Morality, and Civilization: Reflections on Postwar German Etiquette Books." In *Histories of the Aftermath: The Legacies of the Second World War in Europe*, edited by Frank Biess and Robert G. Moeller, 196–214. New York: Berghahn Books, 2010.
Beutelschmidt, Thomas. "Von West nach Ost—von Ost nach West: Irrlicht und Feuer." In *Alltag: Zur Dramaturgie des Normalen im DDR-Fernsehen*, edited by Henning Wrage, 25–114. Leipzig: Leipziger Universitätsverlag, 2006.
Biess, Frank. *Homecomings: Returning POWs and the Legacies of Defeat in Postwar Germany*. Princeton, NJ: Princeton University Press, 2006.
———. "Men of Reconstruction—The Reconstruction of Men: Returning POWs in East and West Germany, 1945–1955." In *Home Front: The Military, War and Gender in Twentieth-Century Germany*, edited by Karen Hagemann and Stefanie Schüler-Springorum, 335–359. New York: Berg, 2002.
Blessing, Benita. *The Antifascist Classroom: Denazification in Soviet-Occupied Germany, 1945–1949*. New York: Palgrave, 2006.
Boxer, Marilyn J., and Jean H. Quataert. *Connecting Spheres: European Women in a Globalizing World, 1500 to the Present*. New York: Oxford University Press, 2000.
Brady, John S., Beverly Crawford, and Sarah Elise Williarty, eds. *The Postwar Transformation of Germany: Democracy, Prosperity and Nationhood*. Ann Arbor: University of Michigan Press, 1999.
Bröckling, Ulrich. "Der 'Dritte Weg' und die 'Dritte Kraft': Zur Konzeption eines sozialistischen Europas in der Nachkriegspublizistik von Walter Dirks." In *Siegerin in Trümmern: Die Rolle der katholischen Kirche in der deutschen Nachkriegsgesellschaft*, edited by Joachim Köhler and Damian van Melis, 70–84. Stuttgart: Kohlhammer, 1998.
Brück, Ingrid, Andrea Guder, Reinhold Viehoff, and Karin Wehn. *Der deutsche Fernsehkrimi: Eine Programm- und Produktionsgeschichte von den Anfängen bis heute*. Stuttgart: Metzler, 2003.
Budde, Gunilla-Friederike. *Frauen arbeiten: weibliche Erwerbstätigkeit in Ost- und Westdeutschland nach 1945*. Göttingen: Vandenhoeck & Ruprecht, 1997.
Buscher, Frank. *The U.S. War Crimes Trial Program in Germany, 1946–1955*. New York: Greenwood Press, 1989.
Carter, Erica. *How German is She? Postwar West German Reconstruction and the Consuming Woman*. Ann Arbor: University of Michigan Press, 1997.
Chin, Rita. *The Guest Worker Question in Postwar Germany*. New York: Cambridge University Press, 2007.
Clark, Mark W. "A Prophet without Honour: Karl Jaspers in Germany, 1945–48." *Journal of Contemporary History* 37, no. 2 (2002): 197–222.
Classen, Christoph. *Bilder der Vergangenheit: die Zeit des Nationalsozialismus im Fernsehen der Bundesrepublik, 1955–1965*. Cologne: Böhlau, 1999.
Crew, David F., ed. *Consuming Germany in the Cold War*. New York: Berg, 2003.
Cuomo, Glenn R. *Career at the Cost of Compromise: Günter Eich's Life and Work in the Years 1933–1945*. Atlanta: Rodopi, 1989.

Davis, Patricia, and Simon Reich. "Norms, Ideology, and Institutions: (En)gendered Retrenchment of *Modell Deutschland?*" In Brady et al., *Postwar Transformation of Germany*, 225–270.
Dittmar, Claudia, and Susanne Vollberg, eds. *Zwischen Experiment und Etablierung: die Programmentwicklung des DDR-Fernsehens, 1958–1963*. Leipzig: Leipziger Universitätsverlag, 2008.
Dussel, Konrad. *Deutsche Rundfunkgeschichte*, 3rd edition. Konstanz: UVK, 2010.
Ehlenbeck, Marianne. *Geschichte des DFDs*. Leipzig: Verlag für die Frau, 1989.
Eley, Michelle René. "Anti-Black Racism in West German Living Rooms: The ZDF Television Film Adaptation of Willi Heinrich's *Gottes zweite Garnitur*." *German Studies Review* 39, no. 2 (2016): 315–334.
Enssle, Manfred J. "Five Theses on Everyday Life after World War II," *Central European History* 26, no. 1 (1993): 1–19.
Epstein, Catherine. "The Production of 'Official Memory' in East Germany: Old Communists and the Dilemmas of Memoir-Writing." *Central European History* 32, no. 2 (1999): 181–201.
Etheridge, Brian C. *Enemies to Allies: Cold War Germany and American Memory*. Lexington: University Press of Kentucky, 2016.
Faulstich, Werner, ed. *Die Kultur der 50er Jahre*. Munich: Wilhelm Fink Verlag, 2002.
———, ed. *Die Kultur der 60er Jahre*. Munich: Wilhelm Fink Verlag, 2003.
Fehrenbach, Heide. "Black Occupation Children and the Devolution of the Nazi Racial State." In *After the Nazi Racial State: Difference and Democracy in Germany and Europe*, edited by Rita Chin, Heide Fehrenbach, Geoff Eley, and Atina Grossmann, 30–54. Ann Arbor: University of Michigan Press, 2009.
———. *Cinema in Democratizing Germany: Reconstructing National Identity after Hitler*. Chapel Hill: University of North Carolina Press, 1995.
———. "The Fight for the 'Christian West': German Film Control, the Churches, and the Reconstruction of Civil Society in the Early Bonn Republic." In Moeller, *West Germany under Construction*, 321–346.
———. "Narrating 'Race' in 1950s' West Germany: The Phenomenon of the *Toxi* Films." In *Not so Plain as Black and White: Afro-German Culture and History, 1890–2000*, edited by Patricia Mazón and Reinhild Steingröver, 136–160. Rochester, NY: University of Rochester Press, 2005.
———. *Race after Hitler: Black Occupation Children in Postwar Germany and America*. Princeton, NJ: Princeton University Press, 2005.
Feinstein, Joshua. *The Triumph of the Ordinary: Depictions of Daily Life in the East German Cinema, 1949–1989*. Chapel Hill: University of North Carolina Press, 2002.
Feinstein, Margarete. "Deutschland über alles? The National Anthem Debate in the Federal Republic of Germany." *Central European History* 33, no. 4 (2000): 505–531.
Fisher, Jaimey. *Disciplining Germany: Youth, Reeducation, and Reconstruction after the Second World War*. Detroit: Wayne State University Press, 2007.
Forner, Sean A. "Reconsidering the 'Unpolitical German': Democratic Renewal and the Politics of Culture in Occupied Germany." *German History* 32, no. 1 (2014): 53–78.
Fox, Thomas C. *Stated Memory: East Germany and the Holocaust*. Rochester, NY: Camden House, 1999.
Frie, Ewald. "The Catholic Church in Germany after the End of the War: its Failure as a Force for Shaping Society." *German History* 13, no. 3 (1995): 373–379.
Führer, Karl Christian, and Corey Ross, eds. *Mass Media, Culture and Society in Twentieth-Century Germany*. London: Palgrave, 2006.

Fulbrook, Mary. *A History of Germany, 1918–2014: A Divided Nation.* Malden, MA: Wiley Blackwell, 2015.
Gregor, Neil. *Haunted City: Nuremberg and the Nazi Past.* New Haven, CT: Yale University Press, 2008.
Grossbölting, Thomas. *SED-Diktatur und Gesellschaft: Bürgertum, Bürgerlichkeit und Entbürgerlichung in Magdeburg und Halle.* Halle: Mitteldeutscher Verlag, 2001.
Gumbert, Heather. *Envisioning Socialism: Television and the Cold War in the German Democratic Republic.* Ann Arbor: University of Michigan Press, 2014.
———. "Split Screens? Television in East Germany, 1952–89." In Führer *Mass Media, Culture and Society*, 146–164.
Hake, Sabine. *Screen Nazis: Cinema, History, and Democracy.* Madison: University of Wisconsin Press, 2012.
Halfmann, Jost. "Two Discourses of Citizenship in Germany: The Differences between Public Debate and Administrative Practice." In Brady et al., *Postwar Transformation of Germany*, 378–398.
Hannig, Nicolai. *Die Religion der Öffentlichkeit: Kirche, Religion und Medien in der Bundesrepublik, 1945–1980.* Göttingen: Wallstein, 2010.
Harsch, Donna. *Revenge of the Domestic: Women, the Family, and Communism in the German Democratic Republic.* Princeton, NJ: Princeton University Press, 2007.
Hearnder, Arthur. *The British in Germany: Educational Reconstruction after 1945.* London: Hamilton, 1978.
Heimann, Thomas. *Bilder von Buchenwald: Die Visualisierung des Antifaschismus in der DDR (1945–1990).* Cologne: Böhlau Verlag, 2005.
Heineman, Elizabeth. "Complete Families, Half Families, No Families at All: Female-Headed Households and the Reconstruction of the Family in the Early Federal Republic." *Central European History* 29, no. 1 (1996): 19–60.
———. *What Difference Does a Husband Make? Women and Marital Status in Nazi and Postwar Germany.* Berkeley: University of California Press, 1999.
Herf, Jeffrey. *Divided Memory: The Nazi Past in the Two Germanys.* Cambridge, MA: Harvard University Press, 1997.
———. "Multiple Restorations: German Political Traditions and the Interpretation of Nazism, 1945–1946." *Central European History* 26, no. 1 (1993): 21–55.
Herzog, Dagmar. *Sex after Fascism: Memory and Morality in Twentieth-Century Germany.* Princeton, NJ Princeton University Press, 2005.
Hickethier, Knut. *Das Fernsehspiel der Bundesrepublik: Themen, Form, Struktur, Theorie und Geschichte, 1951–1977.* Stuttgart: J. B. Metzlersche Verlagsbuchhandlung, 1980.
———. "Das Theater der Bundesrepublk." In Faulstich, *Die Kultur der 50er Jahre*, 35–52.
Hickethier, Knut, and Peter Hoff. *Geschichte des deutschen Fernsehens.* Stuttgart: Metzler, 1998.
Hilgert, Nora. *Unterhaltung, aber sicher! Populäre Repräsentationen von Recht und Ordnung in den Fernsehkrimis* Stahlnetz *und* Blaulicht, *1958/59–1968.* Bielefeld: Transcript, 2013.
Hockenos, Matthew D. *A Church Divided: German Protestants Confront the Nazi Past.* Bloomington: Indiana University Press, 2004.
Hodenberg, Christina von. "Mass Media and the Generation of Conflict: West Germany's Long Sixties and the Formation of a Critical Public Sphere." *Contemporary European History* 15, no. 3 (2006): 367–395.
Höhn, Maria. "Frau im Haus und Girl im Spiegel: Discourse on Women in the Interregnum Period of 1945–1949 and the Question of German Identity." *Central European History* 26, no. 1 (1993): 57–90.

———. *GIs and Fräuleins: The German-American Encounter in 1950s West Germany.* Chapel Hill: University of North Carolina Press, 2002.
Hoff, Peter. "Das 11. Plenum und der Deutsche Fernsehfunk." In *Kahlschlag: Das 11. Plenum des ZK der SED 1965, Studien und Dokumente,* edited by Günter Agle, 105–116. Berlin: Aufbau Taschenbuch, 1991.
Hoffmann, Christhard. "Immigration and Nationhood in the Federal Republic of Germany." In Brady et al., *Postwar Transformation of Germany,* 357–376.
Hong, Young-sun. "Cigarette Butts and the Building of Socialism in East Germany." *Central European History* 35, no. 3 (2002): 327–344.
Hook, Elizabeth Snyder. "Awakening from War: History, Trauma, and Testimony in Heinrich Böll." In *The Work of Memory: New Directions in the Study of German Society and Culture,* eds. Alon Confino and Peter Fritzsche, 136–153. Urbana: University of Illinois Press, 2002.
Jackson, Thaddeus Stephen. *Civilizing the Enemy: German Reconstruction and the Invention of the West.* Ann Arbor: University of Michigan Press, 2006.
Jarausch, Konrad. *After Hitler: Recivilizing Germans, 1945–1995.* Translated by Brandon Hunziker. New York: Oxford University Press, 2006.
Kansteiner, Wulf. *In Pursuit of German Memory: History, Politics, and Television after Auschwitz.* Athens: Ohio University Press, 2006.
Kapczynski, Jennifer M. *The German Patient: Crisis and Recovery in Postwar Culture.* Ann Arbor: University of Michigan Press, 2008.
———. "Postwar Ghosts: 'Heimatfilm' and the Specter of Male Violence. Returning to the Scene of the Crime." *German Studies Review* 33, no. 2 (2010): 305–330.
Kleßmann, Christoph. "Ein stolzes Schiff und krächzende Möwen: Die Geschichte der Bundesrepublik und ihre Kritiker." *Geschichte und Gesellschaft* 4 (1985): 476–494.
Kolinsky, Eva, and Hildegard Maria Nickel. "Introduction." Im *Reinventing Gender: Women in Eastern Germany since Unification,* edited by Eva Kolinsky and Hildegard Maria Nickel, 1–30. New York: Routledge, 2002.
Koonz, Claudia. *The Nazi Conscience.* Cambridge, MA: Belknap Press, 2003.
Kooy, Michael John. *Coleridge, Schiller, and Aesthetic Education.* New York: Palgrave, 2002.
Kucera, David. *Gender, Growth, and Trade: The Miracles Economies of the Postwar Years.* New York: Routledge, 2001.
Kuchler, Christian. *Kirche und Kino: Katholische Filmarbeit in Bayern.* Paderborn: Schöningh Verlag, 2006.
Kurz, Rudi. *Das grüne und andere Ungeheuer: Theater-, Fernseh- und Lebenszeit.* Berlin: Verlag Wiljo Heinen, 2008.
Large, David Clay. "'A Beacon in the German Darkness': The Anti-Nazi Resistance Legacy in West German Politics." *Journal of Modern History* 64, Supplement (1992): 173–186.
———. *Germans to the Front: West German Rearmament in the Adenauer Era.* Chapel Hill: University of North Carolina Press, 1996.
Lee, Woo-Seung. *Das Fernsehen im geteilten Deutschland (1952–1989): Ideologische Konkurrenz und programmliche Kooperation.* Potsdam: Verlag für Berlin-Brandenburg, 2003.
Lindenberger, Thomas. "Looking West: The Cold War and the Making of the Two German Cinemas." In Führer and Ross, *Mass Media, Culture and Society,* 113–128.
Linke, Uli. *German Bodies: Race and Representation after Hitler.* New York: Routledge, 1999.
Logemann, Jan L. *Trams or Tailfins? Public and Private Prosperity in Postwar West Germany and the United States.* Chicago: University of Chicago Press, 2012.
Luhmann, Niklas. *The Reality of the Mass Media.* Translated by Kathleen Cross. Boston: Polity Press, 2000.

Margalit, Gilad. *Germany and its Gypsies: A Post-Auschwitz Ordeal.* Madison: University of Wisconsin Press, 2002.
Mattson, Michelle. "Tatort: The Generation of Public Identity in German Crime Series." *New German Critique* 78 (1999): 161–181.
Meyen, Michael, ed. *Einschalten, Umschalten, Ausschalten? Das Fernsehen im DDR-Alltag.* Leipzig: Leipziger Universitätsverlag, 2003.
Millington, Richard. "'Crime Has No Chance': The Discourse of Everyday Criminality in the East German Press, 1961–1989." *Central European History* 50, no. 1 (2017): 59–85.
Mitchell, Maria. "Materialism and Secularism: CDU Politicians and National Socialism, 1945–1949." *Journal of Modern History* 67, no. 2 (1995): 278–308.
———. *The Origins of Christian Democracy: Politics and Confession in Modern Germany.* Ann Arbor: University of Michigan Press, 2012.
Moeller, Robert G. "Remembering the Past in a Nation of Victims: West German Pasts in the 1950s." In Schissler, *Miracle Years*, 83–109.
———. "What Has 'Coming to Terms with the Past' Meant in Post–World War II Germany? From History to Memory to the 'History of Memory.'" *Central European History* 35, no. 2 (2002): 223–256.
———, ed. *West Germany under Construction: Politics, Society, and Culture in the Adenauer Era.* Ann Arbor: University of Michigan Press, 1997.
Molnar, Christopher A. "Imagining Yugoslavs: Migration and the Cold War in Postwar West Germany." *Central European History* 43, no. 1 (2014): 138–169.
Morina, Christina. "Instructed Silence, Constructed Memory: The SED and the Return of German Prisoners of War as 'War Criminals' from the Soviet Union to East Germany, 1950–1956." *Contemporary European History* 13, no. 3 (2004): 323–343.
Moses, A. Dirk. *German Intellectuals and the Nazi Past.* New York: Cambridge University Press, 2007.
Motekat, Helmut. "Hermann Sudermanns 'Die Reise nach Tilsit.'" In *Hermann Sudermann: Werk und Wirkung,* edited by Walter T. Rix, 9–31. Würzburg: Königshausen & Neumann, 1980.
Müller, Tanja R. *Legacies of Socialist Solidarity: East Germany in Mozambique.* Lanham, MD: Lexington, 2014.
Niven, Bill. *The Buchenwald Child: Truth, Fiction, and Propaganda.* Rochester, NY: Camden House, 2007.
———. "The Sideways Gaze: The Cold War and Memory of the Nazi Past, 1949–1970." In *Divided but Not Disconnected: German Experiences of the Cold War,* edited by Tobias Hochscherf, Christoph Laucht, and Andrew Plowman, 49–62. New York: Berghahn Books, 2013.
Nothnagle, Alan L. *Building the East German Myth: Historical Mythology and Youth Propaganda in the German Democratic Republic, 1945–1989.* Ann Arbor: University of Michigan Press, 1999.
Oertzen, Christine von. *The Pleasure of a Surplus Income: Part-Time Work, Gender Politics, and Social Change in West Germany, 1955–1969.* Translated by Pamela Selwyn. New York: Berghahn Books, 2007.
Olick, Jeffrey K. *The Sins of the Fathers: German, Memory, Method.* Chicago: University of Chicago Press, 2016.
Pence, Katherine. "Labours of Consumption: Gendered Consumers in Post-war East and West German Reconstruction." In *Gender Relations in German History: Power, Agency and Experience from the Sixteenth to the Twentieth Century,* edited by Lynn Abrams and Elizabeth Harvey, 211–238. Durham, NC: Duke University Press, 1997.

———. "'A World in Miniature': The Leipzig Trade Fairs in the 1950s and East German Consumer Citizenship." In Crew, *Consuming Germany in the Cold War*, 21–49.

Perry, Joe. "Healthy for Family Life: Television, Masculinity, and Domestic Modernity during West Germany's Miracle Years." *German History* 25, no. 4 (2007): 560–595.

Poiger, Uta. *Jazz, Rock, and Rebels: Cold War Politics and American Culture in a Divided Germany.* Berkeley: University of California Press, 2000.

Puaca, Brian M. *Learning Democracy: Education Reform in West Germany, 1945–1965.* New York: Berghahn Books, 2009.

Reich, Simon. *The Fruits of Fascism: Postwar Prosperity in Historical Perspective.* Ithaca, NY: Cornell University Press, 1990.

Reichel, Peter. *Erfundene Erinnerung: Weltkrieg und Judenmord in Film und Theater.* Munich: Carl Hanser Verlag, 2004.

Reid, Susan. "Cold War in the Kitchen: Gender and the De-Stalinization of Consumer Taste in the Soviet Union under Kruschev." *Slavic Review* 61, no. 2 (2002): 211–252.

Rinke, Andrea. *Images of Women in East German Cinema, 1972–1982: Socialist Models, Private Dreamers and Rebels.* Lewiston: Edwin Mellen Press, 2006.

Roseman, Mark. "The Organic Society and the 'Massenmenschen': Integrating Young Labour in the Ruhr Mines, 1945–58." *German History* 8, no. 2 (1990): 163–194.

Sabrow, Martin. "Der Apfel von Weibelskirchen. Plädoyer für einen entgrenzten Blick auf die deutsche Teilungsgeschichte." In *Mehr als eine Erzählung: Zeitgeschichtliche Perspektiven auf die Bundesrepublik,* edited by Frank Bajohr, Anselm Doering-Manteuffel, Claudia Kemper, and Detlef Siegfried, 69–80. Göttingen: Wallstein, 2016.

Sackett, Robert. "Pictures of Atrocity: Public Discussion of *Der gelbe Stern* in Early 1960s West Germany." *German History* 24, no. 4 (2006): 526–561.

Saldern, Adelheid von. "*Volk* and *Heimat* Culture in Radio Broadcasting during the Period of Transition from Weimar to Nazi Germany." *Journal of Modern History* 76, no. 2 (2004): 312–346.

Schäffner, Gerhard. "'Das Fenster in die Welt': Fernsehen in den fünfziger Jahren." In Faulstich *Die Kultur der 50er Jahre,* 91–102.

Scheibe, Moritz. "Auf der Suche nach der demokratischen Gesellschaft." In *Wandlungsprozesse in Deutschland: Belastung, Integration, Liberalisierung 1945–1980,* edited by Ulrich Herbert, 245–277. Göttingen: Wallstein, 2002.

Schildt, Axel. "Der Beginn des Fernsehzeitalters: Ein neues Massenmedium setzt sich durch." In Schildt and Sywottek, *Modernisierung im Wiederaufbau,* 477–492.

———. *Zwischen Abendland und Amerika: Studien zur westdeutschen Ideenlandschaft der 50er Jahre.* Munich: Oldenbourg Verlag, 1992.

Schildt, Axel, and Arnold Sywottek, eds. *Modernisierung im Wiederaufbau: Die westdeutsche Gesellschaft der 50er Jahre.* Bonn: Verlag J. H. W. Dietz, 1993.

Schissler, Hanna, ed. *The Miracle Years: A Cultural History of West Germany, 1949–1968.* Princeton, NJ: Princeton University Press, 2000.

Schlosser, Nicholas. *Cold War on the Airwaves: The Radio Propaganda War against East Germany.* Urbana: University of Illinois Press, 2015.

Schneider, Irmela. *Film, Fernsehen & Co: Zur Entwicklung des Spielfilms in Kino und Fernsehen.* Heidelberg: Carl Winter, 1990.

Schneider, Ute. *Hausväteridylle oder sozialistische Utopie? Die Familie im Recht der DDR.* Cologne: Böhlau, 2004.

Schreiter, Katrin. "Revisiting Morale under the Bombs: The Gender of Affect in Darmstadt, 1942–1945." *Central European History* 50, no. 3 (2017): 347–374.

Schroeder, Steven M. *To Forget It All and Begin Anew: Reconciliation in Occupied Germany, 1944–1954.* Toronto: University of Toronto Press, 2013.
Schwab, Ulrike. *Fiktionale Geschichtssendungen im DDR Fernsehen (II): Analyse und Dokumentation.* Leipzig: Leipziger Universitätsverlag, 2008.
Schwartz, Michael. "Frauenpolitik im doppelten Deutschland: Die Bundesrepublik und die DDR in den 1970er Jahren." In *Lieschen Müller wird politisch: Geschlecht, Staat und Partizipation im 20. Jahrhundert,* edited by Christine Hikel, Nicole Kramer, and Elisabeth Zellmer, 27–40. Munich: R. Oldenbourg Verlag, 2009.
Simons, Rotraut. *"Der Pfarrer bleibt vom Bild her problematisch": Ausgewählte Dokumente der Auseinandersetzung mit der Darstellung von Christen in Kinofilmen in der DDR 1956 bis 1989/1990.* Berlin: Staat-Kirche E.v., 2003.
Slobodian, Quinn. *Comrades of Color: East Germany in the Cold War World.* New York: Berghahn Books, 2015.
Spicka, Mark E. "City Policy and Guest Workers in Stuttgart, 1955–1973." *German History* 31, no. 3 (2013): 345–365.
Staadt, Jochen, Tobias Voigt, and Stefan Wolle. *Operation Fernsehen: Die Stasi und die Medien in Ost und West.* Göttingen: Vandenhoeck & Ruprecht Verlag, 2008.
Steinmetz, Rüdiger. *Freies Fernsehen: Das erste privat-kommerzielle Fernsehprogramm in Deutschland.* Munich: UVK Medien, 1996.
Steinmetz, Rüdiger, and Reinhold Viehoff, eds. *Deutsches Fernsehen Ost: Eine Programmgeschichte des DDR-Fernsehens.* Berlin: Verlag für Berlin-Brandenburg, 2008.
Stephenson, Jill. *Women in Nazi Society.* London: Croom Helm, 1975.
Stern, Frank. *The Whitewashing of the Yellow Badge: Antisemitism and Philosemitism in Postwar Germany.* New York: Pergamon, 1992.
Stiehler, Hans-Jörg. "Das Tal der Ahnungslosen: Erforschung der TV-Rezeption zur Zeit der DDR." In *Medienrezeption seit 1945: Forschungsbilanz und Forschungsperspektiven,* edited by Walter Klingler, Gunnar Roters, and Maria Gerhards, 193–208. Baden-Baden: Nomos Verlag, 1999.
Stitziel, Judd. "On the Seam between Socialism and Capitalism: East German Fashion Shows." In Crew, *Consuming Germany in the Cold War,* 51–86.
Suhr, Elke. *Carl von Ossietzky: Eine Biographie.* Cologne: Kiepenheuer & Witsch, 1988.
Sywottek, Arnold. "From Starvation to Excess? Trends in the Consumer Society from the 1940s to the 1970s." In Schissler, *Miracle Years,* 341–358.
———. "Wege in die 50er Jahre." In Schildt and Sywottek, *Modernisierung im Wiederaufbau,* 13–39.
Tent, James F. *Mission on the Rhine.* Chicago: University of Chicago Press, 1982.
Thomas, Nick. *Protest Movements in 1960s West Germany: A Social History of Dissent and Democracy.* New York: Berg, 2003.
Tompkins, David. "Orchestrating Identity: Concerts for the Masses and the Shaping of East German Society." *German Studies Review* 30, no. 3 (2012): 412–428.
Uka, Walter. "Modernisierung im Wiederaufbau oder Restauration? Der bundesdeutsche Film der 50er Jahre." In Faulstich, *Die Kultur der 50er Jahre,* 71–89.
Voigt, Karl Heinz. *Freikirchen in Deutschland (19. und 20. Jahrhundert).* Leipzig: Evangelische Verlagsanstalt, 2004.
Weckel, Ulrike. "The *Mitläufer* in Two German Postwar Films: Representation and Critical Reception." *History and Memory* 15, no. 2 (2003): 64–93.
Wegner, Gregory. "In the Shadow of the Third Reich: The 'Jugendstunde' and the Legitimation of Anti-Fascist Heroes for East German Youth." *German Studies Review* 19, no. 1 (1996): 127–146.

Weinke, Annette. *Die Verfolgung von NS-Tätern im geteilten Deutschland: Vergangenheitsbewältigungen 1949–1969, oder: Eine deutsch-deutsche Beziehungsgeschichte im Kalten Krieg.* Paderborn: Ferdinand Schöningh, 2002.
Welch, David. "Political Re-education and the use of Radio in Germany after 1945." *Historical Journal of Film, Radio, and Television* 13, no. 1 (1993): 75–81.
———. "Priming the Pump of German Democracy: British 'Re-education' Policy in Germany after the Second World War." In *Reconstruction in Postwar Germany: British Occupation Policy and the Western Zones,* edited by Ian D. Turner, 215–238. New York: Berg, 1989.
Wiesen, S. Jonathan. *Creating the Nazi Marketplace: Commerce and Consumption in the Third Reich.* New York: Cambridge University Press, 2011.
Wildt, Michael. "Privater Konsum in Westdeutschland in den 50er Jahren." In Schildt and Sywottek, *Modernisierung im Wiederaufbau,* 275–290.
Willett, Ralph. *The Americanization of Germany, 1945–1949.* New York: Routledge, 1989.
Wolfgram, Mark A. *"Getting History Right": East and West German Collective Memories of the Holocaust and War.* Lewisburg, PA: Bucknell University Press, 2011.
Wyneken, JonDavid K. "Driving Out the Demons: German Churches, the Western Allies, and the Internationalization of the Nazi Past, 1945–1952." PhD dissertation, Ohio University, 2007.
Zatlin, Jonathan R. *The Currency of Socialism: Money and Political Culture in East Germany.* New York: Cambridge University Press, 2007.

Index

1968 student movements, 10, 20, 55, 81, 112, 113, 169

Abendland (Western European Christendom), 4, 107, 158
Adameck, Heinz, 7, 20, 32, 38–39, 77, 96
Adenauer, Konrad, 4, 6, 42, 63, 99, 107
 and 1960 Constitutional Court, 16, 108
Adolf Eichmann Trial, 34, 35, 39, 41, 45, 55, 177
Africans, 70, 162
 Afro-Germans, 157, 158, 167, 169, 179, 186
 African Americans, 18, 144, 156, 157, 158, 163–164, 167, 168, 170
Ahlsen, Leopold, 42–43, 44, 46, 168
Aktion Ochsenkopf (Operation Ox Head), 34
Algeria, 46, 70, 76
American. *See also* African Americans; United States military
 capitalism, 72, 99, 117
 consumers and consumer culture, 7, 96, 97, 98, 99, 108
 imperialism, 72
 racism, 169 (*see also* African Americans)
 television model, 15, 16, 108
 television stations, 12, 14
Andere neben dir, Der (The other [person] beside you), 162–163
Anpassung, Die (The adaptation), 171–173, 175, 179
anti-communism, 5, 37, 64, 73, 82, 165, 178
anti-Fascism (anti-Fascists), 33–34, 36, 40, 44–48, 55, 73, 124, 140, 178, 185. *See also* fascism

 myth of non-Fascist German officer, 47–48
anti-materialism. *See* materialism, anti-materialism
Apitz, Bruno, 37, 38, 39, 177
ARD (Association of Public Broadcasters of the Federal Republic of Germany), 16, 17, 18, 54, 76, 86, 88, 98, 103, 109, 133, 161, 165, 171, 184
Arrangement, Das (The arrangement), 145–146, 148
Atheism, 69, 79
Auschwitz, 33, 34, 35, 47, 51–52, 53, 54, 56, 166. *See also* concentration camps
Ausgangstag, Ein (A day off), 144

Bauer, Josef Martin, 67–68
Bauernecho, 72, 144
Bayerischer Rundfunk (BR), 14
Becker, Karl, 109
Beichte, Die (The confessional), 112–114, 116, 156
Benjamin, Walter, 97
Berlin Wall, 32, 33, 36, 48, 62, 66, 73, 86, 124, 127, 185
Berliner Zeitung, 32, 137
Bild-Zeitung, 19, 53, 65
bishop, 5n24, 21, 98, 108
 Catholic, 108
 Protestant, 68, 98
Bismarck, Klaus von, 7, 20, 35, 61, 109
Blaulicht (Bluelight), 86
Brecht, Bertolt, 9, 75, 97
Buchenwald, 37–38, 39, 40, 44, 65. *See also* concentration camps

capitalism, 2, 3, 4, 34, 97, 100, 101. *See also*
American, capitalism
and the FRG, 3, 4, 99
GDR propaganda against, 36, 70, 73, 76, 77, 80, 99, 102, 108, 136
Carl von Ossietzky (play), 2–3. *See also* Ossietzky, Carl von
Catholicism (Catholic), 20, 34, 37, 41, 64, 98, 100–101, 107, 108, 114, 155, 161
Catholic Broadcasting Committee (Katholischer Rundfunkarbeit), 109
Catholic Center Party, 107
Dirks, Walter, 4
Frankfurter Hefte (see *Frankfurter Hefte*)
Funk-Korrespondenz (see *Funk-Korrespondenz*)
and the Holocaust, 161–162
priest, 112, 113
Censors (Censorship), 9, 11, 21, 31–33, 38, 39, 108, 109, 122–123, 135
Central America, 71–73
Christianity (Christian), 19, 21, 41–42, 51, 79, 80, 97–98, 106–112, 114, 116, 127, 129, 131, 154, 158, 161, 166. See also *Abendland*; Christlich Demokratische Union; denazification, re-Christianization)
Christlich Demokratische Union (Christian Democratic Union of Germany—CDU), 63, 96, 98, 99, 107–109, 126, 137, 158
Cold War, 1, 6–8, 11, 14, 20, 32, 37, 46, 61, 63–66, 69, 70, 73, 76, 78–80, 86–89, 96, 98, 100, 131–132, 138, 140, 147, 158, 185–186
collective memory, 4, 10, 34
East Germany, 61–63, 63–67, 69, 70–71, 71–73, 74–76, 77–78, 79–80, 82–85, 86–87
Ossietzky, Carl von, 2
West Germany, 34, 37–38, 41, 43–44
Columbus 64, 128–129, 140
communism (ideology), 3, 5, 15, 20, 33, 36, 48, 63, 69, 71, 75, 83, 84–85, 86, 109, 116, 129, 135, 160. *See also* anti-communism
communist vs. capitalist debates, 20, 34, 36, 65, 76, 77–79, 99
and family life, 128–129

and gender, 125, 139–140
narrative of resistance to National Socialism, 5, 37–40, 42–43, 44–46, 64–65, 73, 82, 157, 165–166, 178
Communist Party (Sozialistische Einheitspartei Deutschlands—Socialist Unity Party of Germany—SED), 1, 2, 4, 5, 14, 15, 18, 31–32, 34, 37–38, 42–43, 44, 45–46, 48, 52, 62–63, 65, 67, 69, 73, 75, 77, 79, 87, 117, 123–124, 135–136, 140, 141–143, 159, 178, 183. *See also* East Germany; Russia; Soviet Union
Communist International Camp Committee (ILK), 36
and family life, 127
and religion, 98, 114–115
concentration camps, 37, 49, 55, 84, 154, 166. *See also* Auschwitz, Buchenwald
consumerism. *See* American, consumers and consumer culture
Christianity as antidote to, 115–118
East German consumer culture, 96, 183
East German critiques of West German consumer culture, 100
West German consumer culture, 10, 15, 95–99, 101, 106–107, 185
women as consumers, 126–127, 140

Da lacht der Bär (The laughing bear), 31, 95
Demokratischer Frauenbund Deutschlands (Democratic Women's League of Germany), 127
denazification, 6, 7, 88–89, 116
German reckoning with, 4–7, 112–113
political reeducation, 6, 13, 20, 22, 63–65, 74, 76, 88–89
re-Christianization of Germany, 4, 98, 107, 129, 157
Deutsche Film Aktiengesellschaft ([East] German Film Company—DEFA), 38
Deutscher Fernsehfunk (DFF), 2, 12, 13, 14, 15, 17, 18, 21, 31, 32, 34, 36–39, 44, 45, 46, 69–71, 76–77, 82–83, 86, 89, 96, 99–100, 101, 114, 115, 122–123, 128, 130, 133–138, 140–141, 143, 147–148, 159, 162, 163, 165, 167, 177, 179

Index • 211

Dr. Murkes gesammelte Nachrufe (Dr. Murkes's collected obituaries), 93
Dr. Schlüter, 18, 19, 31–35, 46, 48–49, 54–55, 83, 94, 184
Durbidge, Francis, 17, 19, 87, 188

East German/West German Divide, 1, 6, 11–12, 15, 20, 34–35, 42, 66–67, 74–76, 83, 86–87, 88, 98, 101, 128, 146
   ideological gulf between, 5–6
   myth of isolation, 12
East Germany (German Democratic Republic [GDR])
   Christianity in, 114–116
   criticism of consumerism, 96–99, 185
   East Berlin, 3, 71, 81, 83
   and family life, 129, 132, 134
   and gender, 124–128, 135–138
   materialism, 99–103, 117–118
   postwar historical consciousness in, 31–36, 37–38, 40, 46–49, 55
   and postwar integration, 157–162, 167, 176–179
   television, 2–4, 8, 12–13, 15–20, 183, 186, 188
   and women, 140, 142–144, 147–148
economic miracle, 21, 88, 94, 98, 102–104, 115–117, 185
Egel, Karl-Georg, 31, 32–34, 48–49
Egon und das achte Weltwunder (Egon and the Eighth World Wonder), 128, 137
Einladung, Die (*The Invitation*), 74–76
Entscheidung der Lene Mattke, Die (Lene Mattke's decision), 141–143, 148, 185
epd—Kirche und Fernsehen, 19, 42, 80, 81, 94, 110, 111, 165, 167, 168, 176
Erste Lehre, Die (The first apprenticeship), 167–168, 179, 185
Evangelischer Pressedienst (*epd*), 3, 19, 135

Fallada, Hans, 12, 134–136
Fascism (Fascists), 2, 4–5, 35, 38, 62–63, 65, 70, 72, 76, 88, 101, 126, 128–129, 153, 156, 160. *See* anti-fascism
Fassbinder, Rainer Werner, 156, 158, 170
feminism, 147–148
Fetzers Flucht (Fetzer's flight), 17, 73

Flucht aus der Hölle, Die (Flight out of hell), 46, 63, 70–71, 72, 73, 76, 185
Fontane, Theodor, 110
France (French), 14, 44, 46, 71, 83, 107, 114, 158, 168–169, 175
French Foreign Legion, 46, 70
Frankfurt, 17, 46, 51, 70. See also *Mord in Frankfurt*
   Auschwitz trials, 34, 35, 52, 53, 54, 56
Frankfurter Hefte, 4, 97
Frauenredaktion (Mrs. Editors), 128, 141, 143, 147
Frei bis zum nächsten Mal (Free until next time), 153–157, 186
Freie Deutsche Jugend (Free German Youth—FDJ), 34
Funk Korrespondenz, 19, 42, 43, 78, 81, 111, 161, 162, 168, 176

Geboren unter schwarzen Himmeln (Born under black skies), 15, 77
Geißler, Christian, 20, 80–82, 106
Genocide, 112, 154
Gerichtet bei Nacht (Tried by night), 115
German Reconstruction after Nazism, 4–10, 20–22, 76, 98. *See also* denazification
   and armed forces, 47–48, 63
   "correct" politics, 66, 100, 169
   Europeanization, 22
   and gender, chapter 4, 126–127, 129–130, 134, 140
   of German identity, 116
   Germany a victim of Hitler's crimes, 34
   modernization, 4
   morality, 3–6, 15, 20, 31, 78, 85–86, 162–163
   race, 6, chapter 5, 172, 176, 178
   re-Christianization of Germany (*see* denazification, re-Christianization of Germany)
   sexuality, 6, chapter 4
Gewisser Judas, Ein (A certain Judas), 111, 116
Gewissen in Aufruhr (Conscience up in arms), 12, 15, 32, 46, 61–64, 67, 76–78, 82, 84
Gib acht auf Susi! (Pay attention to Susi!), 117–118, 148

Gottes zweite Garnitur (*The Lonely Conqueror*), 6, 18, 144, 168–169, 179–180, 186
Great Britain (British), 16, 17, 68, 107, 125
   British Broadcasting System (BBC), 14
   consumers, 7
   model for television, 15
   soldiers, 44–45
Greifswald, 46, 61, 62, 64
Gröhl, Wilhelm, 124, 142
Grün, Max von der, 101, 103, 104
grüne Ungeheuer, Das (the green monster *or* the green pope), 71–73, 141
Gypsies, 41, 154–155

Hädrich, Rolf, 7, 35, 51–55
Halstuch, Das (The scarf), 8, 17
Hamburg, 12, 13, 15, 40, 70, 167, 176
Heimatfilm, 10, 43, 133–134, 184
Hessischer Rundfunk (HR), 14
historical consciousness, 31–36, 37–38, 40, 46–49, 55
Hitler, Adolf, 3, 9, 68, 83, 97, 126, 127, 128, 153, 156, 166
   assassination attempt in *Ohne Kampf kein Sieg*, 82, 84
Hitler Youth, 50, 104
Hochhuth, Rolf, 41, 161
Holocaust, 20, 22, 34, 43, 44, 45, 47, 55, 84, 112, 153, 161–162, 166, 188–189. *See also* National Socialism
homosexuals, 22, 127
Honecker, Erich, 31, 96, 148, 183
Hubalek, Claus, 79, 80, 163, 164
Hübner, Achim, 31, 33

In der Strafkolonie (In the Penal Colony, 1963 television program), 54
In einem Garten in Aviamo (In a garden in Aviamo), 156, 163–165
industrialists, 21, 34, 36
Infratest, 18–19, 105, 162, 169, 170, 172, 174, 176
integration, 44, 147, 155–158, 165–168, 171, 179, 185–186
international cooperation, 35, 40, 45
interracial relationships, 144, 157
intolerance. *See* tolerance

Irrlicht und Feuer (Ghost light and fire), 14, 101–104

Jews (Jewish), 34–36, 37, 39–41, 42–43, 47, 49, 51, 53, 61, 82, 84, 97, 115, 128, 153, 157, 159–162, 165–167, 177–179, 186. *See also* Holocaust
Jung-Ahlsen, Kurt, 44, 46

Kaltofen, Günter, 8, 77
Katholischer Rundfunkarbeit (Catholic Broadcasting Committee), 109
Katzelmacher, 158, 170
Kette an deinem Hals, Die (The chain around your neck), 79–80, 88, 144, 185
Kleiner Mann—was nun? (*Little Man, What Now?*), 134, 135
Kollegium des deutschen Fernsehfunks (German Television Council), 147, 177
Krimis (criminal thrillers), 85–88
Krüger, Answald, 3, 41, 42, 50, 168
Krupp und Krause (Krupp and Krause), 55
Kurz, Rudi, 7, 71–72, 83–84, 100–101, 141

letters from viewers, 5, 13, 14, 17–18, 40, 46, 49, 72, 85, 102–103, 109, 128, 143–145, 15, 170, 186
Lutheran, 64, 109
Luther, Martin, 109, 189
Luxembourg, Rosa, 141, 159

Mädchen Rahel, Das (The girl Rahel), 165, 166–167, 179, 185
man or woman of conscience, 50, 62, 67, 76–77, 80–82, 85, 185
Marxism (Marxist), 5–6, 15–16, 21, 40, 84–85, 99–103, 114–115, 118, 124, 135–137, 140, 143, 147, 159, 186
Marxism-Leninism, 40, 137, 143
Masculinity, 21, 64, 68–69, 72, 125, 127–128, 133–134, 138–140, 141, 142–143, 146, 185
   emasculation, 73, 125
   Nazi hypermasculinity, 68, 127, 139
Materialism, 10–11, 20–21, 36, 98, 102–103, 107, 115, 117, 143, 185–186. *See also* American, consumers and consumer culture

anti-materialism, 20–21, 97, 98–99, 108–109, 112–114
Matray, Maria, 3, 42, 50, 168
Mechow, Ulf von, 153, 156
Meischner, Dieter, 55, 145–146
Melissa (1966), 87
Menschen helfen Menschen: Zwei Tage von Vielen (People Help People: Two Days out of Many), 49, 161–162
Ministry for State Security (Stasi), 48, 132, 183
moral dilemma, 50, 74, 86, 166, 117, 134, 177
Mord an Rathenau (The murder of Rathenau), 159–160, 185–186
Mord in Frankfurt (Murder in Frankfurt), 51–56, 184
Mörder sind unter uns, Die (Murderers Among Us), 6
Müller-Stahl, Armin, 39, 139
Müncheberg, Hans, 122, 124

Nach Damaskus (*To Damascus*), 99
Nacht an der Autobahn, Die (Night on the Autobahn), 86–87
Nackt unter Wölfen (Naked among wolves), 37–40, 42, 44, 177, 184, 188
Nachtzug D 106 (Night train D 106), 73–74
National Socialism (Nazi), 1, 31, 35, 43, 44, 46, 48, 49, 52, 64–65, 67, 72, 76, 81, 88, 97–98. *See also* Concentration camps; Denazification; German Reconstruction after Nazism; Hitler, Adolf; Holocaust
  Communist Party (*see* Communist Party, resistance to National Socialism narratives)
  defeat of, 21, 40, 44, 112, 125–127
  Gestapo, 42, 45, 76, 84, 110, 161, 163, 165, 184
  masculinity and, 139–140, 185
  moral reckoning with, 37–45, 51, 53, 55–56, 61
  and Prussian militarism, 3
  racism and, 22, 153, 156–158, 161, 162, 165–166, 169, 170, 176, 178
  resistance to (*see* Communist Party, resistance to National Socialism narratives)
  sick man narrative, 4
  and television, 9
  trials of leaders, 6, 34, 35, 52–54, 56
  and women, 125, 126, 128–129
nationalism, 48, 51, 112, 156, 167
North Atlantic Trade Organization (NATO), 11, 44, 47, 66, 89, 103, 116, 131, 132, 163, 167
Neues Deutschland, 19, 32, 40, 102–103, 144
New German Cinema Movement, 56, 156
Norddeutscher Rundfunk (NDR), 3, 15, 17, 40, 50, 79, 81, 104, 109, 144, 163, 167
Norden, Albert, 31, 69, 87, 124
Nordwestdeutscher Rundfunk (NWDR), 8, 14, 15, 16
Nuclear family, 15, 104–105, 109, 126–132, 147, 185.

Ohne Kampf kein Sieg (Without struggle, no victory), 82–85, 88, 185
Ossietzky, Carl von, 1–4

Pacifism (Pacifist), 1, 2, 66, 88
Papas neue Freundin (Papa's new girlfriend), 117, 129–130, 188
Peter Schlemihls wundersame Geschichte (*Peter Schlemihl's Miraculous Story*), 94
Poland (Poles), 17, 35, 40, 154, 177–178
Prisoners of War (POW), 10, 33, 34, 44–45, 47, 62–64, 67–69, 81, 88, 127, 185
prime-time television, 5, 14
Programming, 7, 9, 11–12, 15–17, 20–21, 32, 39, 55, 65, 68, 99, 171, 179, 184, 189
  hours, 11
  radio, 21
  religious, 97, 113
  women's, 141, 143, 147–148
propaganda, 9, 14, 31–32, 65, 79–80, 87, 103, 105, 117, 124, 129, 159
Protestantism (Protestants), 19, 20, 34, 37, 40, 41, 42, 68, 94, 98, 107–109, 114

Radio Bremen (RB), 14
race (racial), 6, 11, 22, chapter 5, 153, 156–159, 185–186
Red Army, 46, 62, 69

Redemption story, 31, 33–34, 35–36, 42, 46, 47–49, 50–51, 53–56, 64, 69, 82, 142, 184
Reise nach Tilsit (Journey to Tilsit), 132–134
resistance narratives, 20, 35, 37, 50, 55–56, 62
   Christian, 107
   Communist resistance to National Socialism, 5, 36, 37–44, 46, 64, 72, 73, 82, 123, 165, 178
   figures, 3
   viewer, 61
Rohrbach, Günter, 7–8, 54, 189
role model, 21, 45, 66, 109–111, 115, 124, 143–144, 178
Roma, 154. *See also* gypsies
righteous fugitive (fugitive), 66–67, 67–68, 74, 76, 88, 185
Russia (Russians), 13, 14, 40, 47–48, 55, 62, 67, 68, 124, 177
   Moscow, 4, 15, 68
   Soldiers, 69

Saarländischer Rundfunk (SR), 15
Sächsische Zeitung, 135, 163
Sakowski, Helmut, 7, 123–125, 141–144, 177
Sansibar (Flight to Afar), 42–43
Schiller, Friedrich, 8–9, 99
Schlachtvieh (Lambs to the Slaughter), 17, 80–81, 109
Schwur des Soldaten Pooley, Der (*The Survivor*), 44–45
Seelenwanderung (Soul migration), 93–97, 99–100, 106, 109, 185
Sender Freies Berlin (SFB), 13, 15, 54
Siberia, 33, 48, 55, 63, 67–69
So weit die Füße tragen (As far as your feet can carry you), 12, 63–64, 66–69, 71–72, 76–77, 128, 140, 188
socialists (socialism), 5, 20, 34, 37, 44, 45, 48, 54, 63, 65–66, 71–73, 78, 82, 85, 86, 96, 100, 114, 116, 123, 125, 137–139, 140–141, 143, 158, 159, 163, 167, 186. *See also* East Germany; National Socialism (Nazi)
Sommer in Heidkau (Summer in Heidkau), 15, 142–144
Sonderurlaub (Special leave), 77–78, 173

Soviet Union (USSR), 12, 14, 15, 33, 46, 64, 67– 69, 72, 101, 125. *See also* Russia
   POW camps, 62, 68, 88
   productions, 11, 124
   troops, 64, 123
   zone, 14, 15, 38, 65, 157
Sozialdemokratische Partei Deutschlands (Social Democratic Party of Germany—SPD), 2, 16, 37, 50, 97–98, 108, 135–136
Spiegel, Der 1, 75
Spur führt in den siebenten Himmel, Die (The tracks lead to the Seventh Heaven), 100
Staatliches Komitee für Fernsehen (State Committee for Television), 114
Stadtpark (City park), 78, 104–106, 140
Stahlnetz (Steel net *or* Dragnet), 86–87
Standgericht (Court martial), 50–51, 54, 168
station directors, 7, 8, 10, 32, 96, 172, 177
Stauffenberg, Claus von, 83
   conspiracy to assassinate Hitler, 37, 82, 84
Steine im Weg (Stones in the way), 104, 123–124, 130, 140–143, 148, 185
Stellvertreter, Der (*The Representative*), 41
Stellvertreter scandal, 116, 161–162
Stern, Katja, 40, 125, 144
student activists. *See* 1968 student movements
Süddeutscher Rundfunk (SDR), 14, 42, 72, 78
Sudermann, Hermann, 132–133
Südwestfunk (SWF), 14, 74, 99, 103, 109, 111

Tagebuch einer Verlorenen (Diary of a Lost Girl), 9
Tagesspiegel, Der, 137, 171
Tal der Ahnungslosen ("Valley of the Clueless"), 12
Tatort, 86, 88
Tempel des Satans (Satan's temple), 77
Thein, Ulrich, 139, 162, 163
Third Reich, 20, 50, 63, 68, 104, 115, 128, 131, 184–185
   anti-Semitism, 76
   crimes of, 34–35
   defeat of, 21, 112, 125

and gender, 125–127
and materialism, 78, 82, 99
media and, 9, 49, 98, 157
racial imaginary of, 159, 169, 180
resistance to, 37, 44, 55
sick man metaphor, 4
similarities portrayed by FGR between the GDR and, 81–83, 89
Tinzmann, Julius, 131, 134
tolerance (intolerance), 3, 4, 22, 35, 128
racial tolerance, 133–137, 160, 163, 164–166, 169–170, 173, 175–177, 178–179, 185–186
Toxi (1952 film), 6

Ulbricht, Walter, 6, 15, 38, 75, 78–79, 96, 124, 126, 127, 129
Umgelter, Fritz, 68–69
Unbrauchbare an Anna Winters, Das (The incorruptible Anna Winters), 130–132, 146, 148, 173
Unfall, Der (The accident), 174–176, 179, 186
United States military, 39, 45, 50, 51, 63, 64, 72, 78, 83, 84, 89, 165
Unterm Birnbaum (*Under the Pear Tree*), 110

Vergangenheitsbewältigung, 56, 112–113, 116, 156, 177
viewer letters. *See* letters from viewers
Volksgemeinschaft. *See* National Socialism (Nazi); *Volksgemeinschaft*
Volksstimme, 85, 125

Wahnmörderin, Die (The crazed murderess), 114, 116
Waldhausstraße 20 (20 Waldhaus Street), 40–42, 44, 109–110, 184
Waldmann, Dieter, 174, 176
war criminals, 44, 46, 50–51, 54, 68, 83
Warsaw Pact, 40, 44, 163, 176, 177
Wege übers Land (Ways across the country), 55, 82, 143, 176, 178, 179, 186
Wehrmacht, 20, 45, 62, 67, 68, 88
Weimar Republic, 1, 2, 3, 9, 36, 61, 82, 86, 97, 107, 115, 117, 135, 159
Werner, Oskar, 111–112
Westdeutscher Rundfunk (WDR), 7, 8, 17, 51, 54, 63, 93, 99, 109–110, 144, 189

Western European Christendom. *See Abendland*
West Germany (Federal Republic of Germany [FRG])
censorship, 108–109
Christianity and television in, 21, 107–108, 111–114, 116–117
Communist opposition to, 2
consumerism, 96–98, 99, 101–103, 108, 116–117, 158, 185
criticisms of communism, 62–63, 65–69
Deutscher Frauenrat, 127
East German criticisms of, 1, 4, 44, 45, 70–71, 74–80, 82–85, 86–89, 124, 136
economic miracle of (*see* economic miracle)
and gender, 126–128, 132, 136, 138, 140, 147–148, 185
and the Holocaust, 5–6, 153–154
number of television sets, 8
and race, 156–157, 163, 167–168, 170–171, 179
redemption theme in, 20, 33–37, 40–42, 46, 48–51, 53–55, 93
religion and television, 98
self-criticism, 80–81, 94–96, 172, 176
television, 12, 13, 15, 16, 17, 100, 186, 188–189
and women, 132–134, 140, 144–145
Wie verbringe ich meinen Sonntag? (How do I spend my Sunday?), 144–145
Wilhelmsburger Freitag (A Friday in Wilhelmsburg), 106–107, 144, 185
Wittlinger, Karl, 93–95
Wolf unter Wölfen (*Wolf among Wolves*), 12–13
Wolffhardt, Rainer, 42–43
women
equality and liberation, 21, 124–128, 130, 143–148
interracial relationships (*see* interracial relationships)
in modern society, 140–142morality and national strength, 87, 107
paradox of women's lives, 133
programs for, 11
sexuality, 21
in the workplace, 21, 131

working classes, 2, 40, 77, 82, 100, 103, 106, 114, 139, 159–160

xenophobia, 153, 157, 170, 174, 179

Zauberer Gottes, Der (God's magician), 114

Zentralkomitee, 69, 138, 143
Ziem, Jochen, 75–76
Zweites Deutsches Fernsehen (ZDF), 13, 14, 16, 18, 19, 35, 49, 76, 77, 78, 88, 98, 112, 114, 130, 131, 133, 134, 144, 145, 153, 161, 168, 171–172, 173, 183–184

www.ingramcontent.com/pod-product-compliance
Lightning Source LLC
Chambersburg PA
CBHW071158070526
44584CB00019B/2837